LOVE THAT DIRTY WATER

THE STANDELLS

and the Improbable Red Sox Victory Anthem

By CHUCK BURGESS AND BILL NOWLIN

ROUNDER

Published by Rounder Books

an imprint of
Rounder Records Corp.
One Rounder Way
Burlington, MA 01803

Cover illustration: Gordon S. Stanley
Back cover "dirty water" photo: Bill Nowlin
Back cover: *Billboard* chart courtesy of Billboard; Standells album cover
courtesy of Universal; photo of Tony Conigliaro by Chuck Burgess
Cover design: Steven Jurgensmeyer
Interior design and composition: Jane Tenenbaum
Color insert design: Rachael Sullivan

Cataloging-in-Publication Data

Burgess, Charles D., 1946–, and Nowlin, Bill, 1945–
    Love That Dirty Water—The Standells and the Improbable Red Sox
    Victory Anthem
    1. Love that Dirty Water (Popular song) 2. Boston Red Sox (Baseball
    team) 3. Standells (Band) I. Title

First edition

2007924456
796.357

ISBN-13: 978-1-57940-146-7
ISBN-10: 1-57940-146-5

♪ ♪ ♪

ACKNOWLEDGEMENTS

Roger Abrams, Cindi Adler, Todd Anton, Kearney Barton, Jerry Beach, Bruce Belland, Peter Blecha, Bruce Brown, Catherine Burgess, Cathy Ann Burgess, Charles Dismas Burgess, Gregory Blaise Burgess, Chris Cameron, Dick Camnitz, Christian Campagna, Ernie Campagna, Larry Cancro, Gene Carney, Ken Casey, Tom Catlin, Tina Cervasio, Mark Chambers, Lennie Sorensen Cobb, Matt Cobb, Bill Coleman, Susan Coleman, Jim Conners, Bill Cooper, George Denham, Jon Dick, Dick Dodd, Jane Dodd, Dottie Douglas, Mike Dugo, Dan Duquette, Chris Durman, Barrie Edwards, Mark Felsot, Paul Foley, Alan Foulds, Kevin Friend, Matt Gelso, Kevin Gertsen, Jon Goode, Ray Harris, Mickey Hatcher, Jim Healey, Mark Heimback-Nielsen, Rich Herrera, Dave Heuschkel, Jeff Horrigan, Geoff Iacuessa, Brian Interland, Heather Cobb Isbell, Burt Jacobs, Jonathan Jacobs, Paula Jacobs, Steve Jurgensmeyer, Megan Kaiser, Maxwell Kates, Ralph Kent, Terry Kitchen, Buzz Knight, Graham Knight, Kevin LaRose, Mike LaVigne, James Leroux, Henry Ly, Dan Lyons, Lincoln Mayorga, Dave McCarthy, Andy McCue, Peter McDermott, Sarah McKenna, Edie McMillan, Gary McMillan, Jacob McMurray/Experience Music Project, Ryan Nadeau, Peter J. Nash, Steve Netksy, Dennis O'Malley, Bruce Patch, Ed Penney, Matthew Philip, Richie Podolor, Jacob Pomrenke, Michelle Quimby, Rene Rancourt, J J Rassler, Marty Ray, Kalen Rogers, Stewart Ross, Charles Runnells, Brad San Martin, Scott Schleifer, Dave Schlichting, Chaz Scoggins, Dan Shaughnessy, Nick Shields, Elaine Shipley, Floyd Sneed, Lyle Spatz, Gordon Stanley, Dr. Charles Steinberg, Armin Steiner, Todd Stephenson, Gene Sunnen, Michael Tamada, Glenda Chism Tamblyn, Larry Tamblyn, Amy Tobey, Tony Valentino, Bill Vermillion, Bill Wanless, Chris Wilson, Al Yellon.

♪ ♪ ♪

For Dylan, Quinn, Annie,
Rock and Roll, and the Red Sox

♪ ♪ ♪

♪♪♪

CONTENTS

"DIRTY WATER"

(Ed Cobb)

I'm gonna tell you a story
I'm gonna tell you about my town
I'm gonna tell you a big bad story, baby
Aww, it's all about my town
Yeah, down by the river
Down by the banks of the river Charles (aw, that's what's happenin'
    baby)
That's where you'll find me
Along with lovers, muggers, and thieves (aw, but they're cool people)
Well I love that dirty water
Oh, Boston, you're my home (oh, you're the Number One place)

Frustrated women (I mean they're frustrated)
Have to be in by twelve o'clock (oh, that's a shame)
But I'm wishin' and a-hopin', oh
That just once those doors weren't locked (I like to save time for my
    baby to walk around)
Well I love that dirty water
Oh, Boston, you're my home (oh, yeah)

Because I love that dirty water
Oh, oh, Boston, you're my home (oh, yeah)
Coda (repeat to fade over intro riff):
Well, I love that dirty water (I love it, baby)
I love that dirty water (I love Baw-stun)
I love that dirty water (Have you heard about the Strangler?)
I love that dirty water (I'm the man, I'm the man)
I love that dirty water (Owww!)
I love that dirty water (Come on, come on)

♪

Opening Day 1998. It was the bottom of the ninth. The Red Sox had squandered a 2–0 lead and were down 7–2 with just three outs to go.

They scored once on Bragg's double. 7–3. Nomar's single scored another. The bases were loaded and a hit batsman forced in a third run. 7–5. The sacks stayed full and slugger Mo Vaughn was at the plate. Vaughn had already struck out three times in the game. He took a called strike, but slammed the second pitch past the Pesky Pole in right for a walk-off grand slam as the Red Sox won in the most dramatic fashion imaginable, 9–7.

"It was an incredible, euphoric scene," remembers Kevin Friend, who chose that perfect moment to launch the song that instantly became the Red Sox victory anthem. Friend was in charge of the music played in Fenway Park. He punched up the sound, and the unmistakable "Ah— rum, dum, dum—dum da dum. Ah—rum, dum, dum—dum da dum" electric guitar introduction of the Standells' 1966 hit song "Dirty Water" instantly blasted out over the public address system and another fabulous Fenway tradition was born. "Dirty Water," written by Ed Cobb and sung by the Standells, has been the victory anthem of the Boston Red Sox ever since.

Now, within one second after every Red Sox home victory, "Dirty Water" is pumped throughout Fenway Park and jubilant fans proudly join in on the chorus—"Aw-oh Boston, you're my home!"

♪

Aw-Oh Boston, You're My Home

Home of the American Revolution, Boston has always been a proud and quirky town. Right from the start, this once Puritan settlement has been home to numerous oddities and contradictions that have given the city its character:

The Pilgrims banned Christmas in Boston as too showy.

The famous Battle of Bunker Hill was actually fought on another nearby promontory called Breeds Hill.

Many of Boston's streets were laid out following the meandering paths that cows took as they grazed in the hills that used to dot today's downtown Boston. Many routes were established almost 300 years before the automobile, producing quite a few peculiar streets patterns. Then there are public ways like Quaker Lane, which crosses itself at right angles, running east and south and even runs parallel to itself at one point.

Boston is the city of the Bean and the Cod—how many cities celebrate baked beans? How many states have a "Sacred Cod" hanging in the State House? The five-foot long wooden sculpture of a codfish has hung in the Massachusetts legislative chamber since the 1700s.

That same legislature adopted the Constitution of Massachusetts in 1780, nine years before the United States was formed under its own constitution. It is the oldest written working constitution in the world. And, of course, Massachusetts is *not* a state; it is a Commonwealth.

Boston was the birthplace of vaudeville, and burlesque queens reigned at the Old Howard Theater in Scollay Square while the city censors made the phrase "Banned in Boston" an ambiguous badge of honor for countless books, plays, movies, and music. The last of those censors (literally, chief of the licensing division of the mayor's office) was Richard J. Sinnott—pronounced "sin-not."

The harbor-side city suffered a disastrous flood in 1919 that killed and injured scores of people—but it was a torrential flood of *hot molasses*—a key ingredient used for Boston's famous baked beans. In the Great Molasses Flood, some 2,320,000 gallons of molasses swept through city streets after a manufacturing plant explosion, dealing a strange and tragic death to 21 citizens and injuring 150 more.

Bostonians elected a candidate to the Board of Aldermen while he was in prison serving a term for fraud. James Michael Curley was nonetheless beloved by the common men and women who put him in office. Curley was then successively elected to the United States Congress, as mayor of Boston, as Governor of Massachusetts, and then to a final term in Congress—during which he was convicted again, this time on federal charges.

Boston also had a subway system that made you pay to get *off*—a practice memorialized in song. (Remember poor old Charlie on the M.T.A.?)

Reverse logic still prevails for a bunch of ocean swimming devotees, the "L"-Street Brownies, who take a celebrated dip in the bay from the frigid and often ice-covered South Boston beach every New Year's Day!

One of the most striking skyscrapers in the modern city's skyline—the John Hancock Insurance building—was covered with 60 stories of plywood for a stretch in the 1970s, as ill-fitting windows kept popping out and falling to the ground. The 60-story high-rise bore the moniker, the Plywood Palace.

Problems of the beleaguered skyscraper in Copley Square pale in comparison to Boston's most celebrated and controversial ditch—The Big Dig tunnel project—the biggest and costliest public works venture in the history of the United States (and perhaps the world). When proposed in 1985, the expensive plan to dig a new tunnel under Boston Harbor, depress the elevated downtown expressway, and build another bridge across the Charles River was projected to cost $2.5 billion. By 2006 that amount totaled over $14 billion for a project fraught with water leaks, cost overruns, and fatal material failures.

Then there are the Boston Red Sox.

For 150 years or so, Boston has been one of the best baseball cities in America, and the Boston Red Sox have a most unusual, storied, and fascinating history, one that has linked generations of fans over time and distance since the establishment of the franchise in 1901.

Everyone knows that Sox fans are a strange and different breed of sufferers, destined for decades to see their team go down in flames, often at the very last moment. Until the memorable 2004 season this was the team that last won a World Series in 1918 (after winning six times in the league's first 18 seasons), but managed to be eliminated in the seventh game of the Series in 1946, 1967, 1975, and 1986 while losing the pennant on the final day of the season in 1948, 1949, 1972, 1978, and 2003.

The seeming predictability of Sox swoons was fertile ground, and when sportswriter Dan Shaughnessy wrote *The Curse of the Bambino*, everyone in New England knew just what the book was about. For nearly 20 years after publication, people tried every which way to exorcise the Curse and free the Sox from the spell supposedly put on them by Babe Ruth for selling him to the New York Yankees.

It's only fitting that the Red Sox play in baseball's quirkiest ballpark, too—a park that turns 100 years old in 2012. The oddly-shaped ballpark is as far from a symmetrical cookie cutter park as one can have—with Fenway Park's 37-foot tall "Green Monster" looming over left fielders (and casting its figurative shadow all the way to the mound) because the park was built up against a city street. For its first 20-some years, the playing field rose as it approached The Wall, creating an incline known as "Duffy's Cliff" named after Boston's star left fielder Duffy Lewis who had mastered playing on the irregular field.

Fenway's flagpole used to be on the field of play, and in play, though that's been remedied in recent years. Fenway has another pole—the Pesky Pole—marking the very short right-field foul pole, named after infielder Johnny Pesky who pulled a very few home runs just around the pole in his years with the Red Sox. The ballpark, built so long ago, was erected in the days before motor vehicles were common. The first equipment truck was Pat Daley's horse-drawn wagon. Pat Daley is still the company that transports team gear to and from the airport. It was not until the first years of the 21st century that Fenway had its first loading dock; before 2003, all deliveries had to be hand-trucked in and down the ramp at Gate D.

And finally, in 2004, citizens of Red Sox Nation entered new and uncharted waters when they pulled off the *greatest comeback in sports history*, coming from a deficit of 0–3 against the powerful New York Yankees (and a 19-run Yankee onslaught in Game Three) to take four games in a row, and the pennant, and then sweep the World Series from the St. Louis Cardinals with four more consecutive wins. The Red Sox became World Champions, something the Yankees haven't managed in the 21st century. It's a topsy-turvy world.

It is probably no wonder, then, that the legions of fans which comprise "Red Sox Nation," the far-flung tribe of followers of the Boston baseball franchise, have adopted a song called "Dirty Water" as the team's venerated victory anthem. The song was first sung by a bunch of 1960s pre-punk rockers from Los Angeles called the Standells. No one in the band had ever been to Boston when they recorded the song. It was first played over the Fenway Park public address system more than 30 years after its debut simply because the lyrics mentioned Boston.

How did this song capture the imagination of Red Sox fans, and so quickly become the institution it is today? That is the subject of this book, which we hope will earn its own modest niche in chronicling the unpredictable lore of the City of Boston.

First There Was "Tessie"

A storied early Red Sox rally song was heard in the early 1900s before the team was even called the Red Sox. The club played its first seven years known as the Boston Americans. The designation distinguished them from the other major league club in Boston, the more senior club known as the Boston Nationals. Beginning in 1901, the new entry—the American League team—played its home games on the Huntington Avenue Grounds, situated less than a mile from the present Fenway Park, across the Fens parklands and the meandering Muddy River, which flows into the Charles River and on out to sea. The Muddy River is not to be confused with the dirty water referred to in the Standells' song, although the Muddy joins the Charles quite near the area where the incident said to inspire the song occurred.

What was this first rally song? It was a popular song of the day named "Tessie." This quite unlikely ditty became the first "official" rally song of the Boston Americans supporters, introduced in 1903 during the very first World Series when the pennant-winning Boston Americans battled the National League champions from Pittsburgh.

The shouts, cries, chants, and songs of fans at ballparks have a long tradition. Author Peter Nash notes of Boston fans of the day: "The Royal Rooters, products of Irish immigrant parents, no doubt were influenced by the many centuries old tradition of crowd chants at Ireland's soccer and hurling matches."[1]

"Tessie" was a song from a Broadway musical, with the most insipid of lyrics (see the Appendix for a full discussion of the "Tessie" phenomenon, lyrics and all), and the most unlikely basis for a rally song.[2]

After losing two of the first three games, loyal Boston fans who'd traveled to Pittsburgh for the games there were looking for something to rally the boys. Tom Burton, one of the Rooters, secured sheet music of the popular song, and the Royal Rooters wrote their own parodied lyrics needling the Pittsburgh players. They hired a band that played it—and prompted a ninth-inning rally in Game Four. Even though the rally fell one run short, they felt the music had spurred on their players. So they redoubled their efforts the next day. They played it so often and delivered it with such vigor—incessantly, relentlessly, *ad nauseam*—that it began to take its toll on the opposition. Even decades later, Pittsburgh's third baseman Tommy Leach said, "I think those Boston fans won the Series...We beat them three out of four games, and then they started singing that damn Tessie song…Sort of got on your nerves after a while. And before we knew what happened, we'd lost the Series."[3]

It may be difficult to believe that a show tune ditty could turn the tide and help win a world championship but, even at the time, sportswriters covering the games felt that "Tessie" had a real impact, and may truly have unnerved the Pirates enough to cost them the World Series.

"Tessie" was trotted out again for the deciding games of the 1904 pennant race (won by Boston), and the 1912, 1915, and 1916 World Series (all similarly won by Boston.) Neglecting "Tessie" a bit during the 1918 World Series win, and abandoning her altogether afterward, may have been one of the reasons the Red Sox had to wait so long to win another World Championship—which they only did in the year they finally revived "Tessie"—2004.

Another song performed during the 1903 World Series was "The Star-Spangled Banner"—played before the final game on October 13. The Letter Carriers Band first played "Tessie" and then "The Star-Spangled Banner." Most agree, though, that the ritual playing of the song that would become the National Anthem in 1931 first began prior to the first Boston home game in the 1918 World Series.

John Kiley and the Organists

Since the days of the original "Tessie" and the Royal Rooters, many other songs at Fenway Park have become special to loyal fans. In the 1950s and 1960s, organist John Kiley both exhorted the fans and punctuated the dull moments of games with his versions of pop music and old standards on the great Hammond organ in the park. His rendition of "Take Me Out to the Ball Game" is a seventh-inning stretch tradition that continues to this day. Kiley also entertained at the Celtics and Bruins games at the old Boston Garden, providing the soundtrack for Boston sports fans all year long. A favorite trivia question among Boston sports fans remains: Who is the only man who played for the Red Sox, the Celtics, and the Bruins? The answer, of course, is John Kiley, who played *the organ* for all three teams.

"Actually, that answer is not correct," says Rene Rancourt, a good friend of the late Kiley and the man who has given voice to the National Anthem at almost every Bruins home game for decades and at countless other venues. "That is actually an incorrect answer to an incorrectly-worded question—because John also played for the Boston Braves when he was in his teens, so the question should be: Who played professionally for *four teams*? The answer to that question is of course: John Kiley."

Kiley played the Hammond X-66 organ at Fenway Park from 1953 through 1989, passing away in the year 1993. He was a Boston institution, hired personally by Boston Red Sox owner Tom Yawkey after Yawkey had reportedly heard him playing pipe organ. One of Kiley's successors at the Fenway organ was Ray Totaro whose family owned the Boston Organ and Piano Company (originally Hammond Organ Studios of Boston.) Totaro says, "My recollection of the story is that John was playing at some function and Mr. Yawkey was at the function and heard him, and asked him if he would be interested in playing at the park. I believe he was the first organist at the park. Boston Organ and Piano is a family business, about 48, 49 years old. John Kiley started here. He was involved with Boston Organ and Piano in its first year. He was a staff organist and he also was a teacher. He taught me. As a kid, I would go into Fenway once in a while with John, after a lesson. As I became older and could go in myself, I was always welcome to the organ booth and I would go up and visit with John. John was like a grandfather to me. Sometimes I'd call him Uncle John."[1]

Kiley played professionally in Boston's top theaters from the age of 15, and put in a full 10 years at Keith Memorial Theater. He spent 20 years in radio,

John Kiley. Courtesy of Ray Totaro.

as program director and staff organist for radio station WMEX. With five years work at Braves Field before the team moved to Milwaukee, John truly did play for four major league teams. His Boston Garden gig lasted over 25 years. Bill Gilman of the *Leominster Champion* admits that as a kid he wanted to *be* Kiley, and writes of the man, "Kiley was awesome. He was there at every game, never missing a shift, never going on the DL [disabled list] and never being yanked late in the game for a defensive replacement. And doubleheaders? Here's a guy who would play at Fenway in the afternoon and catch a cross-town cab after the game to get to North Station in time for the start of the Bruins' or Celtics' nightcap."[2]

After Kiley's 36-year reign at the Fenway Park keyboard, organist Jim Kilroy took over for about five years before being followed by the team of Ray Totaro and Richard Giglio beginning in 1994. Giglio did about 50 or 60 games a year while Totaro worked as his backup filling in the other dates during the 81-game home season. The tag-team of Totaro and Giglio, behind a modern Yamaha digital electronic organ, remained in their perch high above the press box behind home plate until the current Red Sox management team brought in Josh Kantor in 2003.

Like Totaro, Richard Giglio was no stranger to baseball park organ music or to Fenway Park. In the 1970s while living and studying in San Diego, Richard was the organist for the Padres for two years before retuning to Boston to work with Ray at Boston Organ and Piano. He came back home to share with his father, Kelly, a deep attachment to the Boston Red Sox. "My father died in 2005 at the age of 90. Thankfully he did live long enough to witness the Red Sox's most glorious moment since he was a four-year-old child! At the time of his passing, he was the longest season ticket holder to the Red Sox on record—since 1935."[3]

Totaro and Giglio were the first Fenway organists to work in conjunction with the recorded music which was introduced into the park in 1998, an innovation that provided the opportunity to add familiar pop music to the mix that gave fans that special Fenway Park experience. It was this development that would give rise to the introduction of a now 40-year-old rock and roll hit to Red Sox Nation as its victory anthem. Ray Totaro had this take on the introduction of recorded music into one of baseball's most conservative parks: "I think the Red Sox are really doing a wonderful thing. What they're doing is providing a vehicle by having both the CDs and the organ, where everybody can be pleased. No matter who you are, how old you are, what your musical taste may be between the two." During the time that he and Giglio worked the games, he remembered a few times when the organ was the most appropriate entertainment for the situation at hand. "There was one time when the game was delayed. It wasn't a rain delay; it was a snow delay! There was snow on the outfield and they were shoveling it, so I played an hour and forty-five minutes straight. I don't know if anybody else thought it was funny, but the second thing I played was "White Christmas" and this was in April. I thought it was amusing."

Totaro made the case for the spontaneity of a good organist at the ballpark: "Basically, we're on call for whatever is needed when it's needed. The other thing that's cool about it, I think, is that we can shift if there's a shift needed. I'll give you an example. Oftentimes, there'll be a presentation of the colors by some military branch. It will be the Air Force or whatever the case might be. What I liked to do, and I remember John [Kiley] doing it, is to play their theme song. Anyway, there was this one holiday—I think it was a Memorial Day—and I found out that all four branches were there. Well, I knew two of them by heart. The third one I had in music, but at the time I did not know the Air Force song. Couldn't remember it. What I did is I went down into the park and found a guy in an Air Force uniform. He hummed the beginning of it, which triggered in my mind how it went. I went back up to the booth and figured out enough of it so that I could do a few bars of theirs like the others. That's the kind of thing that live music is going to do and no other music is going to do, and that's the kind of thing I think is valuable. To me, that's what's really terrific about having [organ] music on spot."[4]

The National Anthem and
Boston's Star-Spangled Tenor

Was it at Fenway that the National Anthem was first played before a sporting event? Not strictly speaking. For one example, it was played before the final game of the 1903 World Series, and that was at the Huntington Avenue Grounds. The launch of a new tradition, though, came on September 9, 1918 before Game Four of that year's World Series (the first Boston home game), when the band played "The Star-Spangled Banner" to the crowd. The tune had previously been played occasionally during the seventh-inning stretch, and there was that 1903 rendition. But in terms of a ceremonial playing before the game, most agree this is where the tradition began.

Red Sox Senior Vice President for Fenway Affairs Larry Cancro reports, "We've always taken the Anthem very seriously. Fenway Park was the first place the National Anthem was played before a sporting event. It has since become a national and worldwide tradition. During the previous ownership, we predominantly used the organ, and brought in certain people on special occasions." Larry recalls memorable performances by George Strait, Huey Lewis and the News, Susan Tedeschi, Jeffrey Osborne, and many others.[1]

The Red Sox have never had a regular singer of the National Anthem. Besides having the standby option of the park organist to play the song, typically a different person performs it each day, though some return to the park microphone more than once a year.

Marty Ray coordinated Anthem singers at Fenway for parts of three seasons — 2003 through 2005 — and recalls many figures who sang either the Anthem or other patriotic songs at the park during that time: "One of my favorite ones of all time was Daniel Rodriguez, the former NYPD officer who became a symbol of post 9/11 recovery through his daily performance of 'God Bless America' in Yankee Stadium. He performed the Anthem in 2003. One of the less memorable ones was during the '03 American League Divisional Series when Michael Bolton faltered mid-Anthem and had to check the lyrics, which were scribbled on the palm of his left hand. Disgraceful.

"Lou Rawls sang the Anthem on Opening Day 2003 with Ray Charles who performed 'America the Beautiful.' In 2004, we had two Irish tenors at Fenway, John McDermott ('O Canada'—Opening Day 2004) and Anthony Kearns. Of course, that was the first year that Wayne Naus, a professor at Berklee, started performing the anthem solo on trumpet. He is a regular fixture here.

"Five-year old Jordan Leandre, our friend from the Jimmy Fund, made his debut in 2004, as did the Dropkick Murphys. John Castillo from the Perkins School for the Blind sang on Opening Day 2004. We had the cast of *The Lion King* sing here that year. In the post-season, we had the singing State Trooper, Sgt. Dan Clark sing 'God Bless America' in Game Three of the American League Championship Series, the Kingston Trio performed the Anthem in Game Four, and Jo Dee Messina sang "God Bless America" in that game. In the World Series, we had Steven Tyler for the Anthem in Game One and Kelly Clarkson for 'God Bless America.' James Taylor did the Anthem for Game Two and Donna Summer did 'God Bless America.'

"In 2005, Alison Krauss sang in April. Jay Rodriguez from *Queer Eye for the Straight Guy* also sang here. Tracy Bonham sang here that year as did the casts of *Phantom of the Opera, Little Shop of Horrors* and Sara Kramer from the Broadway production of *Mamma Mia*. Young country singer Ashley Gearing from Springfield, Massachusetts is now a regular fixture as well. We have had a bunch of country stars sing here. Billy Dean did last year and this year. Little Big Town sang this year. Herb Reed and the Platters sang last year. Lonestar sang this year as well."[2]

Michael Bolton was by no means the only performer to experience difficulty. That's part of the reason why most performers lip-synch their renditions. As former Red Sox Vice President Jim Healey explained, "The old sound system at Fenway was a central cluster system where all the sound came from speakers in the centerfield bleachers. The delay in hearing the sound from a microphone behind home plate or in the press box is approximately one second. This can be very confusing for the speaker (or singer) especially for someone who is not accustomed to hearing the delay. We used to require almost all Anthem singers to pre-record the Anthem before the game so they would not be confused by the delay. I know we did this as early as 1976. There was someone who tried to sing it live and became very confused by the delay but I don't recall the name of this singer."[3]

Rene Rancourt is best known today for his inspirational and magnificent performances of "The Star-Spangled Banner" before Boston Bruins hockey games. But Rene, a classically trained opera singer, has also sung the National Anthem for over 37 years at nearly every significant sporting event in New England ranging from countless college events to Celtics, Patriots, and Red Sox games. In fact, Rancourt began his career as iconic Anthem singer at Red Sox Opening Day 1969, thanks to none other than the late John Kiley.

Rene Rancourt was born in Lewiston, Maine to French Canadian parents who came down from Quebec to work in one of the many shoe mills of Lewiston. With a voice developed in church choir, Rene looked up to classical singers and opera stars like Mario Lanza for inspiration, not the early rock and roll singers of his 1950s youth. "I totally missed the whole rock thing. I went into classical music as my first choice." His very powerful voice, with its rich

Rene Rancourt. Courtesy of Rene Rancourt.

vibrato timbre, attracted early attention from local ice hockey promoters. "It seemed like I was forever being asked to sing the National Anthem."[4]

After high school, young men in Lewiston faced two typical career choices—go into the Army or get a job in the mills. A high school teacher encouraged a grateful Rancourt to audition at Boston University for a fine arts scholarship. Accepted, he studied under Sarah Caldwell, founder of the Boston Opera Company, trained in theater, then did graduate work at the New England Conservatory. "But it seemed everywhere I went, even then, I still found myself in venues where I was asked to sing the National Anthem. I sang for the BU hockey team when I was in school."

Eventually in the Army nevertheless, Rancourt entered the Army entertainment corps competition to join special services and win his category—Classical Singer. He performed in variety shows that toured army bases in the west and southwest. Rene was always fortunate enough to be able to support himself with his art, and not have to work a dual career—selling cars or something—as so many in music must. He worked in musical comedy, dinner theaters, summer stock, and musicals. After meeting his wife, they formed the Rene Rancourt Orchestra, which was very successful playing weddings, bar mitzvahs, and the like.

Rancourt's road to Fenway Park and his renown as Boston's voice of the National Anthem began in a most curious way and was the direct result of his continuing love for opera and classical music. In 1969, he entered the New England Regional Metropolitan Opera Auditions and won first prize. As John Kiley was driving in his car, he heard the finals of the competition broadcasted on WGBH radio. Kiley had a tradition of inviting the winner to sing on Opening Day at Fenway. "I became very friendly with John because of his love of opera. He introduced me to all the opera singers when the Met came to Boston. It became a bit of a tradition for John to invite me back to Fenway to sing."

"One day in the '70s, John asked me if I ever considered singing at the Bruins games. When I saw the fan reactions at the game, the pounding on the Plexiglas, and the tremendous enthusiasm of those fans, I thought, 'Boy, that's for me.' It's like early opera in Italy or something, where they are throwing food at the stage—I mean, I thought, this is for me. I've been showing up at Bruins games ever since, and I've never signed a contract or anything because I said to John after that first performance, 'Hey, this is great. The hockey games are great. Maybe I should call up the Bruins management and see if they will let me sing some more here.' He said, 'No. Don't call 'em, just keep showing up!' So I did. I recently celebrated 30 years singing for the Bruins."

After Rene began performing regularly at the Bruins games and occasionally for the Celtics, his appearances at Fenway Park became less frequent. One thing that rankles him are singers who attempt to re-compose the National Anthem. As he puts it, they "try to be a song 'stylist' and it comes across that they are more important than the song itself. They are putting across their own agenda." He had tried it once himself. "I had an idea once to change one or two notes of the National Anthem to make it more dramatic. Well, John Kiley went through the roof. He went crazy and said, 'What are you, nuts?!!! Would you ever change a note or a word of a Franz Schubert song or a Leonard Bernstein composition, or an opera—Verdi or Puccini?'

"The song itself is so difficult, so un-vocal. It was originally composed as flute melody, not really meant to be a song. They took that flute melody and made a drinking song out of it, 'Anacreon in Heaven.' It became popular and Francis Scott Key used that tavern drinking song as the melody for the song that's become our National Anthem. It's so difficult to sing that I like to say Francis Scott 'Off-key' did it."

Rancourt's most memorable experience performing the Anthem for the Red Sox before a game was in 1975 before Game Six of the World Series. The Red Sox always had a famous singer lined up to sing the National Anthem for an event as big as this. Kate Smith was scheduled to sing Game Six. Smith became ill and could not make it, so the Sox asked John Kiley for Rancourt's number.

"At the time, I was in the process of developing perhaps the worst cold of my life! Here it was—a performance at Fenway Park, a broadcast that would be seen worldwide, and I'm coming down with a cold. But I didn't tell the Sox that. There was *no way* I was going to miss this opportunity. I asked them if there was some way that I could record the Anthem ahead of time. They said, 'Sure, come on in and we'll record it; we prefer to do that, so that there won't be any slip-ups. We will just have you lip-synch it tomorrow.' I said, 'Great.' and went into Fenway Park that afternoon and we taped it in the press booth. I had just one take. That's was it, because I gave it all I had and after I sang it I *completely lost my voice!*"

"The next day, with 150 million people listening and watching, I had no voice. And that was the only time, in my entire singing life—60 years of singing—that I have lost my voice. That was the only time and it occurred on the most important day of my career at the time." After his 1975 World Series performance, Rene's association with the Red Sox, "just petered out, as I got busier with the Bruins" but he has been pleased to do an occasional Opening Day—"always an honor and great thrill."

"Sweet Caroline" in the Can—
Good Times Never Seemed So Good

Tradition-bound Fenway Park was one of the last major league ballparks to incorporate pre-recorded or "canned" music (in the form of tape recordings, compact discs, and now downloaded music) into its game day presentation and is one of the last baseball venues to retain a live organ. Today, every Red Sox game at Fenway features both classic ballpark organ music and an eclectic selection of pre-recorded music over the public address system that are integral parts of every fan's experience. A variety of pop, rock, and rap music is heard between innings, when a batter takes the plate, when a relief pitcher leaves the bullpen, and at other timely moments. Perennial favorites like "Louie Louie," "Twist and Shout," "Tequila," baseball-specific songs such as John Fogerty's "Centerfield," and the seventh-inning stretch favorite "Take Me Out To The Ballgame" have all been a part of the happening over the years. An occasional cut with local significance is mixed in as well, such as Jonathan Richman's "New England."

Megan Kaiser is the Manager for Advertising Production of the Red Sox. She is also the current programmer of recorded music played over the public address system at the park. As someone who grew up in Connecticut where the border wars rage between Red Sox and Yankees fans, she explained why Richman's song is a candidate for the play rotation at Fenway. "'New England' is a great song. I just play that little chorus, because we're New England's team. Connecticut is a divided place, a tough area; it's like the Mason-Dixon cuts through your state. It's tough to be either fan, but it's tougher to be a Red Sox fan. The nature of the beast is those ugly 86 years shadow over…growing up, the '70s and '80s wasn't so easy. For those people in New Hampshire and for Western Mass., when they come to the games it's nice to hear a little 'New England.' It's a little shout out. Jonathan Richman, I'm sure if he ever comes to a game, might be a little appreciative. We're New England's team."[1]

When the Red Sox ran onto the field on May 11, 2004 to take their positions, the first one out of the dugout was Manny Ramirez, waving a small American flag. He had become a naturalized American citizen in ceremonies in Miami on May 10. When he came up to bat, the team played the song "Proud to Be an American" and he received a standing ovation.

This was a prouder day than another Manny moment, September 8, 2002. As reported in *Day By Day with the Boston Red Sox:* "As Fenway's organist became further relegated to just brief interludes, the Red Sox tried to honor ballplayers who liked to have a favorite song played over the park's sound system as they strode to the plate or came in from the bullpen. Manny Ramirez requested 'I Get High' by the group Styles, and it was indeed played when he approached home plate during the game hosting the Blue Jays. Trouble is, there was a 12-letter expletive uttered early in the song. First, the artist discussed how he needed drugs, then he came out with the word. Second base umpire Angel Hernandez called upstairs after Manny's fly out, and said he would report it to the commissioner's office. 'I think we'll have a CD burning ceremony,' said Sox VP Dr. Charles Steinberg. 'Whatever that song was, you won't hear it again at Fenway Park.'"[2]

An incredibly popular Fenway favorite song always played in the middle of the eighth inning is Neil Diamond's pop hit "Sweet Caroline (Good Times Never Seemed So Good)." Here we have another song that inexplicably worked its way into the hearts of Red Sox Nation. "Sweet Caroline" was a Top 10 and platinum-selling single for Diamond in 1969 and one of 38 Top 40 hits for the singer-songwriter over his career according to *Billboard* magazine. Like "Tessie" in 1903, "Sweet Caroline" is simply a popular song that found its way inside the ballpark and is now considered an integral part of the Fenway Park experience even though the only thing about it that even remotely suggests a connection to baseball is the singer's last name.

It is closing in on 10 years now as a Fenway standard and it is more popular than ever. The introduction of "Sweet Caroline" into the rotation at Fenway on game day began in 1998 when a local video and communication company called BCN Productions was awarded a contract to program the recorded music played at the park. BCN (Boston Convention Network) Productions—not to be confused with the Boston FM radio station WBCN—started out as an audiovisual production company for the many trade shows and conventions in the Boston area. When the old Boston Garden was replaced by the Fleet Center (now renamed T.D. Banknorth Garden), BCN Productions was contracted to provide the installation and operation of the sound system, electronic scoreboards, and the Center's "Jumbotron" video screen. Kevin Friend, the company's president, recalled that at the time, "We also were doing the same thing at McCoy Stadium in Pawtucket for the PawSox and at Foxboro Stadium for the Patriots."[3]

It was only natural that they pursued a contract with the Red Sox as well. At Fenway, BCN just ran the music, keeping the infusion of modern stadium entertainment somewhat understated in the historic ballpark.

Amy (Sill) Tobey, production manager for BCN Productions, was given the responsibility for programming the recorded music and coordinating its play with the traditional organ music at the park from 1998 through 2004. Ray Totaro and Richard Giglio of the Boston Organ Company were the organists in the park at the time Amy and BCN Productions came on board, and Ed

Brickley was the public address announcer. Amy, Ray, Richard, and Ed were located high above home plate on the fifth level—the media level—that houses the park's press box. Amy, Ed, and the organist were all located in separate booths and were physically unable to see each other from their respective locations, but very quickly a coordination of duties evolved. Ed's player introductions and announcements led the way and with three-way communication via headsets, Amy and the organists could smoothly integrate the music that became the game's soundtrack.

Amy selected music "that put energy into the game." As to any one particular selection, it was simply a matter of the music fitting in to a program of uplifting and "fun" songs for the games. Why did she introduce Neil Diamond's hit? "I just liked 'Sweet Caroline.' I had heard it played at other sporting events and simply thought it was a fun song to play," she said. Amy was quick to read the reaction of the fans to her musical selections and noticed a great response to the tune and so it became a permanent part of the rotation.[4]

Many Boston fans were already very familiar with the sing-along nature of the song. Perennial Boston performers and bar bands like Jim Plunkett, D. J. Sullivan, and J.D., Billy & Ken had been entertaining the patrons of the Improper Bostonian and clubs all over Cape Cod with the song as a staple of their repertoires for years. Jon "J.D." Aldrich, of J.D., Billy & Ken recalled the way audiences would sing back at them when they played the song. "I don't know exactly how it started. I'd like to say we invented the audience participation on the song. You know after we sang the part that goes, 'Touching me, touching you, Oh, Sweet Caroline…' and the audience would sing, 'Whoa, whoa, whoa' and then after 'Good times never seemed so good' when the audience would go 'So good, so good, so good!' I'd like to say it, but I'm really not sure where that began. Maybe they first did it at a Neil Diamond concert. I'm not sure but, no matter what, it's a great 'good time' song no matter where you hear it."[5]

"Sweet Caroline" was also a favorite closing song of the many downtown Boston nightclubs along Boylston Street known as bar-alley during the 1980s and '90s. When the club Deejays played the song it was time to go home, so the connection between the song and having a good time was firmly entrenched in the minds of many Red Sox fans even before it became a Fenway staple.

Amy Tobey made the decision to play "Sweet Caroline" at the Fenway Park *only* in anticipation of an impending Red Sox victory, somewhere between the seventh and ninth inning if the team was ahead. "I considered it a good luck charm and would play it if I felt that the team was really in position to win the game. I wanted to wake up the crowd in anticipation of a win, even if I just had a gut feeling that they had the victory in hand." Amy's idea reminds one of legendary Boston Celtics coach Red Auerbach, who would light up his victory cigar near the end of a game that he *knew* his team would win. "I wouldn't play it every game, or when they were hopelessly behind, and certainly not at every game at a set time like it's done now. It was always meant to be in anticipation of a win."

The new Red Sox management team suggested playing the song during the eighth inning of every game, regardless of the score, and that is when you will hear it at Fenway Park now—perhaps because Sox fans have come to believe that, even when the team is far behind, miraculous finishes are never out of the question!

When Megan Kaiser assumed the music programming responsibilities at Fenway in 2003 she recalled that, "Amy Tobey was a big fan of the song, and there was also a fellow in the control room who had a daughter born. Her name was Caroline. So it's two-fold. Amy liked the song very much and this fellow had a newborn named Caroline. So Amy would play the song occasionally because we were winning and they would also play it occasionally because this man had a new daughter named Caroline. When I first came in 2003, in my first days, we weren't playing it every game. It wasn't all the time. In 2004, it was every game.

"Towards the end of 2003, I noticed that people were singing along to the 'Ba ba ba' ('whoa-whoa-whoa' according to other ears) part, so I would bring [the volume] down just for 'ba ba ba.' In 2004, I brought it down for 'so good, so good, so good' and, let me tell you, the first time was *not* so good, so good, so good (very few people in the stands responded). In fact, my producer Danny Kischel looked over at me and said, 'What happened right there?' He freaked out. I said, 'I thought I would try something new.' He said, 'Omigod, that just scared the crap out of me.' You could hear a couple of people singing it. The only thing I was responsible for [in the evolution of 'Sweet Caroline' in the park] was bringing down the sound. Amy Tobey and Kevin Friend were the ones who started playing it. The fans are really responsible for making it what it is. People are like, 'Who started that?' The fans really [did], they were the ones who really made it go."[5]

In baseball circles, the song has become so strongly associated with the Red Sox that when the Tampa Bay Devil Rays overcame a 6–2 deficit after six innings of play to beat the visiting Red Sox in 10 innings on August 6, 2006, the Tropicana Field sound system operator took advantage of the moment and played "Sweet Caroline" to rib the many Red Sox fans who had flocked to the field.

"Dirty Water" 1966—
The Times They Were A-Changin'

"Sweet Caroline" now makes the home crowd feel "so good," near the end of each game, just as "Tessie" did when it was the rally song in 1903 (and again in its new incarnation in 2004). Countless other popular songs have enlivened the fans in the old Fens ballpark over the years, but "Dirty Water"—that 1966 hit song by the Standells that follows the final play of a Red Sox victory—is the most anticipated and most exciting Red Sox song of all. You are going to hear "Sweet Caroline" at every game, no matter what. If you're a Sox fan at Fenway, though, the song you really want to hear is "Dirty Water."

Why? Because "Dirty Water" is the VICTORY anthem of the Boston Red Sox—the song that you joyously hum or sing exiting the park, in your car, or on the "T" as you make your way home after the game. It is the song you sing in the bars, pubs, and restaurants that tune into the Sox game. When you unexpectedly hear it on the radio, you smile at happy memories of when you were at the park with someone special—a best friend, your spouse, a son, a daughter, or your grandchild—when you witnessed the good guys in victory. And "Dirty Water" is *only* played when the Red Sox win, it is *never* played after a Red Sox defeat. Should the unspeakable happen, then the home fans will hear an alternate musical selection played, appropriately wordlessly, on the organ—such as the old 1950s hit "Goodnight Sweetheart," after a night game.

"Dirty Water" is simply written, but absolutely unique—a rock and roll song that has an unmistakable guitar introduction and an unforgettable refrain that begs to be sung-along with. It may be a simple song but, when heard or sung, it becomes an expression of pure delight for every Red Sox fan who has ever savored a victory at Fenway Park.

When you come right down to it, of course, "Dirty Water" is a curious song for the Boston Red Sox to have adopted in the first place. The lyrics to the Standells' 1966 hit song do not gush with wide-eyed, unalloyed love for the city of Boston. In fact, the song refers to the city's major waterway as polluted. Then the women of Boston are branded as frustrated because they had to be in by midnight (a common curfew rule in most of the women's college dormitories of the city at that time.) Next the city is vilified as a home to muggers (some heard the word as "fuggers") and thieves. There is even a reference to the infamous Boston Strangler thrown in for good measure near the end of the song! But as vocalist Dick Dodd sings, it is a "big bad story" of a song.

In Boston, though, all this negativity just makes the song that much more attractive. Bostonians must be a very self-deprecating, good-natured bunch of fans to sing a seemingly derogatory song about themselves and their city. Honest, too. In 1966, when the song was first popular, the water in the Charles River *was* very dirty, polluted, and often smelled offensively from years of abuse. Thankfully, the Charles has been restored and is now one of the most beautiful urban waterways in the country. It is clean enough that a fully-clothed Massachusetts Gov. William Weld startled news reporters by jumping into the Charles during an August 1996 news conference on signing a rivers protection bill into law. Perhaps it is the reference in the song to the lovers who also populated the banks of the river Charles—along with those muggers (fuggers) and thieves—that endears the song to Red Sox supporters. But more likely it is simply because it provides the opportunity for thousands of partisan fans standing in the Fenway Park aisles after each home victory to sing out, over and over again, loudly and proudly, and in heavily accented Boston voices, the defiant feel-good refrain—"I love that dirty *wattah*, (aw)-oh, Baw-stun, you're my home"!

♪ ♪ ♪

The year 1966 began with the début of the campy primetime television show *Batman* while Nancy Sinatra was singing that her boots were made for walking. Songwriter Neil Diamond penned "I'm A Believer," a #1 gold record for the made-for-television rock and roll quartet the Monkees. Beatle George Harrison married Patti Boyd while John Lennon was criticized in the press and in the pulpits for proclaiming the Beatles more popular than Jesus Christ. U. S. Army Special Forces Sergeant Barry Sadler sang about the heroic soldiers that

wore the green beret, while the war in a place called Vietnam was escalating and the Selective Service System was imposing new stringent draft rules on college students not maintaining at least a "C" average. Peter Max's psychedelic poster art hung on the walls of dormitories at every college in the country, often illuminated by black lights and lava lamps. The Federal Drug Administration declared that *the pill* was safe, and girls with dark blue

Professional dancers "Sophia" and "Raul" of the Peppermint West nightclub in Hollywood demonstrate one of the latest dance crazes that the kids in Boston were doing in 1966. Courtesy of Edie McMillan.

The Swinging Sixties. Courtesy of Edie McMillan.

eye shadow, white lipstick, and miniskirts wore Emeraude or Shalimar per-
fume. Guys with crew-cuts, white tab-collar shirts and skinny ties co-existed
with others beginning to wear tie-dyed tee shirts, long hair, and Sonny Bono
caveman vests. The Boston skyline was being reworked with the recent completion of the 52-story Prudential Center Tower in the Back Bay, and ground-
breaking ceremonies for the World Trade Center Towers in New York City
took place in August.

In sports, the Boston Celtics won another National Basketball Association
Championship—their eighth in a row—by defeating the Los Angeles Lakers
in a seven-game series. Rookies Bob Cappadonna from Northeastern University and Canadian-born Bobby Orr joined the Boston Patriots and the Boston
Bruins respectively. Cappadonna became the football franchise's Rookie of
the Year. Orr became a sports legend. The Red Sox were a .500 team with a
losing record going into the All-Star game. Getting a great seat in Fenway Park
minutes before the first pitch was easy. In fact, you could get hundreds of great
tickets to almost any game all season at the often sparsely attended park. Only
811,172 fans came to Fenway in all of 1966 when the Red Sox roster featured
names like Yastrzemski, Conigliaro, Petrocelli, Radatz, and Lonborg.

It was a long hot summer. A July heat wave with temperatures as high as
100 degrees saw young Bostonians fleeing to the beaches in Revere and Nan-
tasket during the day and into the rock and roll ballrooms—Wonderland and
the Surf—at night. It was also pretty hot in Vietnam where American GI's were
dying in an escalating and undeclared war that was rapidly dividing the nation
between young and old, rich and poor, and black and white.

In the South, James Meredith started a civil rights protest march in Memphis and was shot by a sniper's bullet. Shortly afterward, Stokely Carmichael made his "Black Power" speech in Berkeley, California.

John, Paul, George, and Ringo came to Boston at the height of Beatlemania to play at the Suffolk Downs racetrack where tickets to the show were expensive at seven bucks each. Bob Dylan crashed his motorcycle in Woodstock, New York. Medicaid began, drive-in movie theaters were still ubiquitous, and Vespa motor scooters were popular modes of transportation for teens who couldn't afford a car—although a Vespa wasn't much good for a drive-in movie date.

The Los Angeles-based Standells broke into the pop charts for the first time with "Dirty Water" and were close to having the song become a national Top 10 hit by June. In Boston, "Dirty Water" received a lot of airplay all summer long. Most listeners assumed that the Standells were a local group that had suddenly made it big. After all, they sang "Boston, you're my home." But nobody in Boston knew much, if anything, about them.

Gradually it came out: the Standells were a Los Angeles lounge band. They had never even been to Boston. Their producer, Ed Cobb, was a former singer with the Four Preps and was the writer of the song. Finally, the band was going on a national tour that summer with the Rolling Stones—including a stop in the Boston area.

"Dirty Water" was heard as a "Pick to Click" on Boston radio stations in the middle of one of the worst Red Sox seasons ever. The Sox were on a losing streak that would see them finish in ninth place in the then 10-team American League. They hadn't had a winning season since 1958. The only consolation to the disastrous 1966 season was that the Yankees were just as bad. In a battle for last place, the New York team won that dubious honor at the end of the season. The Yankees were the 10th place team.

When "Dirty Water" debuted in Boston there was absolutely no connection between the Standells and the city, and certainly no connection between their raucous rock and roll song and the Red Sox at the time. But the Red Sox had their own aspiring rock and roll star in 1966—a young player named Tony Conigliaro.

Tony Conigliaro—
The Red Sox' Singing Slugger

Tony Conigliaro, or Tony C as he soon became known, was a phenomenally talented Red Sox outfielder and batting star. A local kid with roots in Revere and East Boston, Tony was signed to the Sox as a 19-year-old right out of St. Mary's High School in nearby Lynn. Conigliaro was an outstanding baseball player; he hit a home run in his very first home plate appearance (at Fenway April 17, 1964) and went on to lead the American League in home runs the next year. He was the youngest batter ever to reach 100 home runs, and he was blessed with movie-star handsome looks and a great personality. Young and exuberant, he'd sometimes hop on a local nightclub stage and sing a few songs. It wasn't long before savvy local music promoter Ed Penney talked with him about cutting a record.

In a tradition exemplified by other big leaguers like Mickey Mantle, who once teamed up with Teresa Brewer in 1956 on the song "I Love Mickey," sports and show business were not that far apart. Stan Musial tried his hand at recording once, and Milwaukee Braves outfielder Lee May had a hit song called "Gloria" when he sang with a popular doo-wop group called the Crowns in 1956.

Tony might have been encouraged in his musical pursuits by Red Sox stadium announcer and radio personality Sherm Feller. Not only was Feller the legendary voice of Fenway Park for years but he was also a successful songwriter. His composition "Summertime Summertime," sung by a local Boston group called the Jamies, hit the national pop charts at number 26 in 1958 and the song re-charted again as a Top 40 hit in 1960. Feller also wrote and scored the "John Kennedy Symphony." Red Sox outfielder Fred Lynn was very good friends with Sherm, and provided Feller $5,000 to help score the work. "I was very pleased when Sherm was honored for his fine work with this piece," recalls Lynn. The symphony was performed on the late President's birthday by the Boston Pops Orchestra.[1]

Tony became friendly with Brian Interland, who worked as a statistician for WHDH-TV (Channel 5) at Fenway Park and had a season's pass from Red Sox PR man Bill Crowley. He and Tony became friendly during Tony's rookie season, just around the time Brian got his first job in the music business as New England rep for Merrec Distributors, handling Mercury and its associated labels Philips, Smash, and Fontana. "We'd go out and we'd get a bite and just

Tony Conigliaro publicity photograph. Courtesy of Ed Penney.

hang around," Interland says, explaining that Conigliaro was always interested in the music business. "Athletes then, they had no access, and they loved just even going to shows. Now these guys, they need an entourage. In those days, it wasn't the case at all. He wasn't a singer. He had no concept of that at the time, but he always loved music, was always singing in the shower. We'd go see bands like the G-Clefs. They had a regular gig a couple of nights a month at The Escape out in Hopkinton. On a Saturday night after a day game, we'd go out there. It was just one of those little things that became a fun thing. Who would have ever thought that Tony would be influenced by someone like them?"[2]

The Boston based G-Clefs recognized Tony as a fan, and invited him up on stage to sing a song or two with them, and Tony was pretty fearless, just as he was at the plate. "He just wasn't afraid to embarrass himself." He found he enjoyed it and Interland realized he had a good voice. "Not that he had a great voice, but he was great on stage with the G-Clefs." Interland worked for branch manager John Penney at Merrec, and John's brother Ed was an independent producer in the business with a country single of his own out.

Ed had been a DJ at Cambridge's WTAO for 12 years, but started his own business in 1959, Ed Penney Productions, promoting records and concerts and doing PR work. He had an office in the St. George Hotel (now the Buckminster) and was hosting a cocktail party in the lounge for the Supremes, when Brian brought Tony to the party. "At some point we went back up to my offices—Tony and I and Brian. I think one or two of The Supremes came with us. Just to talk about music. It all led to him coming in to sing. I listened to him and I got the idea...with his popularity. We decided to form a record company and I would produce him and we'd see what happened. Just locally, I figured with the cost of the session and the cost of pressing a few thousand records, we'd sell enough in Boston to at least break even."[3]

Tony's first songs, on double-sided 45-RPM records, were released on the Penn-Tone label, a private label created by Ed Penney. Ed had a lot more experience with an older generation of artists such as Vaughn Monroe, and the

music of the Mills Brothers and the Ames Brothers. He became particularly
friendly over time with Tony's father Sal.

The label name plays on Penney's last name and Tony's first; the two men
co-financed the label, and recorded Tony in New York during December 1964.
The record company was a 50/50 deal between the two. Penney later became
Tony's business manager. For Tony, it was from the NY-Penn League baseball
fields to the Penn-Tone record label, the debut date of the first single being January 19, 1965. At a preview party in Boston, there was a little promotional
overkill: the two tracks were played over and over for $3\frac{1}{2}$ hours!

Tony was known for his music. He even carried a battery-operated 45-rpm
record player on club flights, to the dismay of many of the older players. Now
he was a recording artist himself. His first single was released early in the 1965
baseball season. David Cataneo tells how Tony came into the clubhouse extra
early and placed a copy of his new disc in every player's locker, then went out
to the field to work out. When he returned, the clubhouse was bustling with
players, but there were no Tony C singles to be found. "What happened to the
records?" Tony asked. "Someone pointed to the trash barrel. Tony walked over
and found the records—all of them—in the garbage. The clubhouse erupted
in laughter, and no one laughed harder than Tony."[4]

"Playing The Field" was an up-tempo romantic song written by Ernie
Capp (the pen name of Ernie Campagna, the music director of radio station
WMEX) with many deliberate baseball puns thrown in, presumably to take advantage of Tony's fame. "I'm no rookie at love," "I'm getting tired of striking
out," and "I'm going to try a brand new pitch," are a few examples of the lyrics.
Backed up by a female chorus singing "I'm gonna, gonna play the field, a huh-
huh" (sounding a little like Bobby Rydell's "Swingin' School"), and a rock and
roll saxophone—it was not a bad song for his debut. For Campagna, this was
the first song he'd ever had recorded. The flip side of the record was Tony's version of the 1958 hit by George Hamilton IV, "Why Don't They Understand."

Tony's new songwriter Ernie Campagna had already encountered the baseball star once before, when Ernie was a Pony League ballplayer in East Boston.
He was now working as music director of Boston radio station WMEX. As such,
he was often called upon during "record day" at the station by Ed Penney and
others promoting this record or that. Ernie remembers well the day Penney
told him that he was going to have the Red Sox star cut a song Ernie himself
had written: "I was always pitching Ed on my songs. Ed Penney had the 'Little Red Scooter' song, and told me he was [going to] record it with Tony. I was
excited and went home and wrote 'Playing the Field' with Tony in mind and
brought it to Ed the next day. He loved the play on words and said he'd include it in the New York session."[5]

Campagna was in a potentially conflictful situation, and WMEX program
director Mel Miller was concerned. "I told Mel I would use the pseudonym
Ernie Camp. There was a typo on the Penn-Tone 45 that listed the writer as

Ernest Capp; the RCA Victor releases were corrected. Mel was clear with Ed (who may well have had second thoughts about my involvement at this point) that we would only add the record if WBZ added it first."

Ernie traveled to New York and watched the sessions from the control booth, renewing the acquaintance of arranger Charlie Calello, to whom he'd been introduced by Brian Interland during an earlier visit to Boston by the Four Seasons. WBZ music director Ed Logue added Tony's record the first week, and WMEX added it to the WMEX Good Guys Top 40 the following week. The WMEX offices were located in the Fenway Park structure itself, on Brookline Avenue where NESN offices were located in recent years.

Ernie Campagna was still the music director at WMEX in 1966 and saw The Standells' "Dirty Water" added to the nighttime show of the immensely popular disc jockey Arnie "Woo Woo" Ginsburg. It wasn't long until it was added to the station's overall playlist. Before the year was out, Campagna found a position in promotion at Mutual Distributors, and one of the lines he handled was Capitol's Tower label.

Campagna's tune "Playing The Field" did well enough for Tony C as his first record, getting some good local write-ups in the Boston press. Producer/manager Ed Penney knew Merv Griffin and got Tony on Merv's show and also on the *Tonight Show* with Johnny Carson (Johnny had Yogi Berra on as a guest the same night.) Tony's next release on Penn-Tone was called "Limited Man" and it was a big departure from the style of his first releases. "Limited Man" sounded a lot like Johnny Rivers' "Secret Agent Man" and had slightly psychedelic undertones, which made it very identifiable with the times. The other cut on the record was "Please Play Our Song," another unusual tune. Rather than picking up on contemporary styles, this song was unusually reminiscent of a Jazz Era song.

George Denham, co-host of the "Yesterday's Memories" Saturday evening Oldies show on Boston's South Shore radio station WADT-FM, has what he believes is the most comprehensive collection of original of Tony C recordings—which he still broadcasts occasionally on his show. Denham has been on the radio for more than 20 years. His show is heard locally on the air and worldwide, every Saturday night, on the Internet. As a big Red Sox fan, Denham said he really enjoys it when a listener requests a Conigliaro song. "Tony's songs were never hits nationally, so if they ask for one of his songs, I know right

RCA Victor Inks Red Sox Rookie

NEW YORK—Boston Red Sox rookie star Tony Conigliaro will be wielding a microphone as well as a baseball bat since inking an exclusive pact with RCA Victor Records.

The 20-year old slugger who hit 24 homeruns for the Sox last season marked his debut for the diskery with "Why Don't They Understand" produced by Ed Penney and Al Kashea and now being distributed nationally.

Cash Box—March 13, 1965

away that the caller is not only a Red Sox fan but that they really know their oldies. I am really happy to play them...to keep his memory alive and honor his love of music."[6]

Denham observed that after his first two records, Conigliaro seemed to be searching for a style and the best vehicle to get his musical career off the ground. "Playing the Field" sold out its first pressing, somewhere around 10,000 to 15,000 copies, and Tony was doing well enough with the Penn-Tone label to leverage a deal with major recording company RCA Victor and a sizable $25,000 advance. "I Was There" was his first RCA Victor release and with it Tony had the opportunity to work with two of the industry's biggest songwriters at the time—Gerry Goffin and Carole King. "I Was There" was a very sweet, love lost, romantic ballad with pizzicato strings and full orchestration very similar to King's own 1962 Top 40 hit, "It Might As Well Rain Until September." The B-side was called "When You Take More Than You Give," an up-tempo number with a British Invasion feel to it mixed in with a little rhythm and blues.

A kind of novelty song, "Little Red Scooter" b/w "I Can't Get Over You" was released by RCA Victor in 1966 and as if to underscore the fact that his recording career was not undermining his baseball career, Tony was named to the American League All-Star Team that July. "Little Red Scooter" was another Ernie Campagna song.

None of Tony's songs ever reached the Top 40 or even the national charts but they were big hits in Boston, and teenaged girls swooned over Tony like Elvis or the Beatles whenever he made a personal appearance—but then they did the same thing at the ballpark! "Little Red Scooter" was a cute up-tempo song with a tenor sax providing rhythm and a guitar picking bridge with a "go-go" dance beat. "Scooter" was a sort of local version of the 1964 Top 10 one-hit-wonder song, "Little Honda" done by a group of Southern California studio musicians who called themselves the Hondells. "I Can't Get Over You" was probably Conigliaro's best song—with a great cha-cha rhythm in the tradition of a vintage Ricky Nelson song (think "Travelin' Man").

Tony gave priority to his baseball career and would only work the music side during the off-season; this hurt his chances in another equally competitive industry, and record sales were disappointing by major label standards. Penney recalls that they were not allowed to portray Tony in his baseball uniform, which might have helped from a marketing perspective, "so we had to have pictures of him wearing a cardigan with a baseball glove." RCA promoted the records nationally, particularly in American League cities, but sales were not sufficiently strong and they dropped their young artist early in 1966. The reigning home run champion was probably not greatly disappointed.

Ed Penney said the two agreed on priorities: "We both agreed that he would not promote the record, wouldn't go anywhere during the baseball season—which, of course, with spring training and all, took up most of the year."[7]

Although Tony was enjoying tremendous success and admiration both on and off the field in the summer of 1966, his good fortune and his very life almost came to an end just one year later on the night of August 18, 1967, when the 22-year-old All-Star was hit on the cheekbone by a fastball thrown by pitcher Jack Hamilton of the California Angels. While Red Sox fans watched in horror, their young hero lay motionless at home plate until he was rushed to the hospital. The injury nearly cost him his eyesight and he was out for the rest of the season and the entire next year before making a successful but very brief return to the Red Sox in 1969 and 1970. Ed Penney was at the game that fateful August day, sitting with Sal Conigliaro. Ironically, the very day before, Ted Williams had taken Penney aside, when Ed was visiting his sons in Lakeville, Massachusetts at the Ted Williams Baseball Camp. Ted told Ed that Tony was crowding the plate too much, and he needed to back off. Ed conveyed the message to Tony, who laughed it off: "Do you realize I'm 0-for-12 the last three games? Nobody's going to be throwing at me. They're going to serve it up."[8] Pitchers can't always throw the ball where they intend, and this one unfortunately just got away from Hamilton.

In the winter of 1967, after Tony had been discharged from the hospital, Tony and Penney did put in a fair amount of work on Tony's singing career, with a Merv Griffin concert among the highlights. Merv even spoke at the annual Baseball Writers dinner in Boston, which helped promote the show.

After the 1970 season, Tony was traded to the California Angels, but the deterioration of his sight caused by the injury in 1967 became worse. He only played for half the season.

Tony might have met up with Jerry Kasenetz and Jeff Katz, the "Kings of Bubblegum Music," while living out in California during his brief stint with the California Angels. Kasenetz and Katz had produced the 1910 Fruitgum Company ("Simon Says"), the Music Explosion ("Little Bit Of Soul") and other 1960s pop groups. The two producers formed Magna Glide Records in 1975 and Tony cut a demonstration 45 for them called "Poetry." This was Tony's last attempt at a commercial record—a demo "comeback song" that ironically paralleled his failed comeback attempt to baseball in Boston that same season. Like his 21-game valiant last stand with the Red Sox in 1975, this song marked the end of his recording career. The record was beautifully arranged with soaring strings and gentle vocal backups over a wah-wah electric guitar. It was a moderate tempo love song that had a message, or story to it in the style of artists like John Denver, The Eagles, and Hamilton, Joe Frank & Reynolds. Although "Poetry" may have been Tony's last commercial release, in 1983 two more of his songs were privately pressed and made public in conjunction with a benefit concert held for him at Boston's Symphony Hall.

The story of Tony Conigliaro began like a dream, a Hollywood fantasy that was the envy of many. Fame on the playing field, the opportunity to become a recording artist, even dating models and starlets like Playboy cover girl Mamie Van Doren marked Tony's early career. But after the 1967 eye injury, things never were the same. The Hollywood fantasy soon became a Shakespearean tragedy. In February 1982, Tony, age 37, suffered a serious heart attack and slipped into a coma.

Dionne Warwick had formed a strong friendship with Conigliaro lasting for many years and she, along with a celebrity cast put on a benefit for Tony called "An Evening for Tony C." at Symphony Hall in Boston on April 15, 1983. Others luminaries contributing to the night were Marvin Hamlisch, Frank Sinatra, Ted Williams, Bobby Orr, Willie Mays, and Joe DiMaggio.

The private pressing, *An Evening For Tony C.*, featuring two songs by Tony, was released in conjunction with the benefit that raised $200,000 in his name. The songs on the record had of course been taped before Tony's illness, and were pressed in association with Dionne Warwick's own production company. One side featured "We Can Make The World A Whole Lot Brighter," which was a very late '60s/early '70s sounding song with a Carpenters-style harmony and backup vocals. It started out a bit like Warwick's "I'll Never Fall In Love Again," with muted horns in the beginning and acoustic guitar throughout. Tony had come a long way musically on this upbeat, socially conscious song. The other cut, "You Fill My Life With Music," definitely had the Warwick/Burt Bacharach/Hal David imprint on it. Lots of muted horns and another strong female chorus backup make the love song sound a lot like Warwick's "Walk On By."

Tony Conigliaro never fully recovered after his heart attack and died in 1990 at the age of 45.

That same year the Boston Red Sox established the Tony Conigliaro Award, which is given annually to the major league baseball player "who best

WORC — 1310 ON YOUR DIAL - 5000 WATTS

WORCESTER'S OFFICIAL REQUEST SURVEY
Phone 752-7311 for your favorite songs

BASED 100% ON LISTENER REQUESTS --- WEEK ENDING AUGUST 4, 1967

JULY 15	22	29	AUG 4			
30	8	1	2	LIMITED MAN	TONY CONIGLIARO (Penn)	4
11	4	1	2	AIRPLANE SONG	ROYAL GUARDSMEN	6
4	2	4	3	PLEASANT VALLEY SUNDAY	MONKEES (Colgems)	5
1	5	2	4	ALL YOU NEED IS LOVE	BEATLES (Capitol)	5
5	6	6	5	WINDY	ASSOCIATION (Warner Brothers)	12
7	11	9	6	MERCY, MERCY, MERCY	BUCKINGHAMS (Columbia)	6
8	7	12	7	SOCIETY'S CHILD	JANIS IAN (Verve)	9
-	22	16	8	COME BACK WHEN YOU GROW UP	BOBBY VEE (Liberty)	3
9	12	8	9	LITE MY FIRE	DOORS (Electra)	5
22	21	10	10	THIS IS THE TWELFTH NIGHT	ENERGY PACKAGE (Laurie)	5
2	1	5	11	CARRIE ANNE	HOLLIES (Epic)	8
-	3	7	12	LITTLE BIT O' SOUL	MUSIC EXPLOSION (Laurie)	4
6	9	11	13	SHADES OF GREY	MONKEES/WILL-O-BEES (Colgems)	9
27	26	13	14	THANK THE LORD FOR THE NIGHT TIME	NEIL DIAMOND (Bang)	4
-	33	29	15	BABY YOU'RE A RICH MAN	BEATLES (Capitol)	5
-	-	27	16	SILENCE IS GOLDEN ***	TREMELOS (Epic)	2
19	13	17	17	RUN, RUN, RUN	THIRD RAIL (Epic)	5
16	15	18	18	SHE'S MINE	NIGHT RIDERS (Hills)	6
37	30	19	19	GET THE MESSAGE	BRIAN HYLAND (Philips)	4
-	-	-	20	IT'S THE LITTLE THINGS ***	SONNY & CHER (Atco)	1
-	24	15	21	IF YOU LOVE HER, CHERISH HER	DON & GOODTIMES (Epic)	3
14	16	14	22	A LITTLE BIT SLOWER	JON & ROBIN (Abnak)	9
12	29	24	23	DAY IN THE LIFE	BEATLES (Capitol)	10
-	-	34	24	WHITE RABBIT	JEFFERSON AIRPLANE (RCA)	3
12	10	22	25	VISIT TO A SAD PLANET	LEONARD NIMOY (Dot LP)	4
-	-	31	26	SGT. PEPPER	BEATLES (Reprise)	10
20	27	20	27	THERE GOES MY EVERYTHING	ENGELBERT HUMPERDINCK (London)	8
-	-	-	28	SO RIGHT TO BE IN LOVE ***	ROYAL GUARDSMEN (Laurie)	1
-	-	-	29	REFLECTIONS ***	D. ROSS & SUPREMES (Motown)	1
-	-	-	30	LOOK IN YOUR EYES	SCOTT MACKENZIE	1

SHIFTIN'
31 GOTTA GET AWAY Fantasia (Mala)
32 SUNTAN & WINDBLOWN Bobby Staff (RCA)
33 FORGIVE ME Babs Tino (Kapp)
34 LET THE GOOD TIMES ROLL Sigler (Parkway)
35 MARIANNE 4 Seasons (Philips)
36 ROMEO & JULIET Michael (USA)
37 JILL Gary Lewis (Liberty)
38 YOU KNOW WHAT I MEAN Turtles
39 HEROES AND VILLIANS Beach Boys
40 STAY & LOVE ME ALL SUMMER Jason
(*** Instant Hit)

GOOD GUY GOLD - 2½ Years Ago
THE NAME GAME Shirley Ellis
LITTLE EGYPT Elvis Presley
DOWNTOWN Petula Clark
BYE BYE BABY 4 Seasons
EIGHT DAYS A WEEK Beatles
LAUGH, LAUGH Beau Brummels
ROCK & ROLL MUSIC Beatles
WHOSE HEART ARE YOU BREAKING Connie Francis
YOU'VE LOST THAT LOVIN' FEELING Righteous Bros
THIS DIAMOND RING Gary Lewis

Singer Tony "C" eclipses the Beatles on the local charts! Courtesy of Ed Penney.

overcomes an obstacle and adversity through the attributes of spirit, determination, and courage...." Just like Tony Conigliaro.

In the autumn of 1966, even with their singing slugger Tony C continuing to star in the lineup, the Red Sox once again made their perennial fade from the pennant race. Forty years had passed since the American League pennant had last flown over Fenway.

A 1975 strategy session. L to R: Brian Interland (Director of National Promotion, London Records), Tony Conigliaro, Jack Karney (VP sales, WBCN), Kenny Greenblatt (WBCN), Ed Kleven (Tony's manager), Willis Demalt (New England rep, London Records). Courtesy of Brian Interland.

When the annual migration of the thousands and thousands of college students hit the city that fall, "Dirty Water" was one of the biggest party songs at fraternity houses, area nightclubs and bars, and at every Boston "mixer"—the 1960s collegiate version of a high school record hop—held in the Hub. It remained extremely popular for several years locally, along with songs like "96 Tears," "Wild Thing," "Good Vibrations," "Paint It Black," and lasting party favorites like "Twist and Shout," "Louie Louie," and "Satisfaction."

In 1966, college life was considerably different than it is today. The concept of co-ed college dormitories was as far-fetched as a man walking on the moon. The female college students of Boston had "dorm mothers," usually matronly spinsters or widows who watched every move the girls made—especially when a guy came calling. The young ladies had to sign in and out of the dorms at night, dress in skirts to eat their meals in the dorm cafeteria (no shorts or slacks were allowed except for breakfast on the weekends), and—just like the Standells sang in "Dirty Water"—had to be in by 12 o'clock. If they were late, it was a scandal, and disciplinary demerits or worse were issued to pay for that serious transgression of the rules.

But the fall of 1966, only six months before the celebrated "Summer of Love," was also a time of gradual but inexorable social evolution. Traditional values in America were beginning to be beset by radical ideas in fashion, politics, and just about everything else you could think of, particularly in music. The Standells were on that cutting edge of the musical insurgency that had swept across the Atlantic from Britain and landed in America in the early 1960s. The story of the Standells and the origins of "Dirty Water" began in a place where people had been prospecting for the American Dream for more that a hundred years—California.

Dick Dodd—The Early Years

Dick Dodd, the drummer and lead singer for the Standells, gave us the voice that begins "Dirty Water" by saying, "I'm gonna tell you a story...."

Dodd had an interesting and unusual journey to his date with destiny as a rock and roll singer. A child television star in southern California and a teenage performer in Las Vegas, his story begins at the end of World War II. Born Joseph Richard Dodd to a Mexican mother (Florinda Murillo) and an Irish-American father, Dick Dodd was born on October 27, 1945 in Hermosa Beach, California, though he was raised in the adjacent community of Redondo Beach. His father was in the U.S. Army at the time. "I never did meet my father," Dick admits. "He left when I was just months old. His parents found out that he married a Mexican girl and was going to have a baby. In 1945, that was kind of like a real bad mixed marriage and I never did meet him." Despite having the same name as his father, Dick knows little about his father's family except that they were from Oklahoma, they came to California, and they took his father home with them.

Florinda Dodd worked at a J. J. Newberry 5&10 cent store to help support herself, her mother Juanita Hernandez, and her young son. Dick had no brothers or sisters. Florinda had a brother Leo who worked making aircraft parts. Grandmother Juanita had come from Jalisco, Mexico, immigrating to the United States in 1923. She never did fully assimilate and spoke little English, often asking Dick what this or that person was saying. Dick grew up speaking Spanish with all his relatives and is fluent bilingually to this day. He attended Catholic school through eighth grade, and then went to the public Redondo Union High School.

Dodd was always relatively small for his age (though he's 5' 11" tall today) and found out early that his small stature, charming personality, and particularly his penchant for entertaining endeared him to people. He played a little accordion, but that wasn't where his future lay. "I started out tap dancing and singing. I had the knack of remembering songs when I was little. I don't know why. It just happened and I guess I had a little rhythm going, so I took up tap dancing. Back then it was, you know, OK for a guy to do tap dancing...."

Dick continued to dance and eventually was dancing in the right place, at the right time, and had the right talents to become part of one of America's most famous television programs—Walt Disney's *Mickey Mouse Club*. "I had been dancing for some years and ...we had dance recitals where you would sell tickets and your mom and your aunts and all that would come to see you put on a show. Then in 1955, the Walt Disney Studios sent out a whole bunch of talent scouts checking out all these recitals at all the different dance schools in the Los Angeles area. Back then there was a dance school on almost every corner. This gentleman saw me and came back stage after the show and gave me...my grandmother and myself...his card that said 'Walt Disney Productions' on it. He said we are really interested in you. I thought, 'Walt Disney?

What, am I going to be in a cartoon, am I going to be a voice or something? Wow!'

"We called him back and learned that there were going to be auditions for something called the Mouseketeers and he asked me if I wanted to do it. We didn't even know what Mouseketeers were. I got to go up there to the Disney Studios in Burbank and audition. It was really a big cattle call, there was, like, 300 kids a day and they just wanted to check kids out to see if you would take direction when they told you to sit down and be

Dickie Dodd, Mouseketeer. Courtesy of Dick Dodd.

quiet and so forth. They didn't want any hassles. And Walt; Walt was there every day and he was a part of picking out the kids."

Casting began in March 1955 and little Dickie Dodd successfully passed the many rounds of auditions and became one of the original *Mickey Mouse Club* Mouseketeers. "I was nine that first season," he recalled. "It was 1955. There were 23–24 kids that became Mouseketeers. Twelve kids would be off learning a show, and then another six would be in rehearsal for the next show ...there was a 'red' team, a 'white' team, and a 'blue' team that rehearsed different shows or numbers in support of the main group. Annette, Cubby, Karen, all of them were the main group so it kind of circled around them and different kids would be learning stuff that they would have to learn for the show. While they were learning, this other group would be rehearsing, and this other group was in school. We would be tutored on the set while filming. We had school three hours a day and then we would go back to our local schools after a show was shot."

Dick's mother had to work, so his grandmother took him to rehearsals, traveling on public buses. It wasn't easy. From Redondo Beach to Burbank required two long bus rides, transferring in downtown Los Angeles, but the commitment and sacrifices paid off. It was his first paid job, and he was bringing in $245 a week, much more than the $50 a week or so his mother was earning at J.J. Newberry. Florinda was a clerk and cashier who worked for the company for nearly 30 years, becoming a floor manager in later years.

The whole crew, with Dickie in front row far left. Annette Funicello is in the middle of the third row. Courtesy of Dick Dodd.

Dick was always popular around town. At one point the city of Redondo Beach even crowned him "Prince Charming." He remembers, "I was their favorite little guy. There was always something about me in *The Daily Breeze*; I even wrote for them when I was in high school, just about the game that Friday night, that sort of thing."

The *Mickey Mouse Club* had its television premiere on October 3, 1955, though the Mouseketeers had appeared in a July 17 special celebrating the grand opening of the original Disneyland.

Little "Dickie's" tenure with Disney as a Mouseketeer was limited, yet by the time he was 11 he imagined that he would be in show business for the rest of his life. "I wanted to be a Sinatra or somebody like that. I just wanted to be an all-around entertainer, singer, and dancer. I wanted to play Las Vegas, you know, do that whole bit. After I left the Mouseketeers, I was going, 'Oh my God, I'm eleven and a half and I need to find a job!'"

"I had always been working and when you are that age you think that things are not going to stop. You think that you are just going to go to the studio everyday no matter what, and no matter what they tell you to do, you are going to

Gisele McKenzie with her four little guys. Dick is to Gisele's left. Courtesy of Dick Dodd.

do it. So, when I finished at Disney, I had my mom call up this dance studio where Gisele McKenzie was holding auditions to pick out four little guys. I got to do that. She used to be on a show called the *Hit Parade*, and then she did her own television show called the *Gisele McKenzie Show*. Jack Benny was her mentor, because she, [like Benny,] was also a very talented violin player. Instead of having four big guys dancing with her she had four little guys. We opened her show. We were on a full season on NBC, and we went to Vegas with Jack Benny. I was like 12 or 13 years old. When I started working for Gisele we played lots of clubs in Reno, Vegas, and Lake Tahoe. We would do that circuit. I stayed with her for a couple of years. The first season was the television thing and then we did the Vegas kind of thing with Jack Benny for a couple of years."

As time went on and Dick became a teenager, he did less and less dancing and began to concentrate on singing and playing music. He did get a bit part in a film out of it, though. "I think the last thing I ever danced and sang in was *Bye Bye Birdie* with Ann-Margret and Bobby Rydell. I was in that. Then I started playing the drums—I thought that I was getting serious as a drummer.

I started playing, without really having a drum set. I had a snare I bought from Annette, and a high hat, that was it—that was my drum set." Dick says he first learned to play the drums from Cubby O'Brien, when they both were Mouseketeers. He paid Annette $20 for that basic drum kit. "What she was doing with a snare drum, I'll never know."

Dick joined a local surf band called the Belairs as a drummer and singer. Paul Johnson and Eddie Bertrand had formed the group and actually had a single in 1961 with "Mr. Moto," a tune they recorded, then placed with the Arvee label. It was released after being remixed by Arvee's producer Sonny Bono. They played some clubs around L.A., even earning billing above another new group called the Beach Boys. Co-author of "Mr. Moto" with Johnson was band member Richard Delvy, who quit the band (reminding us how young these guys were) after an argument with Eddie Bertrand's mother! Dick knew both Paul and Eddie and was invited to join the band. Dick had been playing in a band called The Casuals, and was asked to sit in.

The Belairs even became the house band at a club in Redondo Beach that was named after them: it became the Bel Air Club. They also got booked on a number of area television shows, playing for hosts like Wink Martindale, Bob Eubanks, Lloyd Thaxton, and Sam Riddle. They continued to cut some sides, and Arvee gave a half-hearted release to the single "Volcanic Action" in 1962, but Bertrand reports that a rift broke out in the band over musical direction.

As Dick matured, the music scene in his native Southern California was changing as well and he was increasingly attracted to the new instrumental "surf music" evolution in rock and roll. Southern California surfer and musician Dick Dale, the Ventures ("Walk Don't Run," "Perfidia"), the Chantays ("Pipeline"), and the Surfaris ("Wipe Out") were the innovating forces that created the surf sound in the early 1960s. "Around that time, the surf band thing started. It was all-instrumental, and I figured, 'How hard is that?' I started getting into rock and roll, and people started singing on surf records (the Beach Boys, Jan and Dean). Rock and roll was just hittin' it, so I started to go in that direction. Just kept playing."

Both Eddie and Dick were taken with the new surf sound, while Johnson and the others wanted to stick with the older rhythm and blues based rock and roll sound. Bertrand started up a new band, naming it Eddie and the Showmen, and Dick left the Belairs to go with Eddie late in 1962. It was a good move. The new band was much more successful. Dick remembers, "We had a couple of limited hits as the Belairs, and then became Eddie and the Showmen when Dick Dale was doing all-instrumental surf music. We were a big surf band—we packed this place in Buena Park near Anaheim, DJ Reb Foster's Retail Clerks Hall. We used to play there every weekend and we used to drive from Redondo Beach to it...we had gigs every weekend but we were still in high school so that really just became a job to put gas in the car and stuff."

Maybe they liked surf music because they liked to surf. Eddie told author

Robert Dalley that he and Dick had grown up in nearby neighborhoods and spent a lot of time at the beach. "We rode waves every day. We enjoyed the surf and playing the music everyone liked to hear." They added Bob Knight on sax and a couple of members from the Baymen on bass and rhythm guitar, calling themselves The Belltones at first. "We would really get the neighbors mad at us for playing so loud," rhythm guitarist Rob Edwards recalled. "There was more than one occasion where the neighbors sprayed us with the water hose to shut us up!" Their first gig was for Wink Martindale at the Rainbow Gardens in Pomona, backing up Bobby Bare and Trini Lopez. In March 1963, now named Eddie & the Showmen, they cut a couple of songs which Eddie's father Bert produced.

Bert Bertrand had just sold his liquor store to a man who'd recently left Liberty Records. Introductions were made and Liberty's Don Blocker was excited by the music, signing the band on the spot. It was, Eddie looks back, "really funny, as we were signed by Liberty Records about the same time Liberty turned down 'I Want To Hold Your Hand' by the Beatles."[1]

Eddie and the Showmen played every Friday night in Buena Park for nearly two years. They played a number of other clubs in the area, and even traveled as far as Fresno and Bakersfield. The largest audience they played for was the Hollywood Bowl in October 1963, at a YMCA event hosted by Art Linkletter. The Surfaris and the Beach Boys shared the bill. Their December 1963 release of "Mr. Rebel" (named with L.A. deejay Reb Foster in mind) reached number four on the local charts. It was early in 1964 when Dick departed in order to work with Jackie DeShannon. "The rest of the group was very disappointed, because she did not want the whole group to go," Dick recalls. "I had to decide what was best for me, so I left."[3]

Ed Cobb and The Four Preps

About the same time young Dickie Dodd was rehearsing and filming episodes of *The Mickey Mouse Club* in Burbank, four teenaged buddies had just formed a vocal group over at nearby Hollywood High School. The group soon found fame as recording artists the Four Preps featuring Bruce Belland as the lead singer, with Glen Larson, Marvin Inabnett (who later changed his surname to Ingram), and Ed Cobb as backup. Ten years later, Ed Cobb would write "Dirty Water" and have it recorded by the Standells.

The Four Preps recorded pop material in four-part harmony and always maintained a style that was thought to be squeaky-clean and rather "white bread" in its content. Even their name implied that they were clean-cut students—associating themselves with the enviable collegiate fashion look and attitudes of the time, as opposed to the greaser styles of many 1950s' rock and roll groups. Their big hits—1958's "26 Miles (Santa Catalina)" and "Big Man," and 1960's song "Down by the Station"—helped create and foster their image.

But Ed Cobb had a wide range of talent and interests that went far beyond his assigned role as one of the well-groomed and conservative Four Preps. He would later be involved in entertainment management and as a creative singer-songwriter; Cobb was a real hard-charger. Fellow Prep Bruce Belland characterized Ed as "a bulldozer...he would just plow ahead." Even thought it belied the image of his role as one of the clean-cut, middle of the road Preps, it was not really a great departure in 1966 for Cobb to write what later became considered a prototypical punk, grunge, or garage rock hit song.

Ed Cobb died of a rare form of leukemia in 1999, sadly before he could learn that his composition was finding new life and new fans as the victory theme song for Red Sox Nation.

Cobb was born February 25, 1938 in Los Angeles. He told a writer in 1990 that he didn't meet his father until he was eight years old and didn't meet his mother until he was ten.[1] In the meantime, he'd gone to live on a goat farm— or a pig farm or a chicken farm in Arkansas. Friends and associates also agree that Cobb had a real flair for the dramatic. There was unanimity about him living on a farm in Arkansas, but the very fact that three different associates recalled three different barnyard animals Ed said were raised at the farm may have reflected Cobb's penchant for embroidering a good story. He lived with an elderly lady on the farm, he told Peter Van Houten. "We had no electricity or plumbing, so everything was a chore. I liked it. She was the closest thing I've ever come to [meeting] a saint."[2] Her name was Lizzie Sanders and she lived

Ed on the farm with Lizzie Sanders, 1945. Courtesy of Heather Cobb Isbell.

in Fort Smith. A 1945 photograph shows her with goats, a cow, a horse—and a seven-year-old Ed Cobb.

Ed's stepmother Elaine Shipley explains the real story. His birth mother Pauline received custody of little Ed when she and Eddie's father split up, but she was only "about 16, maybe going on 17" and not really well-suited to raise a young child. Pauline's mother took Eddie in. She—the grandmother—remarried and her new husband didn't want a child around, so Eddie was packed off to live with some cousins in Arkansas. His great-aunt Lizzie Sanders visited these cousins, and "she felt Eddie was so mistreated and that life was so bad for him, she offered to take him to live with her on her farm. That was a Godsend for him. He really loved Aunt Liz and really enjoyed life there. She was very into religion and read the Bible every day. She didn't have a farm that was modernized. She was quite elderly but she plowed with a horse. He helped her. He had all kinds of chores, which he enjoyed. He was really good doing things that helped you."[3]

Eddie's father, Ed Cobb, Sr., had a good job during the war as an aircraft and engine mechanic for Douglas, and then worked for a while as a railroad engineer in Winslow, Arizona and San Bernardino, California. When he and his second wife Elaine got engaged, he wanted her to meet his son, only to learn that Eddie was no longer in California. Ed and Elaine wanted to provide a home for Eddie, and were able to obtain custody. Roy Claxton, an uncle from Dallas went out to Fort Smith and talked with Aunt Liz and Ed, and Ed decided he'd like to live with his father so arrangements were made to "carpool" him back to California. Elaine remembers, "He was brought right to the house. This gangly, almost a towhead, sort of sandy-haired blue-eyed kid got out of the car and gave us all big hugs. And that was that—we had a boy!" Ed was 7½ years old.

The family ultimately moved back to Los Angeles to live. Young Ed's best friend and Four Preps founder Bruce Belland shared some memories on meeting the composer of "Dirty Water."

"Ed and I met when I was ten and he was nine. I had just come out to Los Angeles from Chicago. My old man was a preacher who took over the West Hollywood Community Church. About a week after we moved, I was bemoaning the fact that I didn't have anybody to play with, I had no friends.... My mom woke me up one Saturday morning and said, "Get up, get up, a family is moving in across the street and I see they have a son that looks about your age." I went over to my bedroom window and looked out across the street. They were unloading the moving van and stuff and there was Ed. I was always self-conscious that I was shorter than everybody else so I said to my mother, "I can't be his friend." Mom replied, "What do you mean?" I said, "He is too tall! I'll never get along with him."

"I went over and met him...I played the ukulele at the time...and we started learning songs on his front porch. We'd sit around and sing songs on his front porch. As every kid in my neighborhood did, he started going to my dad's church. We had a very active youth group there. We played volleyball on Friday nights and we had a Coke machine in the game room, and it was just a real lively center of the community. Every kid in West Hollywood went to my dad's church and participated in the activities, including Ed."

"My mom talked him into getting into the choir with me...it was a volunteer amateur choir so it wasn't any great shakes. I learned all my music from my mom because she was a piano, choral, choir, and voice teacher. One of the things we did after a while was to go down to the Saint Paul's Baptist Church down in Southeast Los Angeles. Our church service on Sunday nights was from 7:30 to 9:00 P.M. They went on the air down there in Los Angeles from 10 to 11 P.M. every Sunday night on a station called KFWB here in Los Angeles. Their opening song was "I'm So Glad That Jesus Lifted Me...."

"We would get in a bus, 25 or 30 of us kids from my father's church, all chaperoned, and we'd go down to the Saint Paul's Baptist Church....They were all very hospitable to us, all very friendly....They would bring us in and get us seats, and we would listen to that Black gospel music. We just...it was so imbued in our system that both Ed and I always had a feeling for the slightly more raw feeling, the more soulful feeling if you will, from those years with that Black music."[4]

The Four Preps came into existence in 1955 while all four were students at Hollywood High to perform in the schools talent show. There were a lot of girls going out for the show—many more girls than boys—and Bruce Belland and his friend Glen Larson thought it might be a good opportunity to get to know some of the girls. They asked the tall and good-looking Cobb about joining in with them to be part of their vocal group. According to Ed, "The only reason I was asked to join was that I was tall. No one asked if I could sing. We just wanted to meet some girls."[5]

Indeed, 6'4" Cobb added another dimension to the group that became the Four Preps; Belland notes: "He was the dreamboat of the group." The lopsided ratio of girls to boys in the show was the incentive Belland also used to convince Lincoln Mayorga, an extremely gifted fellow student and pianist, to help arrange the nascent group that would become the Four Preps. The quartet worked hard for a week on

Ed's good looks helped Hollywood High's Four Preps meet lots of girls. Courtesy of Heather Cobb Isbell.

"Goodnight Sweetheart" and they took first place in the competition. Lincoln Mayorga would become the group's permanent arranger and was eventually known as the "Fifth Prep."

In time, Ed's family moved from Hollywood and he graduated from South Pasadena High. But the group was launched. Ed's adoptive mother Elaine remembers the boys singing, imitating other groups at first, then entertaining at school functions, and developing their own style. Her stepsister was in the radio business and suggested they make a demo record and take it around. They did, and took it around to agent after agent, ultimately landing both an agent and a deal with Capitol Records in 1956 to record a slow doo-wop number called "Dreamy Eyes." The song reached #56 on the national charts. At the time (this was well before the Jackson Five), it was said that the Four Preps were the youngest group ever signed to a record label. They needed to appear with their parents in order to legally sign the contract. The Preps drove to their gigs in an old beat-up Mercury station wagon the first couple of years, played a lot of college parties around the city and cut a couple of albums, but nothing dramatic happened until they changed their sound to one more their own. The song "26 Miles" written by Belland and Larson became a big national hit and a gold record—they were on their way. The Preps sold over 25 million albums in a short period of time and were the #1 act booked at college campuses.

The money they earned helped Ed indulge in flying lessons and his love of horses—born out of watching John Wayne and Randolph Scott movies as a kid. The several gold records that followed ("Big Man," "Down by the Station," "More Money for You and Me") enabled Ed to buy a ranch in Hidden Hills, California. He later bought a bigger spread in Star Valley, Wyoming, not far from Jackson Hole. "I bought a Corvette and he bought a horse. He was a cowboy," Bruce Belland laughed. Cobb bought his first thoroughbred in 1964 when he was just 26 and he ultimately became expert at breeding. He successfully bred at least two world's record holders: Chigger's Spirit and Bug's Alive Time. In 1997, he was the top breeder of champions in the country, recognized by the Appaloosa Horse Association, having had four horses that had set new track records as well as the two world champions.[6]

Ed's fascination with flying and his love of horses were interests that he shared with his second wife Lennie Sorensen Cobb—who was quite a woman according to Bruce Belland and Ed's other friends. When they first met, Ed told her that he was an airplane pilot and bragged to her that he flew a Cessna 310. She simply said she thought that was nice and modestly mentioned that she was in the transportation industry. He wanted to know more about her career but she demurred. They found they shared an interest in horses, Ed breeding racehorses and Lennie playing polo in her spare time. After dating Lennie for a while, he flew out to Hawaii, where she lived, to watch her at a polo match and kept on pressing to learn more about her work. Finally she told him, "OK, I'm a 747 captain." As it happened, she was the first female 747 captain to fly for Continental Airlines. She laughs, "He said it's the smallest he ever felt in his life."

The material the Preps worked with was chosen out of necessity, fashioned into something that seemed very tame and simple compared to the new rock and roll and rhythm and blues that was beginning to dominate the pop charts and radio play in America at that time.

Belland reflected on the kind of music the Four Preps would concentrate on. "I want to say this in the kindest way possible—when you are in a group like that, in a sense musically and rhythmically, at least, you are reduced to the lowest common dominator. The guy that has the *least* sense of rhythm, you kind of have to go with him otherwise you're not going to ever sing together. Ed, who had a lot of rhythm and feeling, started to get more and more frustrated with the fact that stuff he'd bring in that he had written or had thought about, or even an old song he heard that he wanted to arrange for us with a Black beat...Some guys in the group could never get with it, could never get comfortable with it. The fourth guy with the Preps, Marv, sang in the Mitchell Boys Choir. He was in *Going My Way* with Bing Crosby. He was one of the little boys. He was a rather traditional trained musician so he had some trouble with the rhythmical things, too."

"Ed got more and more frustrated," Belland continued. "Plus, Glen and I were very, very controlling. We had written '26 Miles,' we had organized the group, and had asked Ed and Marv to be in the Preps, so we considered it our

The Four Preps: Marv, Bruce, Glen, and Ed. Courtesy of Bruce Belland.

group and what we said went. Ed got more and more resentful and uninspired because we would just turn down everything he brought in. So then he started to write just for himself."

The Four Preps were making it big in the recording industry for Capitol Records in the late 1950s and early 1960s, appearing as Ricky Nelson's backup group on the *Adventures of Ozzie and Harriet* TV show. Bruce Belland secured a recurring solo role as Rick's comical buddy "Bruce" for several seasons. The Preps also landed a role in the first *Gidget* movie with Sandra Dee and James Darren as the group that entertained the Malibu teens during the big luau scene on the beach.

Aside from his Four Prep responsibilities, Ed Cobb was also developing into an accomplished songwriter and producer and was heading in a direction that would eventually lead him to the Standells—a Hollywood lounge band that would make his yet-to-be written "Dirty Water" a national hit. He was gradually less interested in the four-part harmonies of the Preps, experimenting with writing music that ran the gamut from country to rhythm and blues.

Cobb teamed up with the unofficial "fifth" Prep—Lincoln Mayorga, the pianist, conductor, arranger, and singing coach of the group—to do some creative work that represented a distinct departure from the traditional musical style of the Four Preps. According to Belland, "One year, about 1957 or 1958, Ed took Lincoln aside and said, 'I want start a group called the Piltdown Men.' Ed had read about the whole archaeological hoax that happened about a prehistoric 'Missing Link' allegedly found in Sussex, England, in 1912 and wanted to do some rock and roll instrumental kind of things around it. Ed and Lincoln formed the Piltdown Men and went to Capitol Records, played some demos, and Capitol signed them. Now Ed was writing things like 'Brontosaurus Stomp' . . . rock-oriented instrumentals with Lincoln who was a real genius at getting that Black driving kind of rhythm and blues sound. 'Brontosaurus Stomp' was a bit of a hit, and they had another with 'McDonald's Cave.' It was a real interesting sound, very sax-heavy. You could almost see the dinosaurs dancing. It was a very primal, raw, kind of a rock sound. Ed really got some encouragement from that success. They weren't very big hits in the States but they were huge in England. The Piltdown Men and their music still have a big cult following in England."

Lincoln Mayorga chimed in on the idea behind the rather avant-garde early 1960s recordings he and Ed produced. "It was kind of a very simplistic rock concept. People thought it was a real band. It wasn't. We put it together with studio musicians. It was all Ed's concept. We often did well-known tunes like 'Old McDonald Had a Farm'—we called it 'McDonald's Cave.' These were all presumably prehistoric cavemen in this band. The Piltdown man discovery turned out to be a hoax, so it was perfect for our band name—because we were a hoax. We started in '60 and recorded as the Piltdown Men for Capitol until about 1963. We had two big chart records. 'Piltdown Rides Again'—based upon "The William Tell Overture"—was a hit in England, and 'Brontosaurus Stomp' was a chart record in the States. I've forgotten what position it reached. I was flattered when Ringo Starr told me that the Beatles used to listen to and were influenced by what we did as the Piltdown Men."[7]

"As the Piltdown Men started to happen, Ed started to smell some success and he stopped submitting things to the Preps," Belland observed. "He knew we weren't going to do them anyhow. We did half a dozen songs of his, a couple of which he sang lead on. I remember he wrote one called 'I'm Fallin' in Love with a Girl I Shouldn't Fall in Love With.' He did a kind of Johnny Cash thing. He was writing all different bags...country, but mainly the raw rock sound. The next thing, Lincoln, who for a couple of years had also gone to that Black church with us, got an idea to take the old standard 'Love Letters

Straight from Your Heart' and redo it with a real rhythm and blues gospel sound, a very Black gospel sound. Lincoln and Ed put that together and had a number one record with Ketty Lester."

Billboard charted "Love Letters..." at number five in March 1962 and the song charted for 11 weeks. (The song had been a prior hit for Dick Haymes in 1945 and was the title song from the 1945 movie *Love Letters*, starring Jennifer Jones and Joseph Cotten.)

Mayorga elaborated on this period, "Ed wanted to do something in a Gospel vain. I was trying to think of a standard tune that would work well. 'Love Letters' was actually a tune from a Hollywood movie composed by Victor Young and you wouldn't even recognize it from the way it was done originally. I just thought that the song was simple enough, melodic and very simple yet strong enough that we could put it in a gospel groove with those 'churchy' cords. We didn't have to put it in lush, or harmony, or jazz harmony. We could be very 'churchy' about it. So I developed that arrangement around 'Love Letters.' It became the traditional way to do the song [ever after]. Most people do it that way—the original way is rarely heard."

Belland continued discussing Ed Cobb's transition from a performer to a songwriter and producer, "Now Ed was really on his way. He was a totally instinctive writer. Ed didn't want to know how to write the melody down or how to write the notes down. I would try sometimes to teach him and he would say, 'No, no, no, no, I don't want to know that! Don't tell me that!' I never knew a guy that went more by his gut than Ed—ever. He just wrote what felt good. What he would do was... after he got a few hits... he got a ranch up in Wyoming and he would get on his horse and ride for miles with a tape recorder in his pocket and just sing songs into the tape recorder, and then fly to Los Angeles and get Lincoln to transcribe into music, hire a band, make a demo, and do it."

Lincoln Mayorga was the catalyst for the success of both the Four Preps and Ed Cobb's solo ventures in music. His talent as an arranger was of enormous value to his associates. Mayorga explained exactly what a music arranger does this way: "The term [arranger] is used very loosely. As a professional arranger we take a song or a piece of music, anything that exists in a melody form and we put the harmony to it. We write for the various instruments that we want to have play it—whether it's a solo piano or whether it's full orchestra or whether it's rhythm section and horns. Whatever it is, we prepare the setting. It involves a lot of composition. A lot of creative work is involved putting down these notes, developing the idea, writing a counter-melody, figuring out where you are going to change keys if you are planning to do that, where you are going to have a change in instrumental color, all that stuff goes into arranging. A lot of times people will talk through a song and say, for example, 'I want to go up a half tone at the end of the bridge and I want to do this or that. Those people will then say, well, I arranged it, because I talked it over with my piano player—but real arrangers are those who push the pencil late at night and work damn hard and spend many hours on a song.

"Then there is the difference between an arranger and an orchestrator. An orchestrator takes something that is fully developed and fully written out and expands it for a full orchestra. An orchestrator does much less creative work, he makes decisions about what instrumental colors are used and when. So you have a lot of orchestrators who work on films where a film composer essentially creates the music and then the orchestrator makes all the important decisions and writes it out for the full orchestra. It has changed a lot with synthesizers and midi where the composer can play into a keyboard and store that information. Then it can be printed out. Nobody has to pencil to paper anymore. It's done very easily now, but when you sit down with paper and pencil, it's a different creative process. It's slowed down and for my money is a more interesting. But then again I'm an old fashioned guy."

What Mayorga was able to accomplish from Cobb's vocal ideas could be described as an almost perfect musical collaboration resulting from an abiding friendship. "We had a very strong relationship. We never, we really never fought. There was never disagreement about money or anything like that. It was always just an above-board very comfortable relationship. I really loved Ed. He was like a brother—a very sweet person. He was very macho, very driven. Those were his faults, but he was fair in all his dealings. His word was very good—you could depend upon it."

♪ ♪ ♪

Around 1961, Ed met another collaborator who would partner with him on the business end of his musical ventures. Ed met Ray Harris when the Preps were in Birmingham, Alabama on tour. Harris worked for Capitol Records and was doing a promotion with a radio station there for the Preps' latest tune, "More Money for You and Me." Harris was Capitol's regional promotion director for the entire southern United States and had been for about six years.

"I lived in Atlanta, and I opened their office in Nashville," Harris remembered. "I met Ed when I was [still] with Capitol and soon we decided to put a loose music publishing and development partnership together. I left Capitol shortly after that and Vee-Jay Records hired me and brought me to California. Jay Lasker [the president of Vee-Jay] and Steve Clark brought me out there. I got with Ed and kibitzed a little bit and we just decided to form a partnership. A couple of days later, he said, 'Let's open a publishing company first' and we came up with the name Equinox Music. That was the first thing that we did. He had a couple of things that Motown was considering at the time—productions that he had—and I organized them into some sort of order to present them. Then we presented them to Vee-Jay. He had that Ketty Lester hit, and he said he wanted to do another one. I had given him some [promotional] help with "Love Letters" before, in the South, telling jocks what to do. So then

after we set up Equinox, we were looking for artists for us to do and to promote with Vee-Jay. Jay and Steve knew that I had this relationship with him,
and they said, "Just go ahead and do whatever you're going to do. Just give us
first choice at it—which we did."[8]

Another relationship that Ed Cobb and his new partner Ray Harris developed was with self-employed recording engineer Armin Steiner. Lincoln Mayorga, Harris, Cobb, and Steiner all joined forces on the Ketty Lester project.
"Love Letters" had been a number one record that, Steiner says, "we did with
two microphones at 2:30 in the morning. It just shows that a great song can be
recorded in a really wonderful way if it's all done just perfectly. We turned out
the lights and made one take and that was it and we knew we had a number
one record." It was the first of 10 or 11 number one records Steiner recorded
at his small, home-built studio. "I did most of Motown's records in that room,
and they all thought it was done in major studios," Steiner added.[9]

Harris continued talking about Steiner, "He was just a lovely guy, and a
genius at engineering. He had this little studio that was no bigger than a living
room. He had all this equipment, but it was in his back garage. That was where
we did most of our testing. He did a couple of black artists that we had, and we
presented them to Vee-Jay. They didn't take anything, so I said let's try a couple of other places. We tried Columbia and some other places, but we didn't
have any luck with that and Ed had to go back out on the road. Ed still was with
the Preps. He went out on the road with them until we got the business going."

Steiner was a classical violinist who engineered over 100 albums certified
as gold or platinum, according to Maureen Droney of *Mix* magazine. He has
also scored music for a large number of motion pictures. Artists for whom he
worked include Barbra Streisand, Glen Campbell, Hall & Oates, Johnny
Rivers, Dolly Parton, Heart, the Fifth Dimension, and—of particular interest
because of his later connection to the Red Sox through his song "Sweet Caroline"—Neil Diamond.

The first big hit out of Steiner's studio was "The Mountain's High" by Dick
and Dee Dee. It was a track Armin had recorded just as a demo quickly one
Sunday afternoon, and yet it became a huge chart hit in 1961. Talk about
"garage rock"—Steiner's studio was truly located over a garage, at 108 North
Formosa Avenue in Los Angeles. His grandparents lived in an old Spanish
house and built a smaller studio-style house on the lot for his parents. His
mother was a concert pianist and his father Herman Steiner was an international chess master. The smaller structure housed, first, the Herman Steiner
Chess Club and then Armin's studio. The studio itself was literally the part of
the home he was born in. It was, Steiner recalls, a room with a "phenomenal
sound. What became the control room was actually the bedroom. It had had
a rather large living room and my uncle and I tore out the kitchen so we that
could make a little alcove, and before people were building isolation booths,
I had a wonderful vocal booth."[10]

♪ ♪ ♪

Bruce Belland confirmed Ed's slow but successful shift from singer to producer. "Ed even produced for Motown Records for a while. He wrote a song (arranged by Lincoln Mayorga) called 'Every Little Bit Hurts' that was sung by Brenda Holloway on Tamla Records. It was a big hit, #13 in 1964. There again, it's a Black gospel feel. Ed always had that primal, untrained raw kind of gut way he would write songs."

By the mid-1960s, Ed Cobb and the Four Preps were doing less and less work and their hits were harder to come by, but Ed found growing success in songwriting and production. Belland recalled the way things changed for the Preps: "The British Invasion definitely was the beginning of the end for us. I remember the first time I heard 'I Want To Hold Your Hand.' I said, 'Oh my God!' In our day, when we first started, the respectable thing to do if you were a four-man group was to stand up in tuxedos in front of a microphone and have a 14-piece band playing behind you. The minute you put an instrument on...you strapped a guitar or a saxophone on, you were a *lounge* act. You were a "low-class" *lounge* act. So now here were four guys playing guitars—I remember that Capitol's executives would say, 'You know, four man groups never really get *that* famous or *that* big. They can't because kids don't know who to identify with.' Then suddenly the Beatles happened and we said, 'Yeah, right ...four man groups don't get that famous!'"

"Ed was the very first of the Four Preps to say he wanted to get out of the group and do his own thing," Belland reflected. "I remember very well where it was when Ed approached me about leaving. It was around the swimming pool at a motel in Salt Lake City. We were there to do a concert at the University of Utah. We came back after that show that night—it was a warm summer night—we were sitting around the pool and Ed said, 'Listen, I gotta tell you guys something. I'm going to have to leave the group.' By '65–'66 it was starting to wind down for us as a performing group and by 1969 it was essentially over for the original Four Preps."

Ed Cobb's road to "Dirty Water" truly started when he began to consider life after the Preps. Again, Belland remembers what occurred. "For all intents and purposes, Ed Cobb had two jobs in his adult life. One was being a member of the Four Preps, and the other as a songwriter and producer. He eventually became a partner with Seymour Heller. Seymour Heller was a legend among personal managers at the time, managing Frankie Laine, Helen O'Connell, Lawrence Welk, Jimmie Rodgers, and his biggest client—Liberace." According to Belland, "Heller was the one who put Liberace on the map and turned him into the highest paid act in the history of Vegas at the time— $250,000 a week. After Ed decided that he wanted to leave the Preps, he talked to Seymour Heller. Seymour asked Ed, 'What are you going to do when you leave the Preps?' Ed replied, 'Well, I want to produce records, and I want to get involved with managing acts and stuff.' Seymour said, 'Why don't you come and work here with me and we'll set up a company?'"

He did, but as part of a larger enterprise. By then Ray Harris and Ed Cobb had started Equinox Music, their publishing company, and were beginning to look for acts to "package"—manage, publish the songs, produce the records through another company they set up called Greengrass Productions, and then sell them to the record labels. It would be a few more years before Ed and Ray would join with Seymour Heller in a management company called Attarack Corporation, and still later in American Variety International, or simply AVI. The three also would team up with a street savvy promoter named Burt Jacobs who had done some work with Heller and at the time was the manager of the Standells. Ed Cobb's involvement with the Standells would happen as a result of this collaboration of show business "suits."

Meanwhile the Preps were still in business, at least for a while longer. David Somerville, formerly of the Diamonds ("Little Darlin'," "The Stroll," and a dozen more Top 40 hits) took Ed's place in the Preps, but things were winding down. Bruce Belland and the newest Prep went on to sing as the Belland and Somerville duo from 1969–1972, opening for a lot of big name stars. The two were sometimes jokingly referred to as "The Righteous Smothers" by those who thought their singing ability as good as the Righteous Brothers and the comedy as funny as the Smothers Brothers. Belland recalled the period and the different paths the Four Preps ventured down after the original group disbanded. "Glen Larson went on to a career as a writer selling scripts to TV shows and Marv Ingram had ventured into a non-show business career as a commodities broker."

Cobb, though, was never interested in pure management or the drudgery of setting up road trips, concerts, or personal appearances for the acts he would work with. Nor was he interested in hustling the product he produced to record labels, radio stations, and distributors. Harris would do most of the promotion and marketing. Ed would do the creative work and songwriting in the new agency and he would continue to call upon his old friend Lincoln Mayorga for composing or for arranging the music he created.

The Standells: Tony, Larry, and the Garys

While Ed Cobb, still with the Four Preps, was finding success as a song-writer and through his ventures into the production and management end of the business, Dick Dodd was looking for a new gig. "I left Eddie and the Showmen to be Jackie DeShannon's drummer. I stayed with Jackie a year or two...just before I joined the Standells."

Dick's route to joining the Standells came via the urging of DeShannon, his old acquaintance Los Angeles disc jockey Reb Foster, and Richie Podo-lor—who was to become a major force in the southern California music scene as an independent studio operator and behind the scenes contributor doing everything from recording the hottest stars to sitting in as an accomplished session musician himself. Podolor recorded several surf music albums under the name Richard Allen and went on record and produce major hits by Steppen-wolf and Three Dog Night. A coincidental connection between Podolor and the Red Sox is that he produced and recorded "Joy to the World," a song now also played after every Fenway Park win (following "Dirty Water" and "Tessie").

"Richie Podolor had a little recording studio in the San Fernando Valley called American Recording Studio," Dodd explained. "He produced Sandy Nelson and he was the guitar player on Nelson's instrumental hit song 'Let There Be Drums.' He was there when I first met Jackie...when I became her drummer. Richie also did all of the Standells' recording. Jackie, Richie, and Reb all mentioned to me that there was a group whose drummer was leaving and that maybe I would want to try out."

The group was, of course, the Standells.

The Standells had been formed in 1962 and the first incarnation of the band had Tony Valentino on guitar and harmonica, Larry Tamblyn as the lead singer and organist, Gary Lane (formerly Gary McMillan) on bass, and Gary Leeds on drums. The origins of that group began when Valentino, a recent transplant to Southern California from Italy, was working at a bakery mixing bread dough.

Tony was born Emilio Anthony Bellissimo on a farm in the hills of Sicily. He was a teenager when he fell in love with America and rock and roll. "I always loved music since I was a little kid. I had an imagination of being in a marching band, and symphonies, all this music. I was raised on this farm. I was with cows and goats and horses and all that. We grew grapes and used to make the wine in Sicily up in the mountains. I was playing guitar but [play-ing] Italian music. The guitar players were an inspiration to me, they serenaded people in the piazza in my town. Before I left for America I was looking at magazines in Italy of rock and roll stars like Frankie Avalon, Fabian, and Elvis...Elvis a lot. Elvis was a big influence. Bill Haley, too. I heard that song 'Rock Around the Clock' when I was in Italy and I just wanted to come to America so bad. I wanted to play rock and roll, man."

Sometime in 1959 or 1960, Emilio and his parents moved to America and made their way to Southern California where he landed a job working in a restaurant kitchen. The dark-haired and good-looking Italian teenager couldn't speak a word of English at the time. "Nothing. Not a word. As a matter of fact I took a bus one day ...I was going to work at this restaurant; I couldn't speak not one word of English, nothing. I was supposed to get off at an exit about four blocks from the restaurant, I wanted to tell the driver to stop but

Tony Valentino (Emilio Bellissimo), Longi, Italy 1958. Courtesy of Emilio Bellissimo.

I could not do it. The [expletive deleted] guy kept on going, until two or three stops later."

As with most immigrants at the time, Emilio started picking up the language of his new country out of necessity, at least enough English to communicate with another young musician that he cooked with in a large commercial bakery. "I was working at the Van De Kamp bakery factory. I was working as a [apprentice] baker. I couldn't speak much English so they put me on a dough-mixing machine. There I met this guy—his name was Jody Rich—who played a little bass and he suggested we get together and form a band. We started rehearsing in a garage with a drummer, Jody as the bass player, and me on the guitar. Then we did a couple of gigs with a lead singer named Lanny Duncan." They called themselves the Starlighters.

"Lanny Duncan used to come to my house when we were working on this song called 'Let's Go!' I wrote the middle [guitar] part that went 'ta-da da-da-dum, dum, dum, dum and so on.' We went to Glendale and paid $5 each to make a demo, I played lead on the guitar. We got the name of the song from going to a football game at Burbank High School. I'll never forget we came out of the game and all four of us in the band were clapping our hands like the cheerleaders, and [chanting] "Let's go!"

"Later, when I was with the Standells I became known as Tony—my middle name incidentally; we got booked in Hawaii and I heard the song on the radio and I almost crapped in my pants." Instead of finding success with the song he helped to write, Tony saw the song became a Top 20 hit recorded by another group known as the Routers in 1962, with brothers Lanny and Bob Duncan credited as the writers of the instrumental hit that featured a saxophone, drums, and guitars with a catchy hand-clapping rhythm and the chant "let's go" as the only lyrics. Tony was never credited for his role in its creation. "I was going crazy. I said, 'I wrote this song!' And, stupid of me, I never did anything about it. I could hardly speak English, my parents didn't know about any 'rights;' I just [expletive deleted] let it go. Nobody advised me to take these guys to court."

The Starlighters began their metamorphosis into the Standells with the organist Larry Tamblyn merging into the group. Tony recalled, "I met Larry Tamblyn when I was playing with Jody and Lanny Duncan. This other guy, Gary Leeds, told me he knew Larry as the brother of Russ Tamblyn who we saw on TV. As a matter of fact, I remember also seeing Larry on TV singing a song he wrote about riding the rails or something like that. Larry was on his own. He had a record deal with this other guy. Jody knew his number I guess so we called him and asked him to join us."

♪ ♪ ♪

Larry Tamblyn had a pretty fair pedigree in music and entertainment at the time. His father Eddie Tamblyn was a vaudevillean entertainer and his mother was a chorus girl named Sally Triplett. Larry had two much older brothers. Warren had little interest in show business. The other, Russ was a child actor who later became known for his starring role as Riff in the 1961 film *West Side Story* and successfully continued acting in countless roles as an adult. (Today Russ's daughter Amber Tamblyn has made her mark in show business as the star of television's *Joan of Arcadia* and numerous motion pictures.)

Larry says of his brother Russ and of his own early aspirations as a performer, "I idolized my brother, and he was an actor so I wanted to be an actor like him. I emulated him from the time I was a little kid. I actually had a bit part in a movie myself when I was about nine years old, an old 1950 TV show called *Big Town*. The reason I got the part was that Russ was supposed to play my older brother in it. That was my first real introduction in show business."

His first time on stage, though, came at the age of seven while the family was on vacation, traveling through Oregon. They stopped to see a movie where there was a live talent show before the film and the emcee called for performers to come forward. Larry startled his family by leaving his seat and walking up front. He picks up the story from there: "My two brothers sort of shrank down in their seats. My parents didn't know what to think. The emcee had me come out on stage and asked me what I wanted to sing and I told him 'Four Leaf Clover'—and I won the talent contest. I think I won a couple of bucks. That was my first professional act in show business."

"The first time I realized I wanted to be a rock performer was when I was at a middle school dance. A small jazz band had been performing, but was on break I took the opportunity to walk up on stage, grab a guitar and do a dreadful Elvis Presley imitation. The guitar gave me a feeling of empowerment, which I had never experienced before. After that, I hounded my parents into buying my first guitar. I was actually a session guitar player before expanding on keyboards. The reason I took up piano was that there seemed to be a plethora of guitarists around, but not too many pianists.

"In high school—John Francis Polytechnic High School in Sun Valley— I had several bands. I had a band called the Emeralds and I sang lead and I played guitar. One of the members of the group was Darron Stankey, who later became one of the Innocents. The rest of the Emeralds were Frank Fayad on sax, and Wayne Edwards on drums. Wayne later went on to become part of a group called the Hondells. There was a lot of musical talent around."

Larry counts Chuck Berry as an early idol on guitar, and Little Richard and Jerry Lee Lewis on piano. One of his biggest early influences was Gene Vincent. "I wrote a song that was very similar to 'Be Bop A Lula' called 'Rockin' Joanie' which was the first song I ever recorded.

I went into this recording studio called Valentine Recording Studios in North Hollywood [with some friends]. I was just a kid. We assumed that they would do it for free. They wouldn't give us the recording until they had gotten their money. Our parents had to end up paying for it. I think it was 35 bucks...."

Like a lot of teenaged aspiring musicians of the era Larry and his friends had a lot of interest in recording their songs, hoping for that elusive "big break" to get into show business. "About that time, there were several of us that were trying to audition for record companies. Ritchie Valens was an acquaintance and we did some gigs together. That was before he had the hit record 'La Bamba.' We tried to audition for Del-Fi, the label he signed with, and they didn't even want to talk to us. We set up in the men's restroom and started playing until they had to come out. They finally let us audition. They never signed us, but they got us out of the restroom. We were creating quite a ruckus in there."

"Later on, we met a real promotion manager type of guy, Speed Copp. Speed introduced me to this fellow by the name of Eddie Davis. Davis had one record label called Faro Records and another one called Linda and signed me to my first record deal—as an individual. The first record I made was called 'Dearest.' The flip side was called 'She Is My Baby.' I performed as a single act at different record hops and things, and I was part of the house band at the

Rainbow Gardens club, playing guitar on the weekends. We backed up the Beach Boys, Raul Donner, and Roy Orbison. My biggest thrill was when Eddie got me on a major show up in the San Francisco area with Connie Francis. She was a huge star at that time. Here I was about 16 or 17, still in high school and I flew up to San Francisco with Connie Francis. We were in the airport and Connie asked me to go with her to get a glass of water, but she became faint and actually fainted in my arms. She had just overworked herself and was exhausted. As she walked along, she literally fainted in my arms. Here's a 17-year-old boy with his idol in his arms!"

♪ ♪ ♪

With the addition of the sandy-haired Southern Californian Larry Tamblyn to the Starlighters on keyboard and vocals, Tony (formerly Emilio) saw the band evolve into the Standells. "Lanny Duncan disappeared on us one day, just as we were all set to go to an agency, the McConkey Agency, to get some work. We were standing around the agency's door looking for work all day it seemed. Somehow, because of that standing around at the agencies, we came up with a new name—the Standells. The Starlighters became the Standells."

Now the newly branded "Standells" were Larry Tamblyn on organ, Emilio Anthony Bellissimo on lead guitar, and Jody Rich on bass. They were still looking for work and needed a new drummer. They found both, but not without some problems as well.

"We picked up this young kid named Benny King after we signed with McConkey Agency. I think his real name was Benny Hernandez. He was a drummer, he was like 17 years old," said Tamblyn. "They booked us in several nightclubs, including one in Santa Barbara. That was when 'Mac' McConkey, the owner of the agency, and his wife Gail had a falling out and began a divorce that turned into a real war. The old man knew that several of us were underage, and so he turned us in to the police at that one gig, as a way to get back at his wife who was the actual person to book us there. The police came out and stopped us from playing. Then Gail booked us for what was our first major gig at a club called the Oasis in Hawaii in 1962."

There had been a sudden cancellation, providing an opening at the Oasis that benefited both the agency and the band. Perhaps Gail McConkey knew that by booking them so far away, the chance of the band getting busted for being underage would be greatly diminished and both the band and the agency would be less likely to be harassed by her disgruntled and soon-to-be exhusband.

At the Oasis Club, the Standells alternated performances with a Japanese floorshow. Again Larry recalled, "It was like paradise there. It was my first time away from home. I was 19 at the time. It was great! We alternated with a complete Japanese revue. At that time, there was a Japanese version of everything [in American pop culture]. They had the Japanese version of Pat Boone and they had a Japanese comedian. They performed in [memorized] English. They were directly from Japan. It was kind of like a vaudeville show with chorus girls. And then they had a stripper come on, and we were on after the stripper. Like I said, I was 19, all of the guys were very young, still teenagers except for Jody, an ex-Marine, married and in his 20s, who became the leader of the band."

One of Jody's early edicts was that Emilio change his name to Tony for reasons Tony cannot even recall today. But it was a suggestion that he did not object to anyway. "Jody said, 'well your middle name is Tony, so we are just going to call you Tony—Tony Valentino, from now on.' So, OK, they called me Tony Valentino from then on."

"At first, Jody was just a little dominant," according to Larry, " but in time he became more and more dictatorial, like a little Napoleon. He became an absolute tyrant, making us spit-shine our shoes and press our clothes so we could all look snappier. We had to dress alike any time we went out. It was all just control. Then he put a curfew on us because he got jealous of Tony and me bringing all the chorus girls to our rooms. He was married, and obviously unhappily married. He got jealous and put a curfew on us. Then he started popping pills. Popping uppers, and he was up all night. He'd wake us up in the morning, going crazy frantic, jazzed from the uppers, talking about how he had 20 songs ready. We hadn't even awakened yet, and this guy's going nuts. It was during this period that Jody just went totally bananas and ended up firing Tony and me, and then he realized that he [wouldn't] have a group anymore!"

Larry remembered other aspects of the Hawaiian stay with some amusement particularly the living conditions at the apartment that he and Tony shared in Waikiki Beach. "Unbeknownst to us, there was a third member of our household; a *four-legged* roommate—a small Pacific rat we later named Fred."

Fred presented a big problem to the boys when it came to entertaining their dates in their apartment. "After cajoling the wahines ["girls" in Hawaiian] into entering our small rundown apartment, Tony and I would dim the lights and turn on the record player, which was stacked with seductive music. At this critical juncture Fred would emerge from his hole-in-the-wall behind the oven and create...havoc. The terrified girls would then retreat out the front door, leaving us frustrated and angry."

Larry returned home from the club early one night to relax and have a snack before bed when little Fred made his regular nocturnal visit. "Unlike the previous occasions, my total attention was now focused on Fred...the chase was on! The rat sought shelter in every nook and cranny. Finally he raced into the bathroom and crawled inside an empty Kleenex box. I grabbed the box and threw it into the toilet. I knew that Fred would be forced to sink or swim. The only exit was down the drain and into the sewer, where he belonged. I shut the lid, triumphant in the knowledge that Fred would eventually meet his maker. I crawled into bed, and fell into a peaceful sleep but was awakened by the most wretched scream I'd ever heard! Tony, with his pants down around his knees, stumbled over my bed in absolute hysteria. 'Eet's alive,' he bellowed in his heavily accented voice, 'Eet's alive!'"

Larry got up to investigate and to calm down Tony and saw that little Fred had not yet expired. "Exhausted but alive, Fred still had his two hind feet perched on a corner of the [nearly dissolved] tissue box. After looking at his sad little eyes, I just couldn't force myself to flush the toilet. I wrapped my hands in a towel, [picked him up] and carried him outside, walked a good distance, and released him. He skittered off down a walkway, then stopped, turned, and bared his teeth. He seemed to say *you may have won this time but I'll be back.* I never actually saw Fred again, but on more than one occasion when I had a female overnight guest, I could have sworn I saw movement out of the corner of my eye. Of course, it may have been my mind playing tricks on me."

There were other problems in Hawaii besides Fred the rat and Jody. Benny, their temporary percussionist, quit in the middle of the gig at the Oasis and went back home to his parents. A Japanese drummer from the floorshow filled in, doing double duty. Then the mercurial Jody hired another drummer. "He was this big heavy guy," said Tamblyn. "I don't recall his name. All he seemed to know was polkas."

After half a year, when the gig came to an end, the band came back to California and things got even worse. Larry remembers the comedown: "The McConkeys had booked us in Fresno after our Hawaiian gig at the Oasis—from Paradise in Hawaii to Hell in Fresno. The place was a dive, right next to the railroad tracks. It was terrible, a dumpy nightclub. One night the big drummer fell off the back of the stage. Another night, a 300-pound woman passed out drunk on the bandstand and she was too big to move so they left her there, and we had to step over her. It was just depressing. Totally depressing. At that time, I think we were called Larry Tamblyn and the Standells. That's when we finally broke with Jody."

But now the group was without a regular drummer and without Jody on bass. Fortunately, Larry remembered a couple of guys from a local Southern California group called the Biscaines who just might fill the bill as new members for the now-diminished Standells—bass player Gary McMillan and Gary Leeds, a drummer.

Gary McMillan recalled that his road to becoming a Standell was indeed as the result of that merger but really cannot recall much about it, "Gary Leeds and I were in the Biscaines. I don't remember how it happened but Gary and I somehow got in contact with Larry and Tony and merged into the Standells, although I don't remember *exactly* how that came about."

Gary McMillan, professionally known as Gary Lane after he became a Standell, was born in St. Paul, Minnesota, grew up in southern California,

The Standells

The Standells lineup with Tony, Larry and the Garys. Courtesy of Edie McMillan.

worked in an appliance store, for a construction company, and in various other jobs before hooking up with the Standells in the early 1960s. Always interested in music, he learned to play his bass guitar by ear. Gary always seemed to have friends who played in bands and he recalled just kind of "falling into it" as well. Tall, quiet and handsome, Gary's musical ability made him a welcome addition to any performing rock and roll group. Asked why he adopted a stage name, he simply remarked, "When I was with the Standells, most of the time I used the name Gary Lane, but McMillan is my real name. I just changed my name on my own. I don't remember why I picked Lane. I know one thing; it was easier to sign than McMillan."

After finishing out the gig in Fresno, the band moved back to its home turf. Larry continues the chronology: "Next we played in Hollywood. It was kind of a rough place. Just one cut above Fresno. They had fistfights there every night. Most were outside, but there were a few inside, too. One night, the cops came in and asked us for our IDs. I was still underage so I told them I left my ID at home. So the cop said, 'I'm going to come back tomorrow night and you better have it. Now if you're not 21 and come clean now, it'll go a lot easier on you.' The following day, Tony and I drove down to Mexico and we bought fake IDs, draft cards, and hurriedly filled them in, roughed them up and made them all dirty to look old. We barely were able to make it back in time to do the gig. Sure enough the cop showed up and I showed him the fake ID and he went for it. I was peeing in my pants I was so scared. He said, 'Yeah, I thought you were 21. Nobody would bluff like this.'"

"We played in that club for a while. After that a club up in Eureka called Club Esquire. We played there for about a month, in January and February 1963. That was an experience, what with all the lumberjacks up there! They booked us from there to Sacramento at the Trophy Room. Then we were booked back in L.A., in Pasadena. We played there for a while and then we heard they were looking for a band at the Peppermint West."

The band had aspirations of bigger paydays and better venues and was fed up with playing dives. Back east, the Peppermint Lounge at 45th Street in New York City was the in spot for the beautiful people of the mid-60s. Joey Dee and the Starlighters was the house band there and had a smash number one hit with their recording of the "Peppermint Twist." California's answer to the New York hot spot was the Peppermint West nightclub in Hollywood.

Larry and Tony heard that the Peppermint West was looking for a band and the boys went there every day trying to find someone to give them an audition. Their persistence paid off and they were hired. They got the steady gig but were still able to squeeze in a few side jobs as well. As the house band for what was considered the hippest night spot in L.A., the boys were allowed to shed the clean-cut image that Jody Rich had forced on the group and after about a year at the club, began to sport longer hair—inspired by an unknown British group Tony had seen in an Italian magazine. "This was before the Beatles ever arrived in America," according to Tony, "I was getting all of the Italian teen-age music magazines because they were easier for me to read. In them I used to see all of these European acts with the long hair—including the Beatles. We thought that it was pretty cool and different so we tried it ourselves when we were at Peppermint West."

The eccentric dress designer Marusia was the owner of Peppermint West. "She was Hungarian or something by birth," as Larry recalled her exotic accent. "'I *vant* to....' She talked like that." Gary Lane remembered how she

Zsa Zsa Gabor flanked by Gary Lane, Gary Leeds, Larry, and Tony at Peppermint West. Courtesy of Edie McMillan.

used to stop the band to request a favorite song. "One time she stopped us, right in the middle of the set, and she said, 'I vant you to play "Tvist"'—so we played 'Ooh Poo Pa Doo'—it wasn't The Twist, but you could twist to it. 'NO, NO, NO! No 'Ooh Poo Pa Do!'—I vant "Tvist!"'" she shouted as one of her fake eyelashes was coming off and her makeup was dripping down her face."

"She just kind of had this *air* about her, this diva way," Larry added. "She wore a lot of long dresses. She wore a lot of veils, a lot of flowing dresses, a lot of bizarre things. She reminded me of an aging leading actress with that heavy accent—she could have been Marlene Dietrich."

Larry also recalled one memorable night at the club, an unusually cold night in Hollywood when the Standells were playing at Peppermint West, which was not equipped with much of a heating system, if it had one at all. "I remember this night, it was freezing cold. The club was like a huge converted garage...so we wore gloves and overcoats right on the stage. It was so cold in there. Marusia threw a fit [about our appearance in coats]." He elaborated about the club, "They had a lot of stars coming in. The manager of the club Mario had an accent, too and he was a transvestite. He was very, very much gay, back before it was fashionable. He had performed at Finocchio's in San Francisco. He came up to me one night and started talking with me. I don't know how we got in the discussion. He said, 'You know, I don't tell too many people

No, this is not an early photo of the "Village People," it's Thanksgiving at the Peppermint West. Tony, Gary Leeds, a skeptical Larry, and Gary Lane. Courtesy of Edie McMillan.

this...' I thought, 'Oh, no. He's going to try to hit on me.' He said, 'I get visitations during the night. I get spiritual visitations.' I thought, 'Oh God, where is this going?' He says, 'I don't ask for them, but they visit me, and one of the people who visited me was your father.' He told me all about my father. My father had passed away years ago. He said that the band was going to have a big change in our lives, that my father was my guardian angel, and that we were going to have a big change for the better with some great things happening soon."

"It was during this time that we met our manager Burt Jacobs," Tamblyn continued. "Mario would promote these 'Hollywood Stars Nights' as a way to get people in the club to see and mix with the stars. The place was always so packed and smoky in there that you couldn't tell who was there anyway. He'd stand up on stage and say, 'Now in the back, way in the back, June Allyson. Come on, stand up, honey!' Everybody's looking around, everybody's clapping. But she wasn't there! He used to say things like, 'With us tonight is the famous painter, Larry Watkins,'...all this kind of stuff. I mean what Hollywood 'star' would actually come to a nightclub when they were advertising it as a 'Hollywood Stars' night?"

But the stars of Hollywood did come to the club—just not too often on Mario's contrived "Hollywood Stars Night"—and the Standells met and played for many of the "beautiful people" of the early 1960s. They began to grow their hair longer, they broadened their repertoire and before long, as the British Invasion was taking place, the club hung a big sign out front reading "Beatle-mania here!" The Standells performed a number of Beatles songs. *Tiger Beat* magazine came and ran an article on the band, showing them with the long hair that was on its way to becoming emblematic of the day. "We were the first American group to have long hair. People were really getting into it," Larry remembered of the Standells' nights at Peppermint West in Hollywood.

Burt the Bookie, and
America's Answer to the Beatles

After the McConkey Agency, the next booking agent and first manager of the Standells was Burton "Burt" Jacobs of B-J Enterprises, at the time a wannabe Hollywood manager working out of a rented suite on Sunset Boulevard. Jacobs, born in Brooklyn, New York, was allegedly involved in some small-time gambling activities as his primary endeavor and his only experience at "booking" before he met the Standells was in "bookmaking"—as in running a numbers racket.

California law is very clear about the difference between a musical booking agent and a personal manager for a group or artist. According to Ray Harris, Ed Cobb's first business partner and eventual principal in the production of the Standells' music, a personal manager "primarily advises and makes choices for the artist to consider," while "an agent is a guy who is a solicitor, or can make a booking for an artist or a group. He can go to a concert promoter and sell the group or package, or go to a film company and sell his client for a motion picture or make a deal. A manager primarily advises and makes choices for the artist to consider. An agent is like a...and I hate to use this word but will anyway...like a [pimp working a] prostitute. They don't care. As long as you're hot, they book you and move you. They don't care if they book you in San Francisco two days later after you played New York City and you've spend all your money on transportation." Burt Jacobs blurred the line between being a manager and an agent. He would do a lot of the legwork setting up gigs. He would seek out gigs and get ahold of people but never could actually book the act. It was like looking for real estate on your own and then getting a real estate agent just to do the paperwork."

Jacobs had the reputation of operating on the fringes of acceptable business norms and of being connected to unsavory characters. Ed Cobb's partner in the Four Preps, Bruce Belland, was a little more frank in his assessment of Jacobs: "He was just a stereotypical ...Hollywood schemer, you know. I know who he was and how he operated." Lincoln Mayorga concurred, "He had the aspect of a hood about him." Restless Records CEO Jerry Heller, talking about his early days in the music business, said that Jacobs' "major claim to fame was that he was point shaving and fixing some basketball games in the '60s. He wound up managing Three Dog Night and Steppenwolf."[1]

Despite the harsh characterizations of Jacobs by many people in the music

The Standells at the Thunderbird in Las Vegas. Courtesy of Edie McMillan.

business, many of the individuals from bands he managed have fond regards for him. A strong bond developed between the bands and the man they relied on for their day-to-day needs in the often-zany world of rock and roll. Drummer Floyd Sneed of Three Dog Night had nothing but kind words for Jacobs. "Sure he could be loud and crass sometimes, but he was a tough guy for the band. He always trying to make sure that he got the best he could for us...he was always for the musicians."[2]

Jacobs, born in 1927, was quite a bit older than any of the Standells, in his mid-30s when he became their manager, and was a colorful character to say the least. The impulsive, cigar-smoking, loud-dressing, talent manager with his dark horn-rimmed glasses was indeed a stereotype of what Hollywood often portrayed as a show business manager. He sometimes wore a bad toupee and sometimes dispensed with it. He was a character that could have been in a 1950s black and white B-movie. Phil "Sergeant Bilko" Silvers could have played the role.

Tony Valentino remembered meeting Jacobs for the first time. "When were playing at the time at the world famous Peppermint West in Hollywood we didn't have any management or an agent working for us. We had just gotten rid of the McConkey Agency and were getting our gigs ourselves. We really wanted to play at the Peppermint West because it was just such a hip place. We would go there every day and bug them until they signed us as the house band. The Peppermint West was *the* place to go. All the movie stars were going there, everybody. So one night this guy [Burt Jacobs] walked in and he saw us. He said, 'Hey, I want to manage you guys—I know some people here and there.'

U.S. Answer to Beatles Pauses for T-Bird Stand

The famed Standells, in final preparation for "The musical battle of the year" against Britain's Beatles, have been booked by Thunderbird Hotel Executive Vice President Dave Victorson for a special four-night engagement.

The group opened last night. Victorson returned to Las Vegas over the weekend from a special trip to Los Angeles where he was successful in booking the noted quartet prior to their journey to England where they will formally challenge the Beatles.

Stars of Los Angels' Peppermint Lounge the last seven months, the Standells have played to standing-room-only audiences almost nightly with most of movieland's stars seated ringside, including Zsa Zsa Gabor, Jayne Mansfield, Helen Greco and Spike Jones.

At the present time their latest Liberty record, featuring "The Shake" and Peppermint Beatle" has hit the top of the ladder in Los Angeles and New York.

Making up the group are Larry Tamblyn on organ, Tony Valentine, guitar; Gary McMillan, drums, and Gary Leeds, bass fiddle. Each also is a top vocalist.

"With the Beatle craze now in full swing the Standells — long hair and all—are out to prove they can top the British group," said Victorson. "With arrangements for their trip to Great Britain now complete the Thunderbird has been fortunate in signing the group for the four days. This will be their final U.S. appearance before the trip abroad."

The Standells are featured three times nightly, 1:15, 4:15 and 6 a.m.

Courtesy of Edie McMillan.

We got together and then after Peppermint West he signed us and booked us in the Thunderbird in Las Vegas where they billed us as 'America's Answer to The Beatles.' We were at the Thunderbird Lounge for about a month or so. After that, we went to be the house band at P.J.'s nightclub in Hollywood."

Jacobs had connections in the entertainment industry, which were a little less than wholesome, if not downright unsavory. His numbers operation serviced many of the folks working in the offices of Liberty Records and at a number of diverse other Los Angeles entertainment industry establishments. Larry Tamblyn remembers Burt saying "If I can get you a record contract with Liberty Records, will you sign with me as a personal manager?" The band agreed.

Jacobs' contacts were influential enough to help get the Standells a lot of local work and even some limited national exposure, which endeared him to the band. On February 6, 1964 Larry Tamblyn, Gary Leeds, Tony Valentino, and Gary McMillan (now known as Gary Lane) signed the contract arranged by Jacobs and became recording artists for Liberty Records. Larry Tamblyn strongly suspected that it was Burt's bookie activities that got the Standells their first record contract. "Hell, Liberty didn't even ask for a tape or for us to do a demo record. I think our deal was done because some of them owed Burt about $4,000.00 and giving him a record deal for us was the payoff! We signed with Liberty while we were still at Peppermint West and we recorded a song, which was 'The Shake.' He was taking all their bets at Liberty, so that's how he got us on the label. I knew he was their bookie. I knew they had enough regard for him—or fear—that they signed us. We made 'The Shake.' I wasn't happy with the recording. The producer that they put in charge wasn't too hip."

The Fab Four of the West Coast. Emilio (now Tony), Gary Leeds, Larry, and Gary Lane. Courtesy of Edie McMillan.

Tamblyn recalled the prelude to the band's tenure at Hollywood nightclub P.J.'s. It was a booking Burt brought the band. "P.J.'s, they were also heavily mob connected. We were in Burt's office one time and there was this real kindly old gentleman who was just so nice, with a cane and everything. I just really liked him. I was told later that he was like the Godfather of the West Coast. Goes to show you. P.J.'s was on Santa Monica Boulevard. If you went right up the hill, you'd go up to Whiskey A Go Go, up on the Strip up there. The Troubadour was right down the street. It was kind of all within the area there. By the time we went to P.J.'s, they insisted we clean ourselves up [the good fellows who patronized the club were not yet fond of the new fashions]."

Larry bristles at the notion propagated by some writers that the Standells were a clean-cut group that Ed Cobb "dirtied" up. That was, to be blunt, "Nonsense—we had to cut our hair in order to perform, in P.J.'s. We were the house band for a long time. They tripled the size of the room while we were there. We started drawing in people." This was all before they met Ed Cobb.

The band recorded a live album at the club, called *The Standells in Person at P.J.'s*, which was released on the Sunset label later that year. It appeared on other labels overseas—in Germany, the LP came out on Liberty. The album's liner notes, by KRLA deejay Reb Foster, promised "the most electrifying band

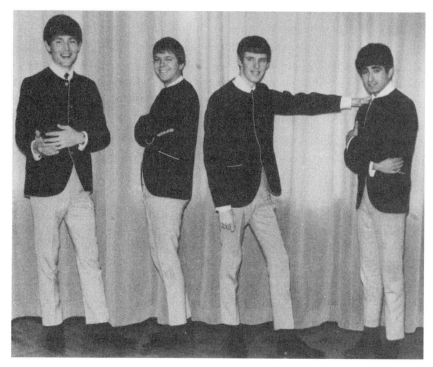

A very deliberate Beatlesque pose. Gary Lane, Larry, Gary Leeds, Tony. Courtesy of Edie McMillan.

in the U.S.A." and advised prospective buyers, "Prepare yourself for a 'shock treatment'!"

Reb Foster's liner notes to the P.J.'s album mentioned all four musicians that are the Standells, as we know them today with the addition of Dick Dodd. Foster wrote, "The driving beat of drummer Dick Dodd, the pulsating rhythms of organist Larry Tamblyn, the crackling tempo of bass man Gary Lane, and flash-fingered guitarist Tony Valentino make up the 'musical miracle' that is known as the Standells."

The Standells had evolved with the melding of individual performers from 1962 onward. The last Standell to join the fold was Dick Dodd. The Standells began auditioning for a new drummer shortly after they landed their gig at P.J.'s. They were all set to record the live album at the club when drummer Gary Leeds unexpectedly decided to leave the group, according to Larry Tamblyn: "Right before we were scheduled to record the album, Gary Leeds left us. So we were really up the creek. So we were auditioning. We tried several people and they weren't right. Then in came Dick and sat in. We knew right off the bat that he was the one. When Dick became part of the group, he was a solid member. He fit like a glove. The only thing was that he was young. He was kind of a punk kid—he'll be the first one to tell you that—and it was kind of an adjustment for him, but we made it work. Soon after he joined us, we recorded that *In Person at P.J.'s* album.

"I had always dreamed of having another voice in the group, especially another lead singer to take some of the pressure off me so I looked forward to having someone else to share the lead signing. Unbeknownst to me, I didn't realize that Dick would be so good that he'd eventually take over most of the leads."

♪ ♪ ♪

When Gary Leeds left the Standells, 19 year-old Dick Dodd was still living in Redondo Beach with his mother. The former Mouseketeer had retained all of his boyish charm but it was now coupled with a worldlier attitude after being on the road and enjoying the attentions of many friendly female fans. With his disarming smile and dark good looks, Dick would be the charming "bad-boy" of the group. The new 1964 line-up of the Standells—Larry, Gary, Tony, and Dick—was the one to eventually record "Dirty Water" and came to exemplify the "punky" image the Standells brought with them on the road after that single hit the charts—the song that has now become a Red Sox fan favorite.

Meanwhile, former Standell Gary Leeds joined up with fellow Californians Scott Engle and John Maus to form the Walker Brothers, who had hit records in 1965 ("Take It Easy on Yourself ") and 1966 ("The Sun Ain't Gonna Shine Anymore"). The Walker Brothers moved to England and met with great success in an unusual reversal of the British Invasion phenomenon that was taking place in America.[3]

With Dodd now on board, the Standells cut the live album at P.J.'s and it enjoyed some local success, but didn't fare that well outside L.A. despite DJ Foster's ebullient liner notes: "Anyone with an ounce of 'soul' will find it impossible not to snap his fingers and to dance when the Standells storm into a song. Other groups may play a song, but the Standells reach into a song and 'grab it,' wringing out of every note the stirring sounds that nightly bring huge audiences shouting to their feet at P.J.'s in Hollywood."

"It is the Standells," Foster's notes continued, "that have made P.J.'s headquarters for the 'watusi elite,' who have made musical addicts of the Southern California 'heavy-beat hippies' and who, through this album, bring to you the thundering excitement and rampaging emotions that will have you talking about it for months. It's a pleasure to know the Standells, because—they're 'out of sight.'"

The pre-"Dirty Water" album was produced by Dick Glasser and recorded by Wally Heider. Glasser was not a good fit as a producer. He'd rearranged Larry's single "The Shake" into something Larry derisively decried as "like a polka." And he took the live P.J.'s tapes and sped them up about 10 percent because he thought it would make the show sound more exciting. These were the days when producers and record companies determined matters more than the artists themselves. "Everything was done by the producer and the group had no say-so," Larry observed. "You just did what the producer wanted you to do."[4] Larry, making a joke about Dick Dodd's old employer, said, "[The sped-up tapes] made us sound like Mickey Mouse." After the band hit with "Dirty Water," the P.J.'s album was re-released as *The Standells Live and Out of Sight*, with a couple of different cuts and at the proper speed.

The P.J.'s album was only moderately successful, but the Standells attracted other attention, too. They also recorded a few singles on Liberty, appeared on some television shows—most notably *The Munsters*—and even in a "B movie" called *Get Yourself a College Girl* during the course of their engagement at P.J.'s. This was a band rooted in Los Angeles and taking full advantage of all that the area offered.

Dick recalled his first few months in the group, playing at the headquarters for the "watusi elite": "The Standells were already formed. They were already playing. At the time in Los Angeles, there was the Whiskey A-Go-Go nightclub where Johnny Rivers was playing and then there was P.J.'s nightclub where Trini Lopez played. Trini had a little lounge in the back of P.J.'s. You would walk in back and hear the jazz, and see the long bar and stuff. You'd look down this long dark hall and you'd open up these doors and there was this huge room where there was a bandstand Trini was performing on.

"After Trini's show left the lounge for another engagement, the Standells started playing as the house band. They played five nights a week and I could make three or four hundred dollars a week with them. In [the early '60s], that was pretty good money so I said, 'Sure.' I auditioned one afternoon and played with the Standells the same night. We were playing dance music...cover music...of whatever was popular like "Linda Lou," "Money," "Kansas City," what was considered popular rock music back then. The Standells were already signed with Liberty Records, which was a big label. Jackie DeShannon was on Liberty Records, so that's where her connection came in, and there was a bunch of other big name people on Liberty then."

Dodd, like Larry Tamblyn, credited manager Burt Jacobs with the group's success at getting bookings. "Some people say he was affiliated with the Mob and some pretty shady characters because he could get us on almost any show even without a hit record. He wasn't really an agent, he was running a numbers game or something around town, I think. But he claimed to have a lot of contacts in the industry."

Jacobs must have had some pretty good inroads to show business indeed. "We did so much TV stuff—even before 'Dirty Water' was a hit," recalled Dodd. "We did an episode of the TV show *The Munsters*, we were on *Ben Casey*, and we were on a Bing Crosby show. We were on a *Shindig* kind of a show that was on TV once a week in L.A. There was always a rock and roll show to play on and we were on those constantly. When we went anywhere, we were always known and noticed. We already had some fame, which fostered the punky, self-assured attitude we projected later on. Larry Tamblyn was the leader of the Standells when I joined the band; he did all the singing all the time until we recorded 'Dirty Water.' They had some local following and very small local hits."

As noted, to become the house band at P.J.'s, the Standells had to trim their long hair and shed the "mod" look they had sported at Peppermint West and in Las Vegas. The management and the clientele at P.J.'s expected a more traditional showbiz look, so it was back to sharkskin suits, skinny ties, and swept-back greaser hair. But as the British Invasion continued to sweep across America, the group was soon back to their "Dry Look" and Nehru suits. After "Dirty Water" became a hit, the band would once again be on the cutting edge of the new fashion look for rockers—longer and longer hair, and outfits where anything went.

Anxious for the opportunity to be considered headliners rather than a cover band, the Standells jumped when the chance for an international gig presented itself. One night at P.J.'s a group of wealthy Nicaraguan plantation owners came in, saw the band and asked if they would be interested in doing a tour in their country. Expecting a tropical paradise with gorgeous women, sandy beaches, and exotic nights the boys in the band got all excited. But the reality of their ill-fated Latin America gig was far from what they imagined.

Accompanied by Burt Jacobs and Reb Foster, the DJ from KRLA, Larry recalls the trip vividly: "Boy, were we in for a shock! We expected a big tourist place with a nice beach. It was *so* bad. When we arrived at our hotel, we actually thought we were in the slums of Managua, until the cab driver told us it was the main drag. I can remember that every place we played, there were soldiers with AK-47s pointed everywhere. Only the super rich could afford

—Por primera vez en JINOTEPE—

Directamente de Hollywood y Las Vegas

Los Standells
LOS BEATLES NORTEAMERICANOS

No se pierda de verlos en su
Unica Presentación en el
TEATRO GONZALEZ
la mejor música de todos los tiempos
interpretada por el mejor conjunto
LOS STANDELLS-Los Beatles Norteamericanos
¡¡NO SE LA PIERDA!!
Unica Presentación en esta ciudad

Courtesy of Edie McMillan.

to see us perform. They thought we were the Beatles because they had never had any entertainment there before. They billed us as 'Los Beatles Norteamericanos.'"

The band was booked to play two or three performances each day. "Our clothes would get soaked with perspiration and we'd have to get them cleaned and get into another set. One time when we were leaving this one place, Dick told this guy to disassemble his drums. He went to do something, and then he got back, and the guy told Dick, 'I deed what you wanted, Señor.' And he had taken apart every screw, and all the skins were laying on the floor... everything was taken apart!"

"While we were there, we did make some money. We were like big stars there. We went to the Presidential palace and met El Presidente. But they also

```
NOTE: ALL PERSONNEL DUE TO FIRE HAZARD PLEASE WATCH YOUR SMOKING & USE BUTT CANS

PROD. #24832                    UNIVERSAL TV          THURSDAY, FEBRUARY 11, 1965
"FAR OUT MUNSTER"                                     SHOOTING CALL: 8:00A
DIR: JOSEPH PEVNEY              "D" UNIT              LOCATION: STAGE #16
ASST DIR: DOLPH ZIMMER/FOSTER H. PHINNEY                       STAGE #17
ART DIR: HENRY LARRECQ
SET DECO: JIM REDD             THE MUNSTERS
PROP: EDDIE KEYES                                     2ND DAY OF SHOOTING
```

DESCRIPTION	D/N	SCS	PGS
INT. MUNSTER'S LIVINGROOM Sc. 32 (LARRY,GARY,TONY,DICK)	D	1	1
INT. ENTRY HALL Sc. 34 (LARRY,GARY,TONY,DICK,BEARD,GIRL,HERMIT,ATMOSPHERE)	N	1	3/8
INT. LIVINGROOM Scs. 40 thru 57 (HERMAN,LILY,EDDIE,GRANDPA,BEARD,GIRL,LARRY,GARY,TONY, 　　　　　　　　DICK,HERMIT,MARILYN,ATMOSPHERE)	N	18	4 3/8
EXT. PORCH Sc. 38 (LILY,HERMAN,EDDIE,GRANDPA,BEARD,GIRL)	N	1	3/8
INT. ENTRY HALL Sc. 39 (HERMAN,LILY,GRANDPA,EDDIE,GIRL,BEARD)	N	1	3/8
INT. ENTRY HALL Sc. 58 (LILY,HERMAN,GRANDPA,LARRY,GARY,EMILO,DICK)	N	1	1
COMPANY MOVE TO STAGE #17 APPROXIMATELY 5:00P			
INT. THEATRICAL OFFICE Sc. 10 (MURDOCK,LARRY,GARY,TONY,DICK)	D	1	1

```
                               CAST CALL
ARTIST                   CHARACTER                MAKEUP           ON SET
LARRY TAMBLYN            LARRY                     7:30A           8:00A
GARY MCMILLAN            GARY                      7:30A           8:00A
TONY VALENTINO           TONY                      7:30A           8:00A
DICK DODD                DICK                      7:30A           8:00A
ZALMON KING       (NEW)  THE BEARD                 8:00A           8:30A
                  (NEW)  GIRL (SC. 39)             7:00A           8:30A
KELTON GARWOOD    (NEW)  HERMIT                    8:00A           8:30A
FRED GWYNNE             HERMAN                     7:00A           9:00A
YVONNE DE CARLO         LILY                       7:00A           9:00A
BUTCH PATRICK           EDDIE  (MINOR)             8:00A           9:00A
AL LEWIS                GRANDPA                    7:30A           9:00A
PAT PRIEST              MARILYN                    7:30A           9:00A
ALEX GERRY              MURDOCK (LOOP 3:00P)       4:00P           4:30P
FRANK KILLMOND          BELLHOP                    CARRY

MUSIC DEPARTMENT:
GIRL WITH GUITAR                                   7:30A           8:30A
MAN WITH BONGOS                                    8:00A           8:30A

ATMOSPHERE:                    REPORT TO STAGE #16
4 STANDINS               7:30A
1 STANDIN                8:30A
7 WOMEN                  8:15A
4 MEN                    8:15A
1 WELFARE WORKER         8:00A
                               CREW CALL
CAMERAMAN                7:30A           RECORDER                 7:30A
CAMERA OPERATOR          7:42A           CABLEMAN                 7:30A
CAMERA ASSISTANT         7:18A           SCRIPT SUPERVISOR        7:42A
GRIPS                    7:30A           WARDROBE MAN             7:30A
```

The "call sheet" for the Standells' appearance on *The Munsters*. Courtesy of Edie McMillan.

schemed as to how they could get their money back. They decided to form a musicians union—actually create one while we were there—and then charge us traveling dues. The day of our departure, our luggage was put on the plane, but they kept us from boarding it and wouldn't let us leave the country until we paid our traveling dues, which was every penny we'd made. We were stuck

THE STANDELLS

Personal Management:
Dick Gabbe-Seymour Heller, Inc.
in association with
Burt Jacobs
Beverly Hills, Calif. - New York

Courtesy of Edie McMillan.

there for about three more days without our baggage, without anything, until
we could clear it all up. We left with just the clothes on our back. When we
finally returned to the U.S., we literally got down on the ground at LAX and
kissed it. We were so glad to be back."

♪ ♪ ♪

The Standells have been described as "one of the great Hollywood club bands
of the mid-1960s." The Standells were doing all right as a lounge act in a popular Los Angeles club, beginning once more to evolve their look and style to
reflect the new British Invasion music that was dominating the pop music
scene in America in the mid-'60s. Rather than following the lead of the early

L to R: Larry, Tony, Herman Munster, Dick, Gary. Courtesy of Edie McMillan.

On the set during the *Munsters* show. The Standells lineup is now Larry, Tony, Dick Dodd, and Gary Lane. The lineup that would record "Dirty Water." Courtesy of Edie McMillan.

THE STANDELLS

Personal Management:
Dick Gabbe-Seymour Heller, Inc.
in association with
Burt Jacobs
Beverly Hills, Calif. - New York

The Standells new line up with Larry in front and from left to right, Tony, Gary Lane, and Dick Dodd. Courtesy of Edie McMillan.

Beatles, though, the Standells fancied themselves as an American version of the wilder, more rebellious Rolling Stones.

Dick Dodd knew that the group wanted to be something more than a house band. "They wanted to become independent, popular in their own right, instead of a cover band. I was with them for a while, and then the Beatles came out. Before that we always dressed very neat—you know, matching gray suits on Monday, black suits the next day. Then all of a sudden everybody's hair is getting long, and you're wearing Levis and leather shirts and all that kind of stuff."

Ironically the Standells' first hit record and biggest success finally came when the increasingly punk-acting and ambitious act settled on Ed Cobb, a member of the "squeaky-clean" Four Preps, as their producer.

The Business of Show Business

This is the point in the story when the Fates converged to bring Ed Cobb and the Standells together.

What makes a hit record was, and is, a complicated process. To most of us a song is a hit when we hear it enough times on the radio, on television, or today on the Internet. We assume that the artist or group singing or playing the song had a lot to do with the record's success and are reaping big rewards as a result. We like to think that it is the talent of the performers that makes a record or a song a success. That is true—sometimes. There has to be something about the music that is compelling, but there has to be a solid business component, too. Most of the time, a record is made a hit through the actions, plans, and promotional activities of people whose names never appear on the record label or the album cover. These are often people who have a very different perspective of the hit-making process than do the musicians who sing the songs. They are the business people of music; in the 1960s, they were in some respects the real rulers of rock and roll.

Ed Cobb and Ray Harris, and their later associates, were just such individuals regarding the Standells and the song "Dirty Water." Cobb and Harris had expanded their partnership to include their production company Greengrass Productions, the next logical step for them as they sought out artists to record. Ed would write the songs and Greengrass would record the acts that sang them under the direction of Ed and Ray, who in turn would use their contacts to sell the completed package to the record companies.

Harris remembered getting a call one day from Standells manager Burt Jacobs. "We had gotten a call from a guy named Burt Jacobs who used to come by Vee-Jay [where Harris was still working for Jay Lasker.] He had had a couple of groups, he was a promoter in a sense, and he had an affiliation with Seymour Heller, who was Liberace's manager. [Seymour] had some little rock and roll things, and he had Jimmie Rodgers and all those people. He had those guys like that, but he [also] had a couple of groups. One of them was the Standells [who were brought to Heller by Jacobs.] Jacobs kept coming by Vee-Jay and talking to me about them. I listened to their stuff and I said, 'This is not a bad group.' They were on Liberty Records at the time. They had an album out called *In Person At P.J.'s*. Ed and I listened to the album and then we went to see them. We went to see them and we met them, but Ed wasn't that impressed at first. He said, 'Well, I don't really know.' I said, 'You know, there's a cohesion about them, Eddie, that I kind of like.' We didn't have anything [for them] at that time. We were just looking at them to see if we might be able to work with them."

Harris told Jacobs that he thought Ed Cobb could do a better job producing them than could any in-house production people at the labels. "They had nobody doing anything with them. But Jacobs was a very impulsive guy and they ended up taking the first deal that was offered, signing directly with Vee-Jay rather than with us as independent producers."

Harris' job at Vee-Jay then was to head up an independent label named Tollie within Vee-Jay. Part of his job was to sway independent Southern producers to come to the label. He tried to convince Vee-Jay to let Cobb record the Standells as an independent and then sell the finished tapes to Vee-Jay rather then have Vee-Jay produce the band in-house. Harris and Cobb were looking for the gig to try to prove their skills at production. They worked on Burt Jacobs, urging him to let them take a shot at independently producing the Standells, but both Burt and some of the people at Vee-Jay were hot on using producer Sonny Bono. In the Vee-Jay studios, the Standells cut four sides for Sonny Bono, the first in-house record label productions of the group, other than the live album, and had some raw master tapes left over after their first sessions.

The timing of the Standells' signing with Vee-Jay could not have been worse for the group. The label was experiencing a lot of fiscal problems and it began to look like it might close down. The newly signed band was in danger of not having their recently produced material released. Harris advised Jacobs, "First of all, I'm leaving Vee-Jay. It's in turmoil and it's going to go bankrupt. It's going to fold. They've got nothing but strife. Jay Lasker and Steve Clark and all the major players that brought its comeback are leaving."

Harris told Jacobs that he and Ed were going to do their own thing full time and that Jacobs should stick with them. Jacobs saw others beginning to leave the company and became anxious, uncertain whether Vee-Jay would release the Standells' material, and worried that he would have to fight to get out of his contract with the struggling label.

Cobb and Harris approached Jacobs and Heller shortly thereafter to discuss the next steps for the Standells. Harris says, "Jacobs and Heller went back to Vee-Jay and told them the contract was null and void. But the label said, 'Oh no, you're not going to do that. We're going to finish the masters off.' And they brought Sonny back in there to deal with it. But Jacobs and Heller finally decided to break the contract. Jacobs and all of them, in a behind-the-scenes move, got their contract out of Vee-Jay so it was all clear and we signed them."

The Standells were free, but back to square one. They needed a new record deal—and they needed a hit song—if they were ever going to be what they hoped to become. Jacobs and Heller made a deal with Cobb and Harris, Ray explained. "They had the management and we had production and promotion, and we started talking, and we said to Jacobs, 'You know, this is silly, everybody's working together. Why don't we form a company and put all of this in the company?'"

Cobb was agreeable to that but Burt wanted to check with Seymour Heller. Heller said OK, his company would take a position, and they agreed to form a company, give everyone stock, and see what they could achieve. In conversation, the lawyer they used came up with the name Attarack and they incorporated as the Attarack Corp.

Heller's company was to handle management of the acts with Attarack getting a percentage. The masters they owned were placed in the company and Heller provided office space. They were tight quarters, though, on Beverly Drive. The office was so small, Harris laughs, that if "one guy wanted to move, the other guy had to stand up. It was a very small office space."

Eventually the management structure became a bit more complex but that didn't really affect the Standells. They kept working, performing, and looking for their first big record. Dick, Tony, Larry, and Gary weren't businessmen— they were kids, rock and rollers barely out of their teens. The only thing that they understood or cared about at the time was that the guy closest to them, Burt Jacobs, was getting them gigs, that they were getting a paycheck, were having a good time, and that the rest of their management team was trying to get them material and a good record deal.

♪ ♪ ♪

The corporation behind the band was a necessary part of doing business. Harris was the businessman—a mover and shaker. "Later, I merged Heller and Attarack together and the company became Attarack-Heller...I then made divisions: Equinox Music Publishing, Greengrass Record Productions, and Seymour Heller Personal Management & Associates. Attarack-Heller issued the stock. When I sold the company to Transcon [Transcontinental Investment Corporation, a big Eastern entertainment concern listed on the New York Stock Exchange], they bought the stock of Attarack-Heller, and then we formed the American Variety International Company (AVI) and went public."

So it was Attarack Corporation—Cobb, Harris, and Heller (who also had another association with Burt Jacobs at the time)—that became the producers and managers of Ketty Lester, Gloria Jones, and the Standells. When Attarack took over management of the Standells, Burt Jacobs was part of the package, so Jacobs became another partner in Attarack and later in AVI, at least in its dealings with the Standells. As with any musical group at the time, the managers/producers were always looking for the right material that could catapult the group to success. Ed Cobb's contacts at Capitol Records from his Four Preps days proved useful, as did Ray Harris' experience in convincing Capitol to sign the band.

Tower Records (not to be confused with the well-known former music store chain) was a Capitol subsidiary label. Capitol, as the parent company, took very few chances with less proven acts, especially in the rock and roll genre. The Tower label was named after the landmark Capitol Records tower, which stood at the intersection of Hollywood and Vine. It was Tower with which the band signed their contract on September 1, 1965. Tower would eventually release "Dirty Water" and the later Standells recordings.

Harris elaborated, "Tower was created primarily so that its records could be distributed through independent distributors. Capitol had its own branch-owned operations, which is where my training came from—Capitol's branch operations in the South. The main reason for Tower was so Capitol could compete with the independents like Atlantic and the rest of them. Warner Brothers was independent before they created their own branch operation. The whole idea was so that [Capitol] could be more flexible and hire more independent promotion people to work with so that they could get into the independent market."

♪ ♪ ♪

The Standells, now managed by Attarack Corporation, consisted of the exotic European Tony, the all-American looking Larry, tall and quiet Gary, and the impish bad-boy Dick Dodd. The band would soon have a date with destiny. As a singer-songwriter/producer, Ed Cobb had some ideas for the group that went far beyond anyone's imagination. One of his earliest ideas for the Standells was the song that would become the group's biggest hit—"Dirty Water."

Creating "Dirty Water"

By all accounts, the inspiration for Cobb's composition of "Dirty Water" came when he was on one of his last college campus and nightclub tours with the Four Preps.

According to Preps founder Bruce Belland, touring colleges was the show business domain where the Four Preps found the most commercial success. "We were one of the first groups to do college concerts. It was a brand new field when we started to do it. In '62, '63, and '64, *Billboard* voted us the number one college concert act in the country—over the Kingston Trio, the Brothers Four, over the Limelighters. We were there because of our two hit 'in-person' albums. We were the only act I know of that did three consecutive in-person albums. …*On Campus, Campus Encore,* and *Campus Confidential.*"

After several successful years as a touring act, things began to change for the Four Preps. There was no doubt that the group was on the tail end of a great ride by 1965, but they still drew good crowds at large venues before their eventual breakup. Belland saw it begin to slow down, though. "We were going from 150 dates a year, to 100 a year, to 75 a year. By then, all of us were doing other things. I was selling scripts to TV shows. Glen was selling scripts. Marv was already a commodities broker; he was selling shiploads of grain from Russia and stuff like that. And Ed was off producing Ketty Lester's hits, and working with the Standells and all these people like Brenda Holloway. We all said, you know, before we end up playing a 'class C' lounge in Bakersfield, maybe we ought to move on to other things in our careers."

Before they did, the Four Preps embarked on a national tour that brought them to the city of Boston in the fall of 1965. With Ed Cobb no longer living, it is impossible to ever know *exactly* how he came to write the song "Dirty Water," but the recollections of people closest to him offer some very logical and plausible theories based upon what they remember or came to learn. Everyone agrees—without the slightest doubt—that *something* happened during this visit to Boston that led him to write this unusual song.

Boston's most famous nightclub at the time was Blinstrub's Village in South Boston and Belland recalled that when the group was performing there, Cobb had an experience that inspired his famous rock and roll song. "I remember an incident," Belland reflected, "We were playing at Blinstrub's and there was a road company of dancers on the program with us, like a version of the New York Radio City Rockettes, so we had 20 girls in a chorus line. . . . Well, we were all young guys and you can imagine how we jumped on that! After the last show, Ed had a date, so we didn't see him again that night until he returned to the hotel. When he came back to the hotel, he was sort of shaken, from supposedly being mugged, I don't know...Ed did have sort of a flair for the dramatic sometimes, so when he said he got mugged, I don't think he actually did. But I think some guys came up and started to talk rough to him and threateningly to him, and he got the hell out of there. I don't actually think he got mugged."

Knowing about Ed's penchant for embellishing his stories, it's not surprising that other people involved with him at the time, or close to him in the ensuing years, all have slightly different opinions on the song's exact beginnings.

Ed Cobb's son Matt thinks the inspiration for "Dirty Water" may have come as a result of a date Ed had with a local co-ed. Perhaps it was with someone he met from the audience of the show in South Boston and not one of the girls from the chorus line. Many years after "Dirty Water" had become a hit record, Matt was talking about the alleged mugging incident with his stepmother, Ed's third wife Lennie. Matt recalled her telling him about Ed's reluctance to clarify what really went on that night in Boston, "He wouldn't 'fess up to actually being mugged for a while. He didn't really want to talk about it ...he was real quiet...my step-mom brought it up [to him] and she started telling me what it was about. The lyrics were essentially the story of his evening."

It was a short evening for Ed and his date as the Californian learned firsthand about Boston's puritanical midnight dormitory curfews for coeds in the 1960s. Again Matt Cobb's conversation with his stepmother may confirm another lyric in the song—the "frustrated women" having to be in their dormitories by 12 o'clock. "Things were going pretty well with the girl, and he may have thought that it might just really work out. But her dorm had a curfew and he had to take her back to the dorm. Not only did he have to walk back kind of dejected along the Charles, but along the way, somebody had taken some of his stuff. All he'd fess up to was showing up with less stuff than he left with. The initial part of it—really thinking that things were going to work out with this girl and being shut out by the curfew, and then having to come back and face the ridicule of the boys: 'Hey, Ed, how'd that work out? You're comin' home awful early.' It added insult to injury, showing up with fewer things than he'd left with, and not voluntarily."[1]

Several years later, Lennie Sorensen Cobb herself tells what she recalls today, the story of Ed and a beauty contest winner dubbed the Snow Queen: "It took a lot to pry anything out of him. I guess there was some sort of contest in Boston that started in the 1940s and was sponsored by the American Legion, of all things. Ed was with the Snow Queen, some beauty queen, and she had to be home by midnight. It was somewhere around 10:30 or 11 o'clock at night. They were walking down the river and they went to the hotel room and Ed got fired up to write a song. She was quite put out because he's there writing a song. I believe it was [written] on some scrap of paper...on toilet paper if I remember correctly. He got her home before midnight, and that was the last he saw of her."

Perhaps the Snow Queen was the inspiration for the line about frustrated women who had to be in by 12 o'clock because of that abbreviated date?

No matter exactly how the song was inspired, Ed's goal remained to get his thoughts down and recorded as soon as he could. Ray Harris, Ed's new business partner at the time, remembered a call he received in California from Cobb while Ed was still in Boston. "About 10:30 one night (well after 1:00 A.M. on the East Coast), I get a phone call. It's from Ed. He says, 'I wrote a song. You got to listen to this.' So he sings me 'Dirty Water' on the phone. He was calling from Boston. He had been down by the river. He sang this song for me on the phone, and I said, 'Ed, it's a hit. Man, that's unbelievable. Where the hell were you?' He says, 'I was down there last night.' I said, 'Who were you with?' He said, 'Well, I was with a lady.... We went down there by the Charles River. It was just unbelievable down there, what you could see.' I said, 'You're kidding. We got to put it down, on tape or whatever. When you get back here, we gotta do that.' He said, 'I have it down. Don't worry about it.' Finally, I said, 'Well, look, maybe we should consider using that band that we've been trying to get something for—the Standells.' He said, 'That's not a bad idea.'"

Harris continued, "So anyway he comes back to town. We go over to Armin Steiner's little studio in his converted garage and he puts it down. Ed never could read music. He had it down in his head. He wrote the lyrics down. He gave me the lyrics, which he had on scribbled paper. He did a little quick demo at Armin's place with it, with himself. He just ran the tape and sang out the beat and tempo 'Buh buh buh buh.' Ed never could write anything. You had to interpret with him. Any time he did any arrangements or anything, Lincoln would come in or whatever, or he would hum to me and I would say, 'OK, I get it.' That's how we worked—we'd always beat the notes out."

At this point Cobb and Harris were ready to try out what they had, with the Standells playing it in the studio. Ray Harris's account of the session differs significantly from the recollections of the band: "We took them over to Armin Steiner's studio to get a feel, to see if we could do it, to see how it would work. The first time, they were either nervous or Ed had other expectations. I don't know what the distraction was, but it didn't come off. I said, 'You know, give them another shot. Maybe they were a little nervous with you. First of all, you're overpowering. They were nervous.' I thought the kid, Larry Tamblyn, did a pretty good job of getting the interpretation. So we went back into Steiner's maybe a week later, could have been three or four days, I don't remember. Dealing with a group instead of an individual singer was kind of a new experience for Ed. He rehearsed them. I mean, he rehearsed them and rehearsed them and rehearsed them and he finally got it down.

"The total arrangement was Ed. Ed had the idea of the [guitar introduction] 'bah bah bah bah ba ba ba bah.' And the way he had it echoed in the mix, too. That was totally his concept.

"He finally got a track. He said, 'I like the track. I dig it, man. It's enough. We've got the performance down.' So then he brought Dick Dodd in for the vocals...we already had the track done...and he worked Dick pretty good. Dick Dodd got the performance that's in there today. Dodd gave an exceptional performance."

♪ ♪ ♪

Armin Steiner, born in 1934, was in his early 30s when he engineered the recording of "Dirty Water." In recording circles he was already considered a genius because of the improvisational and creative work he did in his small studio—which was literally in his garage, a 15 x 25 foot space with 14-foot ceilings. The control room was a bedroom over the garage. He built the recording console from scratch and installed all the soundproofing and air conditioning himself.

Larry Tamblyn appreciated Steiner's talents: "He was really a genius. 'Dirty Water' was done on three-track. [Steiner used an Ampex 350-3.] What we did was we recorded all the instruments first, and then we doubled them. We doubled every one of the instruments. We ping-ponged—you would play the track back and you would record along with it. That was a favorite expression back then—ping-pong. Then we sang along with it and we recorded it.

"But on the second time through, instead of playing the regular bass drum with a foot pedal, Dick did it with a mallet. That's the reason it has such a heavy foot pedal to it. Normally back then, they were very light on the foot pedals on drums. In a lot of the early rock songs, you really didn't hear a heavy bass drum. That's what kind of made 'Dirty Water' stand out. The harmonica solo, I think, was done on a separate track and then ping-ponged in, because there was no way that Tony could put down the guitar and then put that down and pick up the harmonica. When you ping-pong, you're combining both tracks to one track and you still have two open tracks. The one track was background vocals and probably the harmonica solo and the other track was the lead vocals."

♪ ♪ ♪

At their first rehearsal session, Dick Dodd was taken aback at Ed's idea for the song when he presented it to the group. Dick and the rest of the Standells also hold very different recollections of the studio gathering than those Ray Harris described. The Standells, to a man, remembered the session as a collaborative effort—building and contributing on Ed's original idea. Dick says, "Ed had this idea, one day when we were just throwing songs together, putting them on tape. He goes, 'I was in Boston...I got mugged when I was down by this river they call the Charles. The water there is dirtier than anything, and you wouldn't believe the area there. . . .' He was just going on and on and on about this. He said, 'I'm going to write a song about it!'"

Now by this time, according to Ray Harris, Cobb had already conceived the idea, written the song, thought of the opening guitar lick, and created a demo tape of his idea. However, Dodd remembers it being presented to the band during a studio session, and that it was more of a collaborative effort between the band and Ed to create the song. Dodd recalled his reaction to the idea of recording "Dirty Water" when it was presented to the band. "I said 'What? What are we going to do—tell somebody a story about *that?*' and that is where the line 'I'm gonna tell you a story, I'm gonna tell you about my town' came from—I came up with 'my town' just because I thought it might be pretty cool to say it was 'my town.' We all sat down and threw stuff in . . . 'Down by the river, down by the banks of the river Charles'—that was written because of Ed, that's what he had experienced, and then our guitar player Tony came up with the great opening chords 'Ah—rum, dum, dum—dum da dum. Ah—rum, dum, dum—dum da dum.' It was played on a Fender Telecaster, a hard-body played through a Fender Twin amp."

Tony still has the guitar to this day.

Dick contributed parenthetical lyrics and vocal interjections. Much in the same way, Gary Lane added to the mix with his improvisational bass line. "I made it up. It's very simple—just E, A, and B. Just a three-chord change to it." As with the opening riff on the Fender, simple or not, when the various parts combined to create the whole, something special was created.

Although acknowledging that Cobb neither knew how to write musical notation nor to score a work, Harris insisted that Cobb had that opening guitar riff in mind when he first brought the idea for "Dirty Water" to the Standells. Cobb typically left more complex musical arrangements to his friend, arranger and composer Lincoln Mayorga. Cobb would hum, sing, or otherwise vocalize the sounds he wanted. Harris said that's what he did regarding the signature opening guitar chords of "Dirty Water," and that Tony Valentino interpreted Cobb's suggestions on his guitar to produce that memorable riff.

To a man, all of the Standells remember it differently and insist that the opening was entirely Tony's creation. "I wrote that riff," Tony insists. "I am proud that I came up with that riff. I have kids playing that riff; I even met John Travolta once and when he found out that I was with the Standells he started to sing, 'A rum dum dum dumda dum.' He said how he loved that song. I even had a mynah bird once that would do that vocalization of the opening guitar riff—it was the funniest thing, man, when that [bird] would sing that song."

Unfortunately, Tony's experience as he described it was very much the same as with "Let's Go!" where he insists that his contribution was a major one—yet he never got a thing for it. Tony received neither credit nor royalties for his contribution to the development of "Dirty Water." None of the Standells did. This wasn't unusual by contemporary standards, but still does not sit well with band members today.

When "Dirty Water" broke in Boston, the city was still reeling from one of its darkest chapters in history—a murderous crime spree. Between June 1962 and January 1964, 13 Boston area women, both old and young, had been sexually assaulted and murdered by a serial killer the press had dubbed "The Boston Strangler." In 1965, a man with a troubled past had been arrested in Connecticut for robbery and aggravated sexual offenses. While in jail for those charges, Albert DeSalvo confessed to being the perpetrator in the Boston cases and evidence at the time seemed to confirm it, though he never actually stood trial for any of the Boston crimes. The assumed and self-confessed "Strangler" was killed in a prison brawl that some people have theorized was a contract killing to silence him. Recent DNA and forensic evidence in the Boston cases suggest that DeSalvo may not have actually been the killer. In 1966, mentioning the Boston Strangler in a pop song was a radical thing to do, even if it was on a very muddled throwaway line at the end of the song. According to Dodd, a lot of the song was simply ad-libbed, such as the parenthetical lines "That's what's happening, baby" and "Aw, but they're cool people." And then the reference he makes to the Boston Strangler—"I love Boston...have you heard about the strangler, baby? I'm the man, I'm the man" was explained this way: "At that time I knew there was a guy called the Boston Strangler—Tony Curtis did the movie sometime later, I didn't even know what [it was all about] until somebody said to me, 'Do you know who the Boston Strangler is? Do you want that in the song? You're going on saying, 'I'm the man, I'm the man' like you are claiming to be the strangler!' Of course, that was not at all what I was trying to say. The words 'I'm the man, I'm the man' were just meant to be harmless scat lyrics."

Great rock songs often have lyrics that are hard to make out, and part of the appeal of the song comes from attempts at interpretation. Different listeners hear different words. If someone thinks they hear a suggestive lyric, so much the better for the song's success. Many listeners swear that they heard something in "Dirty Water" that caused them to perk up their ears. When Dick sings

That's where you'll find me
Along with lovers, muggers, and thieves (aw, but they're cool people)

any number of people swear they hear the word "fuggers" rather than "muggers."

The way Dodd tells it, the band rendered two versions of the song. "Now the lyrics 'lovers, *muggers* and thieves' are sometimes heard and are sometimes written out as and as 'lovers, *fuggers*, and thieves.' We did two versions of 'Dirty Water'—one with muggers and the other with fuggers, which was our punky way to imply a dirty word that could get by the censors. It was just another thing we did to promote that punk kind of image. I heard later that the 'fuggers' version was the one that the college kids picked up on, kind of like the way they sang dirty lyrics to 'Louie, Louie' by the Kingsmen."

Larry Tamblyn wasn't sure if the Standells actually recorded two versions of the song but he knows that Dick slipped in the word "fuggers" whenever he felt like it during live concerts. "That was Dick. He was the 'bad boy' and that was the kind of thing he would do on stage. I do remember that the kids would sing the word 'fuggers' just for fun."

Dodd continued, "Anyway, that's how I remember how the song came about, When we finally came up with the final take of the song we said, 'Well, that's OK,' and then we went on to other things."

So, in late 1965 the song was recorded in Los Angeles by the Standells in the small West Side garage studio of Armin Steiner and released by Capitol Records subsidiary Tower Records shortly thereafter. Ed Cobb was listed on the label as the sole songwriter, Equinox Music BMI as the publisher, Steiner as the engineer, and Lincoln Mayorga as the arranger. It was Tower #185, "produced by Ed Cobb for Greengrass Productions."

Along with Cobb getting sole credit as the writer, assigning the credit for arranging the song to Mayorga is something that still bothers Larry Tamblyn today. The four band members insist it was a collaborative effort, including Ed Cobb, but question Mayorga's inclusion. "What kind of arrangement could you be talking about?" Larry Tamblyn asks rhetorically. "It was a rock and roll song! I just don't remember him being in the studio, ever coming over to Armin's. He had nothing to do with it!"

Larry is quick to add, though, that he greatly respects Mayorga's musicianship and had the pleasure of working with him on a project in more recent years. "He was a buddy of Ed's. Ed had a clique that he liked and Lincoln was one of them, but he had nothing to do with 'Dirty Water' that I can remember, and I admire Lincoln Mayorga. I think he's brilliant."

There's no dispute here. Lincoln could not agree more with Larry about his lack of involvement. "I stayed away from it as much as possible. I hated it. I couldn't stand it. I did not like their music. I did not like those guys; I thought that they were full of themselves. They didn't need an arranger. Ed was able to talk to them and tell them what he wanted and so I was very delighted that they could make the record without me."

Why then was Mayorga given the credit for the song's arrangement?

"That was Ed's way of being generous. We were partners and he put my name on things. He was very, very generous about that. Ed worked it out as what we call a 'head arrangement.' Nothing was written out. Ed just talked to the band about what he wanted to hear and I am sure that they just began to rehearse it and play it as so many rock bands did. That's another form of arranging where there is nothing really written but the routine is agreed upon — who is going to solo where, what figure we are going to play behind that, etc."

Regardless of whether the respected arranger liked the song or not, "Dirty

Water" became a big hit—though it took so long to break that the band had nearly forgotten the song by the time it did.

♪ ♪ ♪

Armin Steiner credits both Mayorga and Cobb for his start in popular music. When *Mix* magazine asked him about building his studio while lacking a background in pop music, Steiner said, "Two people who were very influential in the commercial rock 'n' roll business helped me and actually went into business with me: Lincoln Mayorga...and Eddie Cobb....They were producing records for other people, and they taught me. I had never really paid attention to commercial music before, only classical."[2]

Steiner's home studio came to an abrupt end in the wake of the August 1965 Watts riots in Los Angeles. Operating a commercial recording studio out of his home was, naturally, not strictly legal. "In those days, you could do that," Steiner recalls. "And then came the Watts riots that devastated Los Angeles. I was working with a lot of black artists. They would work until 3 or 4 o'clock in the morning. It wasn't the music; I soundproofed it very well. It was a big old Spanish house with huge thick walls, but the exuberance of walking down the driveway and getting into their cars and going home, that was a different story. Because of the Watts riots, that produced...I think my neighbor across the street got a little bit paranoid. I was also working at Radio Recorders and one day, my brother called me and said the city inspector just came there and said, 'We know your brother is operating a studio. We know all about it. Just tell him to be out in 24 hours. Otherwise, he'll be fined the likes of which he doesn't believe.' So within 24 hours I moved everything over to Radio Recorders, I continued my career, and the rest is more or less history."

Steiner works almost exclusively in motion pictures and film today, but can look back on a career that produced thousands of recordings, many of them hits.

the
STANDELLS
scrapbook

The young Standells: Gary Lane, Larry Tamblyn, Gary Leeds, Tony Valentino

Original
promotional
single of
"Dirty Water"

Mamie Van Doren dances to the Standells music at the Peppermint West nightclub in Hollywood just before the high profile Playboy cover girl dated Red Sox star Tony Conigliaro

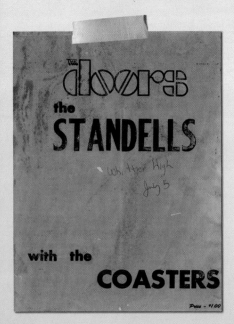

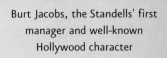

Whittier High School rock 'n' roll show poster - The Doors, The Standells, The Coasters!

Burt Jacobs, the Standells' first manager and well-known Hollywood character

"Dirty Water" hits
#1 in Orlando

Original Tower album cover -
Larry, Tony, Dick, Gary

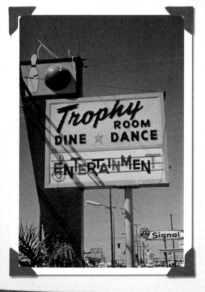

The Trophy Room - you could
bowl a string of 10-pins and
then hear the early Standells at
this Sacramento nightspot

2004 WORLD SERIES PRE-GAME SHOW
FENWAY PARK, BOSTON GAME 2

Three scenes from
the Standells'
performance at the
2004 World Series

The Standells at Fenway, 2006: Larry, Tony, Dick, Gary

Tony

Larry

Gary

Dick

Honorary Standell Dr. Charles Steinberg of the Red Sox at the keyboards,
working out an arrangement of "Dirty Water" with the group.

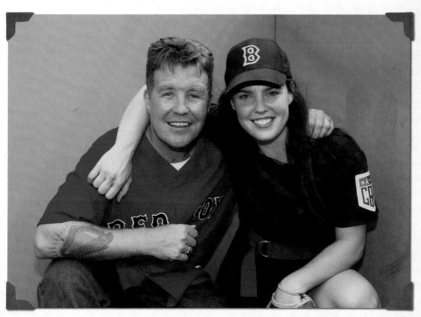

Ken Casey of the Dropkick Murphys with Red Sox employee
Colleen Reilly, "Tessie" in the band's video.

Selling the Song

After the band put a wrap on the "Dirty Water" session, the single came out and got some decent local airplay late in 1965, but it wasn't until the following year that it really attracted much attention. The band went on the road, continuing to play up and down the west coast. Because they did not yet have a hit of their own to capitalize on, they primarily did the popular songs of the day like any good house band. While they were doing dates on the road, mostly booked by Burt Jacobs, the rest of the management team was doing their best to get the Attarack "products" some attention in the marketplace—including "Dirty Water."

Larry Tamblyn recalls that the band had pretty much forgotten about the song and had gone on to other things, including picking up a series of short and one-night stands all across the west and northwest. "We recorded 'Dirty Water' and we actually forgot the song. We recorded it, and we forgot all about it. And didn't even remember what it sounded like when it started hitting the charts. It was also shortly after we recorded the song that Dick left us."

Dick Dodd left the group for a couple of months. Dewey Martin took Dick's place. Larry says, "We played a number of different places with Dewey. We were up in San José and we heard that the song was starting to get play. Dick rejoined the group while we were in San José and we played at least one more week in San José with Dick." Martin later was in the Buffalo Springfield, but never built on his musical career the way that other members of that band did. Tamblyn recalls with regret, "Dewey was never able to get it together after that. Too bad, he was really a nice guy."

The Standells were still playing gigs in some pretty scary venues even after "Dirty Water" was recorded. The Hell's Angels frequented the San José club where the band was booked on a regular basis. "One of them gave me his Hell's Angels business card," Larry remembers. "He [was called] 'F—-Up.' I think the reason he liked me is that I prevented another guy from hitting him over the head with a beer bottle from behind. I distracted the guy with a loud discordant blast from my Vox Continental Organ. His card proved to be an ace in the hole for me later on in the late '60s, after the Standells had broken up. On this one occasion, I was in an alley in a rundown section of L.A., waiting for [a] rehearsal room to open up, when I was approached by a couple of burly biker chicks. They started harassing me and I didn't know quite how to handle them, until I remembered I still had the business card. I pulled out my wallet. The girls were thinking I was going to give them some insurance money, but instead I presented them with the card. They almost fell to their knees in awe. 'F—-Up' was quite a prominent member of the Hell's Angels and was held in high esteem by most bikers."

From San José, the Standells moved on to Seattle for a gig there when they got an unexpected call from Ed Cobb. The band was surprised to learn that "Dirty Water" was showing signs of life, so many months after its release. Dick Dodd remembered it was "like a half a year later, Ed called us up and says, 'Florida is playing the hell out of your song, and they are really getting a lot of response.' I said, 'What, which one?' He said, 'Dirty Water!' I said, 'You're kidding!' I was shocked that it was getting that kind of play. Because of Florida, that song really got kicked into a national hit, then we heard that Boston loved it, too."

Ray Harris was the management partner responsible for promoting the record and was tracking "Dirty Water" after its release by Capitol/Tower. In the record industry, promotional people try to make a song into a hit through personal interaction, constant deal making, visits to radio stations and calls to deejays across the country, as well as working the salespeople for the distributors. Most records fall short, of course, but in the case of "Dirty Water," the improbable happened and—belatedly—it made its way up the charts.

Harris tells the story: "I hired a couple of promotion guys, one guy in particular in Florida. But in the meantime, I had serviced it to a lot of jocks that I knew, from Birmingham and other places—program directors in different spots. I had given them the record and I knew that they were playing it. [I gave it to] a disc jockey by the name of Jim Clark who was on a 10,000-watt clear channel station out of Knoxville, Tennessee, and to his friend Bill Sanders, who was the program director there. But we weren't getting any reaction, no orders or anything, so it was a very depressed time. Nothing was happening. I couldn't think of anything else, so I thought let's just continue on. These guys [the Standells] are still working, so they are OK. It was the holidays, a bad time to get anything going. Then I got a call one day from a guy named Dennis, who used to work with Music City, the independent distributor out of Nashville. He calls me and says, 'Ray, do you have any connections at Liberty?' I said that I knew a few of the guys over there. He says, 'Can you see if you can get me 200 or 300 of that *Standells Live at P.J.'s*? I can sell them.' I said, 'You can sell them there, in Tennessee?' He says, 'Yeah, I can sell them.' I said, 'Well, let me see what I can do.'"

In January 1966, Knox County, Tennessee was just beginning to push for sewer service, and the Clean Water Council was backing efforts to bring service to portions of the county. As someone familiar with local radio in the area for over 40 years, Chris Durman of the University of Tennessee, Knoxville Music Library thinks, "It would be logical for local radio to want to comment on this issue with song."[1] It's only speculation, but perhaps that was why a key station in Knoxville was playing "Dirty Water."

"Dirty Water" became popular in Knoxville as a result of air-play on WNOX. One of the promos had done its job, and Dennis was looking to bring in some Standells material—even if it was their old album—so that he could capitalize on the sudden and unexpected success of the single.

Harris went into action. "I called Jim Clark [at WNOX] and I said, 'That record I sent you, "Dirty Water," have you been playing that?' 'Oh yeah, it's one of our most requested records at night.' I thought that was interesting, that's where this is coming from. They had gotten a reaction there. His station was a clear channel one that reached into the Nashville market at night as well as Knoxville. Stations didn't follow sales of records in stores as much in those days. They were more a listening kind of thing, a reaction to listeners. That's how they played their records. They knew that their station reached way out and that they would influence from there. So I called Ed and said, 'This is really strange, this information from the independents. . . . I don't see anything from Tower. I don't get any calls, I don't get any orders.'"

"Dirty Water" was a grass-roots hit and a heavily requested song on Knoxville radio, but Tower was weak in its distribution in the region and there were no records available there. Ray knew that if he could get copies of the record into the market, he could sell them. Bothered by the news that the Standells' music had found a market but no "product" was available, Cobb and Harris became very upset with Capitol/Tower. The two were without the means to pursue much more in the way of promotion on their own. As it happens, they were down to the last $300 in promotional money budgeted in their "Dirty Water" account—and they owed half of that to a promotion guy in Florida hired months before.

Ray Harris tells about when he learned the record had first broken: "Everyone's depressed. Ed says, 'What are you going to do?' I said, 'Ed, we have $300 in the bank. I owe this fellow in Florida $150 of it. I'm going to let him have it for the next couple of weeks or whatever it is. I'll send him the whole $300. If nothing happens, we're dead meat.' 'It's up to you.' Ed said, 'Send it to him. We may need him later. We've got a good rapport with these guys. You might as well send it to him.' So I wrote a note and sent the guy the $300 and I said this is the last thing I can afford to send you. I appreciate all the work that you've been doing but unfortunately there's nothing happening anywhere else."

"The guy gets the $300 and he calls me a few days later and says, 'Are you out of our mind? It's the #1 record in Orlando, Florida!' I said, What? How come I don't have any business.' He says, 'I can't get any records.' I said, 'You're joking me.' He says, 'No, call Bill Vermillion.' He's the music director at WLOF Orlando. So I call Bill and he says, 'It's #1.' I'm trying to figure out the correlation between Knoxville and Orlando. I ask the promotion guy, "How come all this is happening?" He says, "Ray, it's sort of a competitive thing in the market. WNOX is a 10,000-watt station. It's sort of a local station.'"

Being a 10,000-watt clear channel station, WNOX's signal was coming into central Florida with the strength of a local station. Listeners in Orlando were hearing "Dirty Water" played on the Knoxville station and the music clicked—with a boost from Vermillion, who loved the record and started giving it heavy airplay.

Bill Vermillion had come to Orlando from KXLY Spokane and was the music director at WLOF from 1965 through 1972, and program director thereafter. WLOF was an unusually popular station in the fast-growing Orlando market, exploding in size after Disney's 1963 announcement it would build Disney World there. Vermillion had only been the music director for a few weeks before he started playing "Dirty Water." He says the Standells' single was the first record to ever break out of Orlando, and that some record promotion people hadn't yet learned where the city actually was!

WLOF had a 33% market share on a 24/7 basis, and a 45% afternoon share. Vermillion himself earned a 60% share during his own slot, allowing the station to promo the show thus: "More people listen to Bill Vermillion on WLOF than all other stations combined." Regarding "Dirty Water" in particular, Vermillion recalls, "I remember picking it from a stack of records. I'd go through all the records and pick out ones for possible airplay, and then through those to narrow them down. I put it into normal rotation, and the phone calls took over from there."[2]

The record first hit WLOF's chart the week of January 15–21, 1966. It debuted at #37. Just two weeks later—the week that started on February 5—the record hit #1. "As far as I know, from what Ed [Cobb] said, we were the only station playing it. There were NO copies available for sale anywhere, as the record had been dropped [by Tower] by the time we were playing it." WLOF's principal competition, WHOO, started playing the single, too. Vermillion gave it a few spins, but is clear that it was the listener reaction that drove further airplay. The strong reaction prompted WHOO to add it as well, and truly broke the record.

When Ray Harris heard that the record had shot to the top of the Orlando station's chart, too, and that there were no records in that market, either, he was far from pleased: "I really get mad now. I call up my old boss at Capitol, and jumped all over him. I said, 'I'm going to show you how effective your cocka-mamie label is. You sit there. You didn't want to put this record out. You went through these gyrations. You have a #1 record in Orlando, Florida and a Top 10 record in Knoxville, Tennessee, both of them swinging it away. I talked to the distributor and the promotion guy. They said they couldn't get any product from you. They've got orders sitting down there and they can't get a nickel's worth of records.'

"So he gets on the phone, he calls me back and says, 'You're absolutely right. It looks like a breakdown.' Well, they got on the horn and they were flying records down there and so forth. I go back and tell Ed, 'Tell Seymour, it

Bill Vermilion in Orlando at
the WLOF console. Courtesy
of Dick Camnitz.

looks like we got a spot [on the charts]' It started being programmed on all the
stations in Florida, so suddenly they take up the piece to try to get it in other
markets. It was around February or March or so, somewhere in there, it started
hitting the regional charts around there. Now they're up to about 25,000 sales
but you can't get it anywhere else. It's only showing up in a couple of spots. I'm
frustrated. But I tell Ed, 'Be thinking about an album—something that you
can do quick—if this act starts breaking.'"

Suddenly, a sewer project in Knox County, Tennessee, may have kicked a
song recorded by a relatively unknown Los Angeles, California quartet about
a polluted river, romantic couples, and petty criminals in Boston into becoming a big hit in Orlando, Florida, but it was still not yet well known in Boston—
the city celebrated (so to speak) in the song.

Harris continued his story: "So now they sell all these records. Again, I'm
frustrated. We spent a lot of time trying to break "Dirty Water" in Boston. Nothing happened. The record bounced from city to city, but not in Boston. It was
Cleveland, and then Detroit. It started hitting all these different places. Los
Angeles, it started. It was just going one, to one, to one, market to market to
market."

"So now I'm up in our office. We were in another little office on Doheny
Drive. We were trying to get *Billboard* action. There was a guy coming in there
by the name of Seymour Stein. Seymour was working for *Billboard* at the time,
and we told Seymour, 'Man, we're having a tough time trying to get this record
going. There's no way we can get this thing happening. We always thought it
would break in Boston.' He says, 'Why don't you send a thousand records to the
one-stop up there? Danny Gittleman's. Send him 1,200 records, tell him what
the story is.'"

A record one-stop was a wholesale distribution outlet, a place where jukebox operators and small record store operators, among other people, stocked
up on records rather than buying them direct from each individual label or
distributorship; it offered one-stop shopping. Gittleman had the biggest oper-

ation in the area and Harris needed to go to Capitol to convince them to send the records to Boston. "I went up to Capitol and said, 'I need 1,200 saleable promotional copies.' They said they would let me have them, but charge them back to me if nothing happens. So, I get the records. We sent them up there and in about a week's time, the record started popping up all over the joint. It starts happening. It starts breaking out but it was really a credit to Seymour Stein, who really put me onto it and told me how to do it."

Stein's reply? "Ray gives me more credit than I deserve for the Standells and for Soft Cell, who recorded his copyright 'Tainted Love.'" Years later, Stein's label Sire Records had a huge hit with Ed Cobb's song "Tainted Love."

What Seymour Stein suggested, and what Ray Harris did to promote the song, was called "greasing the skids" or "priming the pump," said Peter Mc-Dermott, another one-stop operator in the Greater Boston area during the 1960s. His business, Peter's One-Stop, was a relatively modest operation compared to the volume that Dan Gittleman did in the mid 1960s. Peter's primarily serviced small independent music stores and the jukebox operators in the region while Gittleman's U.S. Records was known in the business as a "rack jobber"—a huge operation that could afford to handle 100,000 or more records at a time, servicing the big record stores and large discount department store chains.[3]

Dennis O'Malley was the Boston sales and promotion man for Capitol several years after "Dirty Water" became a hit. As a 25-year veteran of the record industry, Dennis called upon many one-stops, big and small, for much of that time. His experience tells him that despite Ray Harris' assertion that Gittleman "broke the record," an operation like Dan's would never buy an unproven record in any meaningful quantity. As the big guys in the business, they followed demand and would buy at volume after a record had begun to chart or was well on its way to becoming a hit. The one-stops would service the smaller customers and the initial demand.

The rack jobbers dealt in volume, and typically waited for their big record department customers to need quantity, truly working the hit songs that the customers were after—a classic demand and supply kind of business. O'Malley explained his thoughts on Gittleman's influence on the success of "Dirty Water" in the Boston market: "Danny Gittleman owned U.S. Records in Somerset, Mass. U.S. Records was one of the largest rack jobbers in the country and supplied all of the Zayres stores and all of the Military P.X.'s in the country. When he bought a record, the sheer volume had an impact. Radio stations around the country would see a 10,000 or 25,000-piece movement in New England on a record and sense that something big was happening. They didn't always associate the buy going into hundreds of discount stores. Danny's singles buyer was a woman named Georgianna Mirragis. She had quite an ego and many record sales people played off this, letting Georgianna think she personally 'broke records.' Her office walls were littered with gold singles given by appreciative labels. To say that U.S. Records broke 'Dirty Water' would be incorrect. If anybody was responsible for its success, it had to be radio stations that took an unknown band and gave them a shot."[4]

Gittleman would not buy a record that was not already solidly establishing itself in the Boston market. A sharp promoter could take a chance on a band, though, offering a quantity of records to a rack jobber at no cost, as an enticement.

Gittleman in turn, could take those records and "seed the market" with them at no risk. Harris had "greased the skids" by providing those 1,200 records. If the seeding got the record in the hands of the stores, jukebox operators, select radio station deejays and programmers, it could create a demand for more—and help make a hit.

The charts of industry publications like *Billboard, Cashbox,* and *Record World* were based on a combination of airplay and sales, and they were by no means as objective as they are today. It was not unknown for an adept operator to manipulate the charts, at least at the lower levels. Pumping over 1,000 records through the system gave a sense of activity on the song.

Stew Ross was the contact person at Peter's for the regional and national chart makers for many years. He'd spent time as the regional representative for ABC Dunhill Records in the early 1970s. "Every Wednesday we would get a call from the various chart trackers from *Billboard*—Hot 100, Country, Adult Contemporary and so on—asking us how a certain song was doing or what songs were moving. Every Tuesday, before those calls, the various record company promotion men would be calling us to persuade us to push their records to the jukebox guys and our other customers so that their numbers would look good. Then a song might start getting up on the charts, or be listed 'with a bullet' meaning it was really rapidly rising. That would create more demand, more sales, and a hit was in the making."[5]

♪ ♪ ♪

"Dirty Water" broke into the *Billboard* Top 40 charts as a hit during the summer of 1966. As we've seen, the record first started getting some airplay in Knoxville but truly broke in Orlando. It was first noted in industry publications when the March 5 issue of *Billboard* listed it as a regionally successful single in Miami, #35 on the regional chart. This no doubt reflected the airplay it was getting out of Orlando. It climbed into the top 10 regionally in the March 19 issue. Come April 2, the single was #2 in the Miami market. On April 23, it reached #1—and, for the first time, made *Billboard*'s national Hot 100 list, ranked at #98.

This was also the week "Dirty Water" first made its mark in Boston, slipping onto the very lowest position on the regional chart, #40. *Billboard* suspended its regional charts after the May 14 issue; the highest the record ever reached in Boston was #39. It was making its mark as a national single by this time,

July 2, 1966   THE BEAT

KRLA Tunedex

DAVE HULL

BOB EUBANKS

DICK BIONDI

JOHNNY HAYES

EMPEROR HUDSON

CASEY KASEM

CHARLIE O'DONNELL

BILL SLATER

This Week	Last Week	Title	Artist
1	7	DIRTY WATER	The Standells
2	1	SEARCHIN' FOR MY LOVE	Bobby Moore
3	6	DOUBLE SHOT (OF MY BABY'S LOVE)	The Swingin' Medallions
4	2	A GROOVY KIND OF LOVE	The Mindbenders
5	10	YOU DON'T HAVE TO SAY YOU LOVE ME	Dusty Springfield
6	3	PAINT IT, BLACK	The Rolling Stones
7	4	ALONG COMES MARY	The Assoication
8	18	PAPERBACK WRITER/RAIN	The Beatles
9	14	STRANGERS IN THE NIGHT	Frank Sinatra
10	13	LITTLE GIRL	Syndicate of Sound
11	9	HOLD ON! I'M COMIN'	Sam & Dave
12	19	SOLITARY MAN	Neil Diamond
13	11	DON'T BRING ME DOWN	The Animals
14	23	OH HOW HAPPY	Shades Of Blue
15	5	WHEN A MAN LOVES A WOMAN	Percy Sledge
16	15	YOUNGER GIRL	The Hondells
17	21	WHERE WERE YOU WHEN I NEEDED YOU	The Grass Roots
18	16	I AM A ROCK	Simon & Garfunkel
19	12	DID YOU EVER HAVE TO MAKE UP YOUR MIND	The Lovin' Spoonful
20	20	OPUS 17 (DON'T WORRY 'BOUT ME)	The 4 Seasons
21	26	DAY FOR DECISION	Johnny Sea
22	17	BAREFOOTIN'	Robert Parker
23	27	HANKY PANKY	Tommy James & The Shondells
24	34	SWEET TALKING GUY	The Chiffons
25	25	BETTER USE YOUR HEAD	Little Anthony & The Imperials
26	22	DIDDY WAH DIDDY	Captain Beefheart & His Magic Band
27	35	(I'M A) ROAD RUNNER	Jr. Walker & The All Stars
28	49	WILD THING	The Troggs
29	29	LOVE SPECIAL DELIVERY	Thee Midniters
30	32	HE WILL BREAK YOUR HEART/HE	Righteous Bros.

"Dirty Water" tops the charts in LA. Courtesy of Edie McMillan.

though, with an extra boost coming out of Cleveland. *Billboard* gave it a "star"—today, that's called a "bullet"—and it was #63 nationally that same week.

By no means was Boston the only town where "Dirty Water" resonated. The song broke in Cleveland as well, its third major market. It was on its way to becoming a national hit. Even way down in the border city of Laredo, Texas, music aficionado Yleana Martinez remembers the song from her younger days and how it seemed to even apply to the brown waters of the Rio Grande. She also recalls the muggers and fuggers controversy.

When things began to break, Ed Cobb flew to Seattle and had the band cut enough additional material for a full album, which was released on June 11. A detailed study of "Dirty Water" on industry charts is contained in the Appendix, but suffice it to say that the record did very well indeed, reaching the top slot in several parts of the country and reaching #8 in *Cashbox* and #11 in *Billboard*.

Tower tried hard to capitalize on the success, but in retrospect one wonders a bit at their approach. Rather than intensely work the one single, they came out with a second single almost immediately. It's hard to fault the timing of that, but by the time 1966 was done, Tower had released three albums! *Dirty Water* came out in June, *Why Pick On Me—Sometimes Good Guys Don't Wear White* came out in September, and *The Hot Ones!* was released in November. One could argue that was overkill, too much too quickly and far more than the market could absorb. It's clear that management was pushing in this direction, too, but it would be hard to find any group that released three LPs in a five-month frame.

The Standells continued to perform, trying to ride the crest of the wave as far as it would take them. They continued to cultivate an image of a bad-boy band and went on to achieve their greatest notoriety in the short few years that followed. "Some people have called us a garage band, or the Godfathers of Grunge," reflected Dodd many years later, "because of my tone, a kind of whiny bitching-about-things kind of tone, and the punk-ish attitude we projected. I don't know, I always thought of us as kind of an American Rolling Stones kind of band."

A Rock Group's Rise and Fall

Ray Harris had called Cobb about the record's success and Cobb then called the Standells. "Dirty Water" was now a hit record. Tamblyn says, "Tower got back to us when they saw the play the song was getting and we had to rush and do a Standells album." Burt Jacobs had booked the band for a couple of months' gig in Seattle at the A-Go-Go club, so arrangements were quickly made for Ed to fly up to join the band and begin work on the *Dirty Water* album. Harris says, "There was a studio up there and I said, 'OK, do the album up there.'" Most of the album was recorded at Kearney Barton's Audio Recording studio at 2227 Fifth Avenue in Seattle. The cover photo for the album was taken in Seattle as well. The Seattle sessions featured several original Standells songs besides "Dirty Water" and included the song released as their next single release, "Sometimes Good Guys Don't Wear White." The recording was done quickly, in just two days, the band playing the club gig at night and working in the studio with Cobb during the days.

Kearney Barton represents yet another link. He recorded the classic "Louie Louie" by The Kingsmen, on Jerden Records. The song, first cut by Richard Berry in Los Angeles, had never been a hit but had become a song that many of the bands in the Northwest featured as a regular part of their repertoire in the clubs. When the Kingsmen wanted to cut it, though, Kearney laughs, "I tried to talk them out of doing it. I told them they'd never get it started in the Northwest. It won't sell. So they recorded it and sure enough six months later it hadn't done anything in the Northwest, and a distributor in Boston got hold of it and started it in Boston and got a little action. What really broke it was this kid in Indiana who called the Governor and told him that if you played it at $33\frac{1}{3}$, you'd get all these filthy lyrics. A guy from the *P-I [Post-Intelligencer]* came down to interview the Kingsmen and me. I said, 'I'll play it any speed you want—sideways, backwards. That's not in there.' But the governor just immediately banned it and the record took off like a banshee. Even after it went nationally, though, it still didn't sell in Seattle."[1]

Barton was taken aback when he first met Ed Cobb. "It was a rather strange session," Barton begins. "Cobb, to me, was one of the worst producers I ever worked with. Jerry Dennon of Jerden Records had owned part of Audio Recording Corporation at that time and he made a deal with Cobb that we'd do it for half price, which was about $\frac{1}{4}$ of what it would have cost them in L.A. Cobb came in and the first thing he said was that he had to sit in the studio for an hour in the dark so that he could get the feel of the studio before we recorded.

Full cover photograph for the *Dirty Water* album. Courtesy of Edie McMillan.

Oh boy! Mister Hollywood! So we started doing the session and all of a sudden the sound was just going berserk and I looked over and he was playing with the equalizers! I said, 'What the hell are you doing?' And he said, 'I don't like the sound on the drums.' I said, 'Well, I usually do the EQ at the end of the thing, when we listen to it back and you can say, "I like that" or "I don't like that"—but you don't change it in the middle of a take!' I said, 'If you're looking for EQ on the drums, you can do *this* . . .' and he said, 'Oh, that's what I'm looking for!' I said, 'All you've got to do is ask.'"

As we have noted, the "Dirty Water" single was pretty much in the band's rear-view mirror by the time The Standells were on the road in Seattle. Except for the initial inkling they heard that something could be happening with the song when they were playing in San José, nothing further got back to the group. Larry remembers, "It was months, literally months. I have the feeling it was almost a year after we recorded it. We recorded it in '65 and it didn't hit the charts until '66. We completely forgot about the song and had to re-learn it. We were up in Seattle when it finally hit the charts. We were performing up there for a couple of months."

When Cobb returned from the Seattle recording sessions with the tapes for the *Dirty Water* album, Tower wanted to release "Sometimes Good Guys Don't Wear White" as the next single release. Cobb and Harris agreed, but there were some technical difficulties with the master that had to be corrected and they were not easy to effect. Harris told Cobb, "We've got distortion here. Heavy distortion. How are we going to correct this? It's going to be terrible. We've got to master it. It's just not going to work. It doesn't sound good." Harris explained the solution: "We found a little studio on Ventura Boulevard called American Sound Studios owned by Richie Podolor, who later did all the Three Dog Night stuff. Armin's studio had gotten very busy so we went to Richie. We told him we had these problems with distortion. So anyway, we cleaned it up and it came out really great. What they did is, they meshed the distortion on 'Good Guys' into the drumbeats. Later, many producers—including Quincy [Jones]—said, 'I loved the way it came out, that drum sound.' He wondered how they did it—it was the distortion. That's how we got it. Total distortion disguised in the drumbeats."

Of course, Richie Podolor was already familiar with the Standells from their days at P.J.'s and with Dick Dodd from Dodd's sessions as a drummer with Jackie DeShannon. From the time he started at his first Hollywood studio in 1959, Podolor's work always reflected a great appreciation for the importance of the drum and drummers in music. "I was one of the first guys to ever put a microphone on a bass drum because I thought it was so necessary. Everyone else was overlooking that." It was natural that he and his long time studio engineer Bill Cooper would look to the bass drum track as a solution to the distortion problem on "Good Guys." Podolor's early work with teenage drumming sensation Sandy Nelson was an indication of his continuing appreciation for the work of percussionists. "I did 'Teen Beat' with Sandy Nelson which went number one, then a year later I wrote 'Let There Be Drums' for Sandy and that record went to number one, and became Record of the Year. I just had a real affinity to drummers for some reason."[2]

There was a bit of an aftermath to the Seattle sessions besides the distortion problem. Kearney Barton wrapped up the recording and gave Cobb the tapes, still shaking his head about the experience. "We got through the thing and I sent him an invoice. One month and a half later, I still hadn't been paid. The thing is climbing on the charts nationally, so I called down to L.A. and asked to talk to him. The gal said, 'Well, he's busy.' I said, 'It's been a month and a half and we haven't been paid for this session.' She said, 'Oh, the checks are going out at the end of this month.' 'Ahhhhh . . . OK.' So I waited another month and a half. Nothing. I called again and I say, 'What's the story? Let me talk to Ed Cobb.' She said, 'He's busy.' I said, 'I don't care what he's doing. Let me talk to him right now.' I got him on the phone and I say, 'What's the story? The record is like number two on the national charts in *Billboard* and we still haven't been paid for this.' He said, 'Oh, I thought you'd be so honored to do us that you'd do it for nothing.' He said that! I said, 'You're out of your cotton-picking mind.' I said, 'Dennon made a deal with you for half price, which I don't agree with. You pay me right now or I'm suing you' and I got a check within a few days. But come on . . . !"

♪ ♪ ♪

As soon as the Standells finished the hurried album to capitalize on the new-found success of "Dirty Water," Larry and the boys were off on a hastily arranged tour put together by Jacobs. The tour took advantage of their hottest market and was launched clear across the country, in Florida where the single had broken.

The transition of Burt Jacobs from bookie to booking agent became complete. "Burt personally booked us from job to job, setting up gigs for us," Larry remembered. "That led to one series of adventures after another. We went right from Seattle after recording the album, right to Orlando. We were met at the airport by hundreds of screaming teenagers. That was quite a thrill. Going from this nightclub—things were a little more refined in the night-club—to screaming teenagers. It was a whole different feel. We went from Orlando up the coast and through the southern states, then into parts of New York and some of the northeastern states. We would do one show per venue. Basically, we did a concert and then go to the next city."

Despite the frenetic welcome, pulling the tour off with Burt booking gigs on the fly did not always result in days of wine and roses. "We'd do a job and wouldn't know where our next job was," Larry told Robyn Flans for *Goldmine*. "We'd drive hundreds of miles and get to where our next job was supposed to be, and it would be a cow pasture. We were so broke. It was during that first tour that Gary Lane decided he had had enough and wanted to be a plumber."

Over the next few years and during the Standells' most productive period, members of the group would come and go.

Larry recalled one night when their newly-found popularity actually got them

Courtesy of Edie McMillan.

out of what looked like a pretty serious jam. "One time we were driving through Tennessee at night and we passed through this town so small we didn't even see it. Tony was driving doing about 80 miles an hour. All of a sudden a red light's flashing behind us and this Smoky pulls us over. The cop got out of his car, came up and leaned on the window and said, 'Where ya'll goin' to, boys, a fire?' The combination of this guy's thick Southern drawl and Tony's inability to speak the language well really confused things. Tony didn't know what the guy was saying but he thought he'd just agree with him. So Tony says, 'Yeah!' And so this guy immediately grabs Tony's license, thinking he's a wise guy, and makes us follow him back into this so-called town. 'Why'd you have to be such a wiseass, Tony?' we said. He said, 'I didn't know what he was saying. I was just trying to agree.' Here we were, all of us with long hair, which they absolutely hated in the South, driving too fast at night with California plates on the vehicle. And here we are going to this town, God knows into what. The cop was the sheriff, the justice of the peace, and the mortician all rolled into one. Everything was in one building. We're thinking, oh God, he's going to lock us up and throw the keys away. Finally he gets a look with us in our long hair, and he says, 'You boys in some kind of rock and roll group?' I started to say no, but Tony speaks right up again and says, 'Yes.' 'What's the name of your group?' the Sheriff asked. I said, 'The Standells.' He says, 'Did ya'll say the Standells? — "Dirty Watta"?' in his heavy southern accent. 'Y'all know what? My daughter's a big fan of y'all.' So we got out of there by giving him an autographed album for his daughter!"

When Gary Lane quit the band during the tour, he told the others, "I just can't do this any more." He was the only married band member and wanted to be home more with his wife. He didn't care for all the traveling, and the uncertainties of haphazard booking. The group was stuck again for another member, needing a bassist. They auditioned several musicians — and even took advantage of their radio success by putting out an appeal over the airwaves. They found someone they'd actually already known — Dave Burke.

"Dave was a real affable guy, real funny, and had a great sense of humor. He was from Tennessee, I think, but he was in Florida at the time. He was just a poor boy, shuffling around doing nothing and we made him part of the Standells and he was making some real money. He didn't know how to handle it...and had some personal problems as a result. He was with us for about a year. We played different places all over and finally returned to L.A. with Dave. Burt and Ray Harris and those people met us at the airport. We went back into the studio to record another album, but we really didn't do much more with Dave. He just didn't know how to deal with the success."

Dave Burke would stay with the band for the next tour but was later replaced by John Fleck (Fleckenstein.) He recorded with the Standells just once — on the *The Hot Ones*, an album of "cover" songs, songs that other groups had made famous. Tamblyn reflected, "...*Hot Ones* was such a bad idea—it wasn't ours…it was just a bunch of songs other groups had done already. We just did what we were told by our managers back then."

Was the album thrown together and rushed to its release simply to have more Standells material in the market? Perhaps. Why weren't the Standells given some original material to record by their producers instead of doing "other peoples' hits"? Ray Harris explained, "Tower said, can we do another album of something? The Standells did not have a lot of their own material ready at the time, they were on the road doing covers and they didn't write a lot. Ed and I said, 'Hey, we don't have material to do another album.' That is when I came up with the idea of doing the material of these other groups. Many of the real successful groups from that period wrote their own stuff, they were bigger groups, and they were able to advance themselves where the Standells did not write a lot of their own things and so we had to find outside material at great lengths…the band themselves were not coming up with new material, and they were never the greatest of writers anyway."

The immediate goal was to capitalize on the success of "Dirty Water" for the band that likened itself to one the world's hottest British Invasion bands— the Rolling Stones. Unknown to the band at the time, as they were working on the *Hot Ones* album, arrangements were quickly being made for them to tour America with none other than the Rolling Stones themselves!

♪ ♪ ♪

Larry Tamblyn remembered how rushed it all was. "Right back after we got back to Hollywood and finished the [*Hot Ones*] album, we went on the Stones tour. Burt made the connection with the management of the Rolling Stones. Back then, tours were never coordinated by record companies. I think they just got whoever was available. We were available and we were on the charts. It was a natural fit. We were compatible. We had even done 'Paint It Black' on the *Dirty Water* album."

The Standells were in perfect company!

According to Ray Harris, the arrangements for the Standells to join the Stones tour were made with the assistance of Seymour Heller's East Coast contact and another partner of his, Dick Gabbe, and the role of Burt Jacobs in the deal was not as significant as Tamblyn thought. "Burt blurred the line between being a manager and an agent. He would do a lot of the legwork setting up small gigs. In the big stuff, like when they were on the Rolling Stones tour, that was a Seymour Heller find. Seymour knew the guy, so did I, who put the tour together. It was handled out of New York and the law in New York is different from the law in California. In California you can be a manager but you can't book an act. In New York you can be anything and make a deal. Same in Nashville, you can be a manager as well as an agent. So the Stones tour was done with an East Coast arrangement we had with Dick Gabbe out of New York. Seymour Heller was originally partnered with Dick in the firm Gabbe

The Standells on tour with The Rolling Stones. L to R: Brian Jones, Dick Dodd, Mick Jagger, Larry Tamblyn, Tony Valentino. Courtesy of Emilio Bellissimo.

and Heller when I merged with them. After Dick passed away, I merged the whole thing with Seymour and that is when it became Attarack-Heller."

The Standells opened up for the Rolling Stones—Mick Jagger, Keith Richards, Brian Jones, Bill Wyman, and Charlie Watts—on their whirlwind 1966 North American tour. The Stones tour only lasted a little more than a month, from June 24 through July 28, yet the tour made 29 stops.

Despite the big venues and head-spinning life on the road with the Rolling Stones, one of the most amazing stops for the Standells was the very first one— on June 24, 1966, at the Manning Bowl high school football stadium in Lynn, Massachusetts, when they played on an opening bill along with the McCoys, who had a number one hit in 1965 with "Hang on Sloopy." Dodd said, "We started playing 'Dirty Water' and everyone went crazy! Everybody was singing it with us, then it started to rain and it made everybody just go crazy—like the song made it rain or something, man! You know—back then, they were all wearing [hippie] beads and stuff…it was a real good ride."

Tamblyn agreed. "The Stones tour was especially memorable. I remember

The Standells appear on Los Angeles TV with replacement bassist John Fleck on board. Courtesy of Edie McMillan.

the one show we did in Boston [Lynn]. Of course, we were huge there. It was an outdoor concert. Anyway, when the Stones finished their set, the crowd rushed toward it. The security rent-a-cops fired off tear gas to keep them back. When our buses left the stadium, we drove through a cloud of it and were all teary-eyed. It looked like a war zone."

It was June 24, 1966. Author Bill Nowlin remembers the night well. "My friend Don Wilcock got us front-row seats, and the Stones said they were so impressed that all their fans stayed through the driving rain that they were going to play an extra-long set. They played 45 minutes instead of the usual 25-minute show that was characteristic of some of the bigger bands back then. I can still recall Brian Jones playing a near-solo version of 'Lady Jane' on dulcimer, but when the band kicked into 'Satisfaction,' everyone knew that was the end of the show and all the people behind us rushed toward the stage. The police were ill-prepared. They had a row of wooden sawhorses in front of the stage, to separate the audience from the performers. That didn't last long, and I can still see police and sawhorses tumbling end over end in the frenzy. The Stones finished fast and bolted from the stage for the security of their limos — but they couldn't leave. There were too many people crowded around the cars. And one or two of us even climbed on top of the cars. I have the clearest of memories of lying across the roof of one of the limos, looking down into the back seat from above at the terrified face of Mick Jagger. The police finally fired off tear gas in sufficient quantities to disperse the crowd and let the bands leave." The bands left to fly to Pittsburgh, the second stop on the tour.

As for the rest of the Standells' tour with Britain's bad boys of rock and roll, Tamblyn went on, "Everybody knows where the Stones came from. That tour we did with them, they were often so stoned they didn't know which way the plane was flying!"

Once when they were with the Stones on a short hop between cities in a small aircraft—one where the pilot was separated from the passengers by a simple cloth privacy curtain—the co-pilot allegedly had to step into the rear of the plane and plead with the band, "You guys have to put that stuff out, or the captain will have to land the plane. We're having a hard time staying in control with all the smoke that's coming forward—we're getting a contact high!"

The Stones tour ended in the Standells' home state of California with concerts in Sacramento, Bakersfield, The Hollywood Bowl, and finally at the famous Cow Palace in San Francisco. But that was not the end to life on the road for the Standells. When "Dirty Water" was still on the charts, and "Sometimes Good Guys Don't Wear White" began doing reasonably well, there was every reason to think they would soon have another big follow-up hit.

♪ ♪ ♪

Unfortunately the Standells' second single did not do as well as it might have on the charts—due to an unforeseen bit of bad timing, Harris explained. "The second single got shot down in the market because at the time there were a lot of radio stations out with promotional campaigns marketing their deejays as the 'Good Guys.' If you were a 'Good Guys' station, they would play the song. If you were not a 'Good Guy' station then they wouldn't play it. They would say 'We don't want to promote the other station because the record says 'good guys' on it." It was a bit confusing for everyone as to which station managers would allow the song to be played and which ones would not. The unfortunate result however was that "Sometimes Good Guys Don't Wear White," the Standells' hoped-for follow-up hit, never got the airplay it needed. It did fairly well on the national charts, reaching #50 at its highest point, but it might have done a lot better.

"It was just one of those things," Harris laments. "Too bad. I thought it was one of the better records that they did. It had all the ingredients. It had Dick Dodd's performance. It had really good performances by everybody. By that time, they now had been playing together for so much that they started to sound really good as a band."

As the Standells became better known all over the country, Ed Cobb assumed more and more control. Tamblyn was not happy with how matters

In the studio, L to R: Ray Harris, Ed Cobb, Larry Tamblyn. Courtesy of Larry Tamblyn.

evolved. "Ed . . . began to take over *all* of the creative processes. At first, he was a real pleasure to work with. He left a lot of the creativity to the group and was able to channel that creativity into our recordings. As time went on, he became more and more dictatorial. Eventually, he wouldn't even let us play on our own recording sessions." Astonishing as that may sound, he elaborated, "I remember, when 'Can't Help but Love You' was recorded, Ed brought in a bunch of black musicians. He wanted the blue-eyed soul sound. When asked why we couldn't participate, he said, 'These guys sound more like the Standells than you do.'" Ed's former partner Bruce Belland didn't hesitate to agree that Ed was dominating, and highly opinionated.

One-Hit Wonders

The management team put their heads together and continued to try to figure out a way to follow up the success of "Dirty Water." The untimely or jinxed release of "Sometimes Good Guys Don't Wear White" fell short. They decided to follow up with another single, another song Ed Cobb had written, "Why Pick On Me." Tower released the single in September and it charted for the first time in mid-October at #93. It stayed on *Billboard* for three weeks reaching #54 before falling off the chart a week later. As on many of the Standells recording, Ed joined with Larry on the background vocals. Perhaps foreshadowing their later single "Try It," Larry says that Cobb slipped in a little sexual innuendo. "On 'Why Pick on Me,' during the chorus, we actually were singing, 'Why ball ball me'." The band didn't find it representative of their sound and didn't really care for the song. Bill Cooper played bass on the recording (the same Bill Cooper who was the recording engineer at American Recording Studios. Both he and Richie Podolor—an accomplished musician in his own right—often sat in as session players for the groups they recorded), but Larry says Cooper "screwed up" during the second verse going into the chorus, and played some wrong notes. Ed didn't notice, or felt it was passable, and it remained on the finished master.

Cooper, however, recalled the session and the Standells in a most favorable light, particularly Dick Dodd. "From the day they walked in, it was a real good feeling. I've been to a lot of sessions, sometimes there's a lot of fighting, a prima donna singer, and things like that. But honestly looking back I don't remember any of that stuff. When we did stuff with Ed Cobb, there was a good atmosphere. Ed was a cheerleader kind of guy. He had a lot of good ideas, a lot of sound ideas, and musical ideas. It was a very positive experience. Usually with a group there might be two guys that are favorites, and one guy is a jerk, and the drummer was uptight, or something else. I'm not trying to sugarcoat it, but I don't remember any bad times with the Standells. It was always just a great fun experience. That's why a lot of stuff came across that way on the records, because that's the way they were. Typically personalities will come across in records. When I first met Dick Dodd one of the things that really impressed me was when we were done with the first thing we did with him, he turned around and gave both Richie and me these English kind of Naval pea coats. At the time they had to have cost 60 or 70 bucks apiece. I thought, 'Wow, here's a guy in a band who just went out and did this—he didn't have to do that. It was way out of the ordinary. It struck us as to what a nice guy he was."[1]

Cooper also recalled that Larry might have been the band member most concerned with the way things were done, how the sessions went. It could explain the differing perspectives on the latter recording sessions. "Larry was the business mind of the band. Of all the guys, if I made a suggestion about the keyboards, Larry would look at me and contemplate it for a long while. Everyone else would respond to a suggestion "Yeah, OK, let's do it,' but Larry was always concerned about the little details and analyzed things a great deal."

Contrary to Larry's implication that Cobb was often indifferent to recording mistakes, Richie Podolor recalled Cobb's attention to details as characteristic—a trait more in keeping with the "controlling" nature most of the band members began to attribute to him as time went on. Regarding one Standells studio session at American Recording Studios, Podolor said, "Dick was sitting playing drums, everyone was doing their thing. Ed and I were more concerned with the bass drum sound because we were both fanatics about fidelity and stuff. I had the opportunity to experiment a lot. I came from that school. Then when the band all went home to go to sleep at two in the morning, Bill and I would sit back and tear the console apart—changing transistors and transistor values trying to get a little more bass drum out of the tapes because you shape the curve of the fidelity of the response by changing certain values in the circuitry. Ed would say something like,' Gee, wouldn't it be great on that bass drum if you could reach down to 40 cycles and really rock the room!' Bill and I would look at each other and say, 'Ah-hah!' and then would call in some electronic genius we knew and he would change things around at four in the morning. The band would come back at noon the next day and we hadn't even slept. But that's what we'd go through [behind the scenes]."

In late 1966, the Standells contributed to the soundtrack of the motion picture *Riot on Sunset Strip*, which was released in May 1967. Even though by this time, many in the business recognized the virtues of groups being granted full artistic control, the Standells were once again shortchanged in that area. One of the songs on the soundtrack album, Larry notes, was recorded on four tracks but when it appeared on the album, two of the tracks were omitted, "so all you can hear is bass and guitar. In those days, everyone was crowded around one mike on a soundstage and they wouldn't allow you in the mixing room. We asked for echo, and they said it was a different union! There was another instance where we did the motion picture theme for *Zebra in the Kitchen* with Jay North, and they did the same thing. It was a very short song and they wanted to lengthen it. They clipped it and stuck the two pieces of tape together and didn't edit on the beat. The beat is messed up where they edited it."[2]

In a recent interview, Dave Aguilar of Chocolate Watch Band seems to confirm the Standells—particularly Tamblyn's—view of working in the studio with Ed Cobb. Aguilar told Richie Unterberger, "Ed Cobb was a studio recording person. We were an onstage performance band.... When we approached an album, we were thinking onstage—for us, a studio performance was performing onstage. The audience was always more important to us than what we put down on vinyl. He just didn't understand what he had with us. He was very bent and focused on his sound. It was his music that he wanted us to record…we just didn't feel it was ours. It didn't feel right for the way we presented music. Going into a studio and everything that went in around it, that was fun. We were not crazy about the songs that Ed had picked for us, but then again we had no background preparation. We didn't go in with songs of our own that we wanted to record, and so we accepted what he did. We didn't know that he was changing them and adding people to it, and adding stuff to the album, 'til *months* after we'd been in the studio and we were gone."

"I remember at one point, one of the albums came in, and we took a look at it, played a couple songs on it, and said, 'What the hell is this shit?' And somebody threw it in the trash. And we went back to rehearsing for a show that we had coming up. I mean, it bothered us that it wasn't us, but we weren"t playing any of Ed Cobb's stuff in performances anyway, and we were right up there onstage with the Yardbirds and the Dead and the Airplane in the Fillmore Auditorium and rubbing elbows and feeling good about it. So that didn't bother us either. We felt that we had arrived, just on a different level. We weren't selling records, but that didn't really matter to us at the time."[3]

Management had a much different view of Dave Aguilar's take on the times and the way the Chocolate Watchband was produced, according to the way Ray Harris remembers things:

"I'm the guy who found the Chocolate Watchband in San Francisco through a little small manager who was up near there. When Ed and I signed them, they were sounding more like the Rolling Stones that anything else. They were a very loose band, and they just played in the local area. When I signed them and put them out on Tower, Tower was a little [skeptical] but said they would go along with us on a whim because perhaps we 'found something.' I was the architect of their first album. I'm the guy that directed the way it was during that that era. If you remember it was really a psychedelic time then and so when I created that album cover with the Capitol art department it was really way out in left field—that is what I wanted. My trick was to put over 2,000 names on it—Aguilar didn't get that. On the back of that cover, you will see over 2,000 names. Most of them were record buyers, independent promotion men, radio station programmers, disc jockeys, people in the industry who suddenly found their name on the back of an album. Everybody started talking about it, trying to see if they were on it. The names were laid out in a maze and you really had to look to find your name. They looked at the album cover, took the record out, and played it! That is what started the Chocolate Watchband as a national entity. Every cover after that was designed to have something special about it. That was the idea to get some recognition for the band in spite of the fact that they were nuts. I mean they were like an 'out' band. Now granted they did do some good things that we recorded, but a lot was Ed's stuff that they didn't use in their own personal appearances. Most of the time they played other peoples' material, then finally some of their own."

Still, Aguilar didn't hold back when it came to Cobb's and Harris's management: "The other thing that bothers me about Ed Cobb and that whole group was, why in the world did they stick us on Tower Records, which was a black label? I mean, c'mon. Why? What in the world was going through their minds at the time? I don't get it. We didn't know how many other groups they had in the can. We were never aware of that. It was never discussed. We thought we and the Standells [who were also on Tower] were it. We didn't realize that they had all these other people on the hook also. It's like buying 16 baseball teams and hoping one of them can go to the World Series. We weren't aware of that."

In fact, Harris and Cobb were not producing many other artists at the time, and there is no indication they regarded Tower as a "black label." It was a subsidiary of Capitol set up to give an opportunity to artists that might not have been able to ink a deal otherwise—whether they were black, white, or anything else. Gloria Jones happened to be a black artist that Cobb produced on Tower at the time, but that did not make the label a race-based one. Harris explains, "At the time we only had three or four groups, and we were recording some outside projects. The Standells were one of our biggest focus groups. Remember when we went to Tower Records we gave them three artists, the Standells being one. I later signed the Chocolate Watchband and the E-Types so we had to find material for all those guys. Gloria Jones had already broken through and we saw her as a very hot female artist."

The Standells also never conceived of Tower as a "black label." They were excited about their signing at first, naturally, but in time came to perceive that the staff at Tower "weren't very powerful and were incapable of promoting their acts." Larry Tamblyn says, "I think the only success they had was with us and Ian Whitcomb. Pink Floyd had an album out on Tower, but they were completely lost there and didn't achieve success until after switching labels." Tamblyn talked with one of the other Watchband musicians at the Cavestomp Festival in 1999 and said, "He was pretty bitter about Ed, especially about Ed removing his vocals and replacing them with his two black friends." These were the same two vocalists Cobb used on some of the later Standells recordings. Compared to the Chocolate Watchband's experience, Tamblyn felt that Cobb allowed the Standells comparatively more creative freedom, at least in their earlier years.

Ironically, the group's biggest hit, "Dirty Water," was never the group's favorite recording. Tamblyn believes, though, that the *Dirty Water* album—recorded well after the single's release—in some ways captured the band at its best. The album "came the closest to sounding like we did on the stage, simply because we didn't have the luxury to add in special effects. It was quickly recorded in three days…it really captured who we were. There weren't any session songs like in some of our other albums."[4]

Larry Tamblyn's personal favorite Standells song was the February 1967 single "Try It" which he believed more than any other was "the song that was synonymous with the Standells sound." Unfortunately, the song's supposed suggestive lyrics and Dick Dodd's bold performance was a little too much for some of the more conservative media bigwigs of the day. Tame as it is by today's standards, the song was banned in many markets.

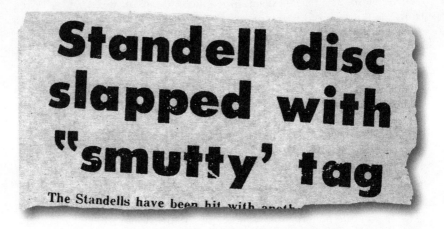

Ray Harris remembered that he and Ed Cobb deliberately used the band's "sex appeal" to push the envelope a bit. "We created a lot of sexual overtones with them like on 'Try It'—it got banned. Ed had gotten the song from Lester Sill, who was a great publisher, one of the finest men I ever met. Ed liked the song, and he produced it in a sexy way with Dick." The problem came with the grandstanding of rightwing media mogul Gordon McLendon, the Top 40 radio king of the day. "McLendon decided he didn't like it because of it sexual overtones and he banned it, from all of his radio stations. That was a big hurt again. It was like 'Good Guys Don't Wear White' all over again." McLendon said his Liberty Broadcasting System required that "all of the record companies provide us with a written copy in advance of the lyrics for a particular song…. We take a look at them to be sure there is nothing suggestive in those lyrics." He objected to rock songs "where it takes you about three days of listening just to get the title of the record, and by the time you've got [it], it's been on the air for three days and you wake up to the fact that you're airing a sex story…. I don't want it done to my children, and I assume that other people don't."[5]

McLendon had a history of controversy. According to the Spartacus Educational website in the United Kingdom, his radio station network gave voice

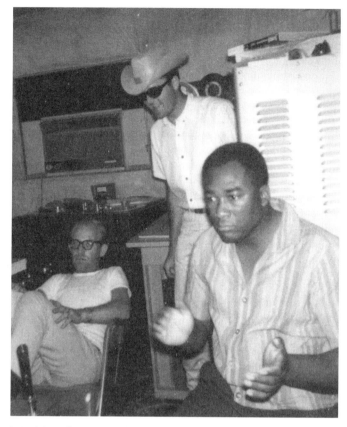

In Armin's studio. L to R: Armin Steiner, Ed Cobb, Hal Davis. Courtesy of Heather Cobb Isbell.

to "his attacks on federal aid to education, racial desegregation of public schools and equal voting rights for all races." He was friendly with Dallas nightclub owner Jack Ruby and "in 1963 rumors began to circulate that McLendon might have been involved in the assassination of John F. Kennedy." Conspiracy buffs suspected many; McLendon wasn't alone in that regard, but his outspoken right-wing positions often acted as lightning rods drawing attention his way.

McLendon made a crusade out of his campaign against objectionable song lyrics, even embarking on a national PR campaign, appearing before the news media, on camera, holding up the Standells' single and claiming the recording contained obscene lyrics. The crusade had an impact. Mark Davison of North Springfield, Virginia wrote a letter to the editor of the *Washington Post* about the reaction he and his parents had to "hi-fi pornography." Davison wrote, "I was glad to find out that the stations I listen to—WEAM, WPGC, and WWDC—don't allow contaminated records on the air, and that each has responsible DJ's who listen to each record before they allow it to be broadcast. Personally I despise the Rolling Stones and most of their lyrics, but I like their sound. I feel the same way about the Standells. These songs about LSD, sex, the draft, etc., are, or should rightfully be, banned and I'm glad most people (teenagers included!) think so."[6]

Other letter writers noted the "questionable" lyrics of other songs like "I've Got My Love to Keep Me Warm," "Temptation," Mitch Miller's "If I Could Be with You" and Frank Sinatra's "Strangers in the Night." The reaction prompted a rejoinder from reader Jim Menzer, who argued, "These nitwits today abuse a college education by wasting their parents' money during four years of campus nonconformity, drugs, sex, orgies, etc. and they regard pop music as relevant." Some of the songs cited, Menzer complained, "were written by famous writers and played by real musicians such as Louis Armstrong, Tommy Dorsey, Harry James, not these jerks who only strum a guitar and shake up a storm."[7]

"Try It" was banned on Los Angeles stations KHJ and KFWB, but received strong airplay on KRLA. The group wanted to sue McLendon, but both record company and management were afraid to do so because of the power McLendon wielded in the business. Larry Tamblyn regrets that timidity: "I still feel today that if we had a stronger company behind us, we could have capitalized on the PR and turned it around." Dick and Pat Moreland suggested editing the master, and they produced an edited version with all the lines that McLendon had deemed objectionable edited out. The record went to #1 in Los Angeles — the edited version — and some DJ's had fun playing both versions and asking listeners, "Do you think it's too sexy?"

The Standells even appeared on national television, debating McLendon. On May 27, 1967 the Standells were guests on Art Linkletter's TV show *Let's Talk*, debating the radio mogul himself. The show was taped at the Hullabaloo club and several members of the exuberant teenage audience lobbed specific allegations at McLendon. Tamblyn remembers, "His face turned bright red as he unsuccessfully tried to zero in on the perpetrators of the outbursts. To this day, we don't know who actually hurled the epithets at McLendon or how they arrived at their information. The catcalls were edited out of the show (as well as some of our best replies to McLendon)." It might have been that Burt and/or AVI fed some of the questions to the young people present, but the band never knew this to be the case.

Pete Johnson, music critic at the *Los Angeles Times*, noted that KRLA was the only station playing the record in the region but claimed, "limited exposure hasn't dampened its sales." Johnson went on to say, "It is mediocre, as is most of the output of the Standells ('Muddy Water' [sic] and 'Good Guys Don't Wear White' are their most notable hits.) I don't consider it obscene, but the group undoubtedly was conscious of its censorship potential when they made it. If the screeners had been cooler and allowed it to compete openly with the rest of the Top 40 records, it probably would have done no better than minor hitdom [sic] but it exploited the sales potential of a predictable reaction."[8]

The debate over obscenity might have generated enough controversy to turn the trick nationally, but it simply wasn't enough to overcome the McLendon machine. Later, suggestions of hypocrisy surfaced raising questions of impropriety regarding McLendon and his proclivities.

♪ ♪ ♪

In retrospect, even with their cutting edge posturing and controversial songs like "Try It," the band never viewed themselves as the musical pioneers they are sometimes described as. Tamblyn named their main influences as The Beatles, The Stones, Motown, and Chuck Berry. The British groups were particularly influential. "The British invasion, they really paved the way for groups like the Standells." What was the Standells' music about? "That's really hard to say. We were really a cover group playing in clubs. I think the history books have painted us as rebels because of the us-against-them lyrics of our music. But we weren't really trying to go in any direction."

Ray Harris reflected about the legacy of the Standells and his firm's other "garage band," the Chocolate Watchband. "The real crux is that the Chocolate Watchband and the Standells are now recognized as the top garage bands of the era. And each one of them has said stuff about Ed or me—that we were interfering with them or whatever. But they didn't realize that Ed and I were a team. We discussed almost everything we were going to do and how to approach things. It was a long-term strategy. The reason other groups made it was because they had a long-term strategy, they stayed together, they put their records out—some were hits, some were not—but it was a consistent flow of product.

"We put out four Standells albums in one year. Why did I want to do that? Because the more products I had in the marketplace, the better shot I had [at getting a hit.] I got that concept from when I opened up Capitol's country operation in Atlanta. I saw how much product the country artists were putting out. When you went into a record store, you always saw a nice bin for each country artist with four, five, or six singles or LPs. That was the idea, because if down the road we got one hit, the whole catalogue would move." Harris lamented that the Standells did not help themselves by creating more good material on their own—for the long haul.

There are music aficionados like J. J. Rassler, who have described the Standells as a "Mount Rushmore band of '60s punk garage."[9] In 1999, Neil Strauss wrote in the the New York Times that the Standells were "one of the most-cited garage-rock precursors of punk."[10] Will Shade questioned the Standells' reputation as a true garage band in an exchange with Larry Tamblyn. Said Shade, "Since the band kind of predates the British Invasion, sometimes 'garage purists' say you were a professional outfit, not a real garage band."

Tamblyn responded to the statement regarding the group's development in its early years: "We were just trying to earn a living. Like the Beatles, playing in clubs helped us to do just that and also really helped to tighten the group."[11]

The band is best seen in its Hollywood context. This was not a four-man group coming out of Liverpool—or Athens, Georgia. As we have seen, Larry Tamblyn came from a show business family and Dick Dodd had a career in television as a child actor that preceded his musical development. Both the band and its managers had familiarity with film and TV, and with its well-connected management, it is little surprise to note the band's frequent appearances in both fields. Among the variety show hosts that presented the Standells on TV— some before and some after "Dirty Water" became a hit—are Bing Crosby, Regis Philbin, and Joey Bishop, each of whom had his own show. They were included in the *Pat Boone in Hollywood* show. The band also appeared as regular guests on shows such as *Hollywood Discotheque*, *Where the Action Is*, and *Shebang*, with appearances on *Shindig*, *Groovy*, and Dick Clark's *American Bandstand*. They appeared in the films *Get Yourself a College Girl* and *Riot on Sunset Strip* and in episodes of TV shows *The Munsters* and *Ben Casey*.

They never became the Beatles, though, and instead of becoming the American Rolling Stones, the Standells became a one-hit wonder group and faded from the national scene into obscurity by the time the 1970s rolled around. The band was still recording after the success of "Dirty Water" but nothing seemed to click and they fired Ed Cobb and AVI as their managers and producers. The Standells, except for Dick Dodd, went back to Burt Jacobs as their sole management. The change did not help at all.

Breakup, Blame, and Bitterness

Ed Cobb saw the inevitable decline of the Standells from a management point of view and thought it typical of a lot of groups of that period, according to his Four Preps partner Bruce Belland. In 1989, when Belland, Cobb, Jim Pike of the Lettermen, and David Somerville of the Diamonds got together to form the "New Four Preps" they began talking about the creation and breakups of a lot of acts they had known. Ed was heard to say with some degree of bitterness about the Standells, "Well, the Standells were just like every other band. You take them under your wing, you nurture them, you mentor them, you train 'em, you get 'em a hit or two, and then they think they know better than you do and that they can do it themselves. The next thing you know you never heard of them again."

Belland added, "Ed had some very hard feelings about the way the Standells related to him and what he had done for them as they progressed in their career. You know, he probably took some degree of satisfaction.... In fact, once they separated from him, they never had another hit. He was a little bitter about his dismissal and I don't blame him."

Not surprisingly, the Standells felt very differently about the breakup of their act and felt it was the divisions and differences amongst their management team that ultimately lead to the band's demise.

According to Dick Dodd, "Internally, our producers Ed Cobb, Seymour Heller and his friend—the assistant V.P. of our production company—Ray Harris were coming to me, 'You don't need the Standells. You're the voice. You can make it on your own. You don't need these guys.' I don't know why ...they were making [the suggestion] that we should break up. I guess because they wanted to make money off of me and keep the Standells the Standells." Dick was urged to stick with AVI as a solo artist, which he did, while Tony and Larry went their way as the Standells with Burt Jacobs. Gary Lane had left the group in 1966, replaced first by Dave Burke and then by Jon Fleck.

Dick regards the move with regret. "It was a dirty thing to do to me, and a dirty thing to do to the Standells. I will always regret it. I was young and naive. I've always trusted everybody. My producers and my managers were ...I'd laid it all out—they were taking care of me. I was taking care of my family and they were taking care of me. I would sing on their records, they would take care of me. And so when they told me that I could do it on my own ...and then we go back to when I was a kid, I always wanted to be *that* entertainer if I went out on my own. I could get out from in back of the drums. I could get out front. That's what I wanted to do."

Dodd's recollection varies, perhaps understandably, from the perspective of the management of AVI as expressed by Ray Harris, the company's Senior Artist and Repertoire (A&R) director at the time: "The Standells' breakup caught us by surprise. When Jacobs decided that he wanted to leave AVI, we tried to convince him not to leave. Jacobs had told the group that he was going to get them out of the contract, get them another deal, a lot of money at Dunhill. Jacobs said to Ed and I, 'I'm going to leave.' I said, 'Why do

Reb Foster and Burt Jacobs listen to playback at the Standell's recording session last week. Burt manages the Standells, and is one of Reb's closes friends.

Clipping showing Reb Foster and Burt Jacobs. Courtesy of Edie McMillan.

that? We've been successful together. It's a little slow now, but why do this?' He was adamant. He was always an impulsive guy. He said, 'I'm going [to partner] with Reb Foster.' So OK, that was that. We worked out the deal with them. He left but the acts would stay with us. But then he went to [the Standells], in a behind-the-scenes thing putting us down, to get them to break the deal. Jacobs, who could be very hateful in a sense, preyed upon them to break-up and leave."

Harris went on, "Dick Dodd actually went to Ed and said what [Jacobs and the band] were doing and I said, 'Oh, boy, I never expected that.' Dick said, 'I'm not going to go with that. I don't think it's right. Let's give you guys the full benefit of the doubt. It's slow, but finish out our contract. Why go through all of this?' He was very straight up about it, so Ed and I talked about it. I went up to Bud Frazier, the president of Tower, and told him the situation. Bud said, 'Can you replace them?' I said, 'I have the lead singer. We can do an album on him by himself.' 'Well, we can do that. The other guys are [just] musicians. We can replace them.' I said, 'That's not the point. It's the cohesion of the group and everything else.' He said, 'Well, as far as we're concerned, they're [just] musicians. You can replace them if you've got the lead singer. That's the bit. I've got the producer and I have the lead singer. But in the meantime, we're going to defend ourselves.'"

"Ed said, 'Well, look Dick is here and he wants to continue on in his career, so we'll do it.' We told Dick that we will put another band around him if the rest of the guys don't want to stay with us, or he could do solo—whatever he wanted. We had several bands around Dick. We had him in Vegas for over a month with Dick Dodd and the Big Train. Once he finished Vegas, Dick then went on to a new group called Joshua and played down in the Long

The Standells performing just before the breakup of the group. Courtesy of Edie McMillan.

Beach area for quite a while. The point is, Dick Dodd worked after he got out of the Standells, under the various groups, and we were constantly trying to find him jobs, and we recorded his album in Atlanta with the support of Tower Records. Tower thought at the time that Dodd could be successful. But he never did find the right element for himself."

Dodd acknowledged the support of Harris and Cobb after the Standells breakup, but still feels that he was misled into making the decision to stick with AVI. "I had a couple of singles out and I had an album, *The First Evolution of Dick Dodd*, that I did in Atlanta, Georgia, with that guy that produced the Classics Four, and Billy Joe Royal, and Tommy Roe, all that Atlanta Rhythm Section thing.... We went there...and it was really a neat album, but it didn't do it." *First Evolution* was also released on Tower, in April 1968.

Larry Tamblyn remembers the end this way: "Burt Jacobs convinced us to leave AVI. But AVI convinced Dick to leave us, thus destroying the core of the group. AVI was not satisfied in just breaking up the group, but conducted a personal vendetta against the remaining members. They claimed that according to our agreement with them, if one member remained signed to AVI, they had rights to retain the name. Burt told us that AVI had destroyed a pending deal

with ABC Dunhill Records by threatening them with a lawsuit. It took a year
to straighten this mess up. By then, we were forgotten about, old news, and
the major labels were no longer interested in signing us. AVI was every bit as
responsible as Gordon McLendon for the Standells' demise."

Once again management had a very different perspective on the events
concerning the demise of the Standells. According to Ray Harris, "I don't know
[about conducting a vendetta.] We didn't do that at all. In fact, I always thought
that they might come back to their senses. The truth is, Jacobs brushed them
off after that. He was stuck with his own thing. He didn't give Larry the time
of day in any fashion. For them to get back together it had to be a reconcilia-
tion between Dick and themselves. We would have probably welcomed them
back and gone back in to record them and maybe put them with some other
management people."

As to AVI keeping the Standells name, Harris continued, "That is correct.
It is common in the business. We had the name in their contract; we had the
rights to their name. So did Tower. However, we let it slide. I didn't want to pre-
vent them from making a living someplace. We could have enforced it and
would have probably won the case, it was in black and white in a contract that
they had lawyers review."

As to the story that Burt Jacobs had told them about AVI destroying a pending deal with Dunhill, Harris was adamant in his reaction and response, "That
never happened at all! We didn't try to kill anything. That was Jacobs's story,
probably to get off the hook [for having no deal at Dunhill.] I would have never
done that in the first place. I was pretty close to the Dunhill people. Remember, Jay Lasker [at Dunhill] was the guy who brought me to California, so I
knew him very well. Jay was a pretty smart guy, he would have called me knowing that I had the lead singer and probably would have said let's see if we can
work something out, see if we could put the group back together—and I would
have been happy to do that. The thing with Larry Tamblyn was, and Larry is
a very smart guy and a sweet guy, I think if he were to have come to the table
or had come to Ed and said, 'Ed, I think we made a mistake, let's get this back
together'—it would have worked out fine."

Larry never did approach Ray Harris, Ed Cobb, or Seymour Heller in that
manner because from his perspective, things seemed very deliberately orchestrated to break up the group. He remembered with some bitterness, "Especially painful was the manner and timing in which we were informed that
Dick was leaving us. We were appearing at the Ice House in Pasadena. Members of Dick's family were there (unknowingly, to witness Dick's final performance as part of the group.) The following day, we received a letter from
Dick informing us of his departure. We were unable to contact him because,
anticipating our calls, he was staying with Ed Cobb at his ranch. On a personal note, over and above the betrayal I felt, Dick's letter came on the day we
were to perform at my high school alma mater. Since it was such short notifi-

cation, we...had to cancel. Either Three Dog Night or Steppenwolf were sent in our place. The school didn't look too kindly on our cancellation, and I had to come up with a written excuse. I obtained a bogus doctor's note saying I was too ill to perform. Actually I was, but not from any medical problem, just the disappointment of not performing at my old high school."

Regarding Dick's activities at this time, Harris counters the assertion that he was trying to avoid the other band members or was betraying them in any way, "The big thing was that...we didn't go solicit [Dick] to remain with us (AVI). He came to us, he was humble, he really had a problem of dealing with the breakup. He felt that Ed would take care of it, that's why Ed took him out to his house and let him stay there for a while. We were really shocked at the fact that the breakup happened. I didn't think that Jacobs would do that. But he did, and he did it for selfish reasons. He wanted to get back at me because I squelched a lot of his ideas. I wished him good luck when he left. The parting didn't kill either one of us. I really never saw him again. He really only had one major act to concentrate on and we had many other interests."

That one big act that Burt Jacobs still managed after the Standells broke up was indeed a major one and was the one that defined the rest of his career until his retirement from show business in 1979.[1]

One of the first "Super Groups" of the late 1960s to the mid-1970s, Three Dog Night had 18 straight Top-40 records, seven of which were Top-10 hits, and three that were charted at #1 ("Mama Told Me Not to Come," "Joy to the World," and "Black and White"). Jacobs later added the pioneering hard rock band Steppenwolf ("Born to Be Wild," "Magic Carpet Ride," "Rock Me") to his stable to provide him with a pretty lucrative managerial career after the demise of the Standells.

The two original Standells—Tony and Larry—tried to make a go of it. They added another band member for a while in Lowell George, but the band known as the Standells had pretty much run its course. "We were actually scheduled to do one more gig at the Ice House when Lowell was with us." According to Larry, "We were rehearsing about a week before the gig, when Lowell announced his new vision for the Standells. He wanted us to revert to a greaser look, a parody of ourselves. I remember he really didn't have a high regard for the Standells or our garage rock sound. At this point, he had almost taken over the leadership of the group and was almost as dictatorial as Jody Rich. He and I argued about our differences. Essentially, he said *my way or the highway*, and I stomped out. The group split up and we did not complete our agreement with the Ice House. Later, we reformed without Lowell, the guys choosing to stay with me."

Capitol/Tower retained control of the Standells masters, until Harris and Cobb regained ownership and in the 1980s put together a reissue deal with Rhino Records. Rhino released several albums, including *Standells Golden Archives* and *The Very Best of the Standells*. But Harris says that AVI had nothing to do with the repackaging, nor did they profit from the first Standells albums on Rhino.

"You know what Rhino's theory was—they were the guys to first put out records that were not available or that were deleted from catalogue, no longer in print. They were the guys that really came up with that formula. Later, they cut deals for mail-order packages like with Columbia House. A lot of the compilation packages were sold through radio. They would tie in with a jock— "Big Joe So and So" or whoever. Wolfman Jack was one of the big names. They sold the packages through the station—the station got something and the dee-jay got something. The original licensing on the Standells was from Tower. We (AVI) would clear the license because it helped the station and the song would be played and promoted.

"Rhino had done some direct deals with Tower before. They were building up their list by licensing product from the major labels who weren't working their own catalog. Years later the majors created their own special marketing departments who started to do that and got into competition with Rhino. But Rhino had already made inroads. With the Standells stuff Rhino put out, we didn't get any of the revenue because we had "offsets of debt" to the label, Capitol, so whatever [revenues] Tower already had, they got to keep."

Rhino's liner notes on those albums offend Larry Tamblyn. He believes Harris and Cobb were responsible for slighting the band. "Even though we were in contact with Ray Harris and Ed Cobb, the band members were given no input into the liner notes on the albums," said Tamblyn, "Thus the fiction [was perpetuated] that Ed Cobb changed our image and sound, and the misperception that Ed Cobb was our *svengali*. Nonsense! I take issue with the notion that Cobb nurtured us. This goes hand-in-hand with much of the mis-information out there. As the story goes, Ed discovered us and changed our image from clean-cut to punk. Nothing could be further from the truth; witness our long hair in 1963. Cobb had absolutely nothing to do with our image. Because we were playing in nightclubs, we were forced to have shorter hair (other than the Peppermint West and Thunderbird Lounge.) It remained this way until we began to do concert tours after 'Dirty Water' hit the charts. Other than in the recording studio, we had very little contact with him."

Not surprisingly, the group's disaffection includes business disappointments as well. Tamblyn again gives voice to the feelings of the four Standells: "When asked about royalties from the record sales, Ray Harris informed us that there were none, even though they kept releasing re-issued material. We finally were forced to contact Artists Rights Enforcement Corp., who represented us in filing suit against AVI. The suit was settled out of court with the stipulation that the terms of the settlement would not be revealed and information about AVI's misdeeds would never be discussed or made public. In return for AREC's participation, the Standells have had to split all royalties with them 50/50. This has amounted to tens of thousands of dollars out of our pockets. Regardless, we have never regretted our relationship with AREC. They've done an excellent job in representing our business interests. This could all have been avoided if Ray Harris and Ed Cobb had been forthcoming and acted responsibly. Ray has lost all credibility with us and we would tend to discount most information coming from him. In our minds, he is a flim-flam man. We do not wish to forgive and forget, and have absolutely no interest in dealing with him."

AVI saw things in a different light regarding the recordings and royalties. After Rhino released the Standells under their deal with Capitol, Cobb and Harris went after the Standell tapes from Capitol for their own use.

Harris said, "We called up Capitol and told them we were going to come by and pick up the tapes. We went over there and they said they couldn't find them! They finally said, 'We threw them away. They were just no good and we just threw them away.' We called our attorney and he said we should sue, which we did for $350,000. Tower and Capitol had control of the Standells licensing and all that stuff—we didn't. We only got whatever our *overrides* were, or any offsets against royalties that were due us. Capitol was not really great on their accounting—so we sued.

"Capitol came back with an offer. They said they would give us the whole catalogue, but no money—we had to assume our own costs for our attorney fees and all that. Capitol said that they would give us back all the unedited masters [not the lost edited ones.] I thought that I could re-use those masters for licensing and putting them in different projects, so we took all them back.

"Now we distributed them ourselves. We really never put out a whole album again as a Standells album because Rhino and Tower had already put it out. We used the basic hit songs in different packages and stuff like that. So it didn't earn a lot, it was just what we call a catalogue item that you can stick in something, and anything for television or anything it was a good throwaway and you earned a couple of grand. That is the way we treated it. We didn't think that anything further would happen with that.

"Everything was OK for a while; then the band went to this artists' rights guy, because there was something that was put out—by Time-Life or somebody, but it was still part of the old Rhino deal (between Capitol/Tower.) I didn't have anything to do with that. These 'rights guys' who used to go around the country finding an old artist[s] . . .or an act that had a complaint, and then go and form these nuisance lawsuits against the record companies. Some of the artists they represented were acts that were originally created as acts for hire. [Producers or record companies] would hire these acts, put them together and give them these phony names and put them out there to perform, members of the groups were interchangeable. One of the members of the group might say, 'I didn't get any royalties.' Well, he had gotten paid on the session and royalties were not part of the original agreement. But sometimes they would win if they got a liberal judge. The unfortunate thing is when the acts would sign up with those guys, they agreed to sign over 50% of all their revenue for life. I think that is an atrocious thing for anybody to do. I could see covering the legal expenses and an agent's commission for 10 or 15 years or something. But they didn't do that."

The Standells didn't have royalties due them because they had an offset of debt in two places—with Cobb and Harris' group and with Capitol/Tower. Any royalties that came in were just automatically "offset" against debts the band had incurred with management and with Capitol. Money spent on studio time, production costs, publicity and distribution costs, even traveling expenses and hotel rooms—all were the sorts of expenditures that could be charged back to the artists' account depending on the nature of their contract with either management or the record company, or both.

Harris went on, "We opened our books to them and there was not much there. At the end of the day it cost us a lot of money and they got [very little.] They could do whatever they want after that because we really didn't care. [The Standells' music] wasn't a big money maker for us anyway. We could have kept the Standells name too, but we let them use it if they wanted. We didn't begrudge them making some money off it in the future. I wished them luck and that is the way it ended up."

♪ ♪ ♪

There were a few gigs for the Standells in the 1980s, Larry Tamblyn recalls. Groups like the Fleshtones and the Pandoras were being compared to the Standells and it offered a bit of a hook to keep playing together. Tony, Larry, and Dick decided to reunite. "We first appeared with the Fleshtones—who were billed as the '80s version of the Standells—at the Club Lingerie. It was quite an event and the place was jam-packed. We then headlined at Harrah's Casino in Reno, but disbanded again. We made several more attempts after that in the '80s but none were earth-shattering."[2] The band also performed at the Golden Bear in Huntington Beach, with guitarist Bruce Wallenstein and bassist Eric Wallengren joining the trio. The next time they performed together was at Summerfest, a 1960s revival concert staged in July 1986 at Glen Helen Regional Park, San Bernardino.

When did the last incarnation of the band finally break up? Co-founder Tamblyn isn't sure:

"The band had several break-ups. The first was when I got together with several members of the original Knack (not the famous late '70s band) and we formed Chakras. Tony acted as our manager. We signed with Warner Reprise Records and released a few singles that didn't do much. That band broke up and we re-formed the Standells with Tony, myself, a British man named Paul Downing, and a drummer—I can't remember his name. It was 1970 and I was pretty burned-out. We were back to playing nightclubs, which I hated. Finally, I could take no more and split from the group. Tony took over as the leader, and carried on for several more years. I don't know when his Standells actually broke up."[3]

In the late 1980s, Tony (Emilio), his younger brother (actually named) Tony, and Larry formed a record label, Telco Records. They recorded two songs: "60's Band," written and sung by Larry, and "Try It", sung by Tony. The first song was a tribute to bands of the '60s, including the Beatles, Rolling Stones, Byrds, and Doors. "60's Band" received quite a lot of play in Los Angeles by Rodney Bingenheimer on his KROQ Sunday evening show, plus several radio stations throughout the country, but the record's sales never amounted to very much.

Ed Cobb. Courtesy of Heather Cobb Isbell.

There were exceptionally few reunions of the Standells. The most notable was the Cavestomp Festival in 1999, where the band appeared and recorded a live album that was released in 2000, *Ban This! Live From Cavestomp!* "The Cavestomp concert was terrific," Tamblyn enthused. "It was the first time we had been together in concert since the mid-1980s. We only had three rehearsals and the event was recorded live. I must say it surpassed our wildest dreams. When we walked on stage before the screaming crowd, it was the '60s all over again—the magic that we once had, returned. Our CD *Ban This!* [recorded at the concert] really captured the moment. The only other concert was in June 2000 at the Las Vegas Grind. Gary Lane, our original bass player, joined us this time, and all of the originals were on stage together for the first...time since the 1960s."[4]

Larry has a sense of wonder that the Standells are still remembered after all these years. "Honestly, when we broke up in '69–'70, I thought that would be the last of the Standells," said Tamblyn, never imagining for a moment that years later they would be considered influential pioneers. When he learned that they were so regarded, he was totally taken aback. "The idea that our group—which I considered to be dead and buried—would be revived and revered as the original punk-rockers, thoroughly astounded me. 'Dirty Water' was basically our big hit, our one-hit wonder. When the group disbanded, we thought that would be the end of it. Little did we know that we would be reborn, and that we would inspire other bands."

Aside from the release of various re-compilations of the original Standells recording, "Dirty Water" has been recorded by a number of groups, from the

Inmates to the Apollos, Bronson Arroyo to the Dropkick Murphys, Joe Gru-shecky, National Razor, Singapore Sling, Thundertrain, and even someone by the name of Jack "Penetrator" Lipton.

"We were shocked, literally shocked, when we started to see things in the news, starting to compare groups like the Ramones, Bangles, and Pandoras to us," Larry mused. "All of a sudden, we started developing this following. I get news alerts every day from Google. Almost every day now, I'm getting alerts from some group referring to us and how they were inspired by us. There was this jazz pianist [Victor Verney] who talked about how he was [influenced] by us, how his father hated us, and that just motivated him even more! At least as amazing are references to us in books such as Stephen King's book *Faithful: Two Diehard Boston Red Sox Fans Chronicle the Historic 2004 Season.*"

♪ ♪ ♪

Interestingly, many years after the Standells had stopped performing, Ed Cobb had an even larger hit than "Dirty Water" as a producer/songwriter. His com-position "Tainted Love," first recorded by Gloria Jones in 1964, broke big again—this time internationally—in 1981 by the British synth-duo Soft Cell and was a Top 10 *Billboard* hit in 1982. It has been said that Cobb offered this song to the Standells, but the band doesn't remember it. If they had recorded it, it would have been considered a cover of Jones' recording.

Burt Jacobs too, went on to greater accomplishments with his management of Three Dog Night and Steppenwolf. He was doing well enough to reside in the exclusive west Los Angeles enclave of Beverlywood near Beverly Hills be-fore his retirement to Orange County where he now resides with his second wife Paula. Burt, nearing 80, is in the early stages of Alzheimer's disease ac-cording to Paula, but still enjoys recalling his past successes in show business on occasion.

After his parting with the Standells, Cobb continued to breed horses and enjoy life. He remained involved with Harris and Heller in one or another en-terprise until Ed took a sabbatical, for what turned out to be about a year.

In the meantime, Ray Harris had acquired a recording studio, Producers Workshop. "A lot of major artists recorded there. I give Ed credit for getting a lot of them in there. *The Wall* (Pink Floyd) was done in there. Ninety percent of *The Wall* was done there. And then *Rumours* [by Fleetwood Mac]."

Ed's third wife Lennie recalled a notorious event that she thinks happened at Producers Workshop when Ed became the only person to ever throw Mick Jagger out of a recording studio. As the story goes, Ed warned his engineer against sharing all the drugs being done by the Rolling Stones entourage. In the morning, the engineer was found OD'd—dead—and Ed told them to leave. Mick Jagger said, 'I'm Mick Jagger' and Ed said, 'I'm Ed Cobb and you'll leave my studio.'" Ed himself didn't smoke–anything—and he would only have an occasional glass of wine.[5]

In 1988, Ed served as executive music consultant to the movie *Liberace: Behind the Music*. That would have seemed out of character, but for the fact that Ed's partner Seymour Heller had served as Liberace's long-time manager.

Seymour Heller passed away in 2002, but quite a few years earlier, Heller and Cobb decided to sell AVI. Among the people they met with was Barrie Edwards, president of Music Sales Corporation, a large international publisher with over 200,000 compositions in its catalog. Edwards met with Cobb and Heller, and expressed interest but the parties could not agree on a price. AVI was sold to an investor named Harry Anger, who set it up as a standalone company. Anger wasn't able to make a go of it, and when Edwards offered him an administration deal, he readily agreed, selling 50% of the company to Music Sales Corporation and one of its in-house publishing companies, Embassy Music, in December 1995. One year later, Music Sales purchased the other 50% and now is sole owner of the "Dirty Water" copyright.[6]

Cobb developed cancer and passed away in 1999.

It is abundantly evident that not everyone was pleased with the way the business wound down. The band felt deals were being done without their consent, and reached some form of settlement regarding their allegations of unpaid royalties. Ed's widow Lennie remains angry about what she feels was a dismemberment of the song catalog that Ed had built up, and the associated businesses such as Nashville-based Woodland Sound, and levels some very strong and heartfelt accusations at Ray Harris. "Tainted Love" was, of course, Cobb's biggest song, and she is pleased that Barrie Edwards and Music Sales now own the rights to both it and "Dirty Water."

♪ ♪ ♪

After the Standells' brief fling with '60s stardom, the band had long been gone from the pop music scene. By the time the new millennium rolled around, and the Standells and their one-hit-wonder "Dirty Water" had largely faded away.

Except in Boston, that is.

Red Sox Nation Loves That "Dirty Water"

"Dirty Water" never, *ever*, faded away in Boston. After its initial success as a Top 40 hit in 1966, Boston's rock and oldies radio stations continued to play it all the time. It was a Boston song, no matter what its roots. Every junior high school kid in a garage band learned it, and every wedding band had the song in its repertoire. At Fenway Park and in Boston Garden, John Kiley's successors would occasionally throw the song into the mix of tunes played on the organ. But it wasn't until 1998, when recorded music increasingly began to supplant the familiar Fenway organ entertainment, that "Dirty Water" truly burst forth on the Red Sox scene.

Recorded music first began to infiltrate into Fenway after Red Sox owner Jean Yawkey died in 1992. The *Globe*'s Dan Shaughnessy explored the initial changes in his July 1, 1992, column, noting that a few oldies had infiltrated the park's set lists, such as "I'm A Believer" by The Monkees and other tracks such as "Louie Louie" and "Summer in the City." John Kiley had played the organ at the park for 40 years. Hearing that rock music was getting its foot in the door, Kiley was philosophical: "I never thought they'd go for it. I guess if the public wants it, you have to give it to 'em."

Larry Cancro, Vice President of Marketing for the Red Sox, told Shaughnessy the idea originated with ownership. "Whoa. Ownership?" Shaughnessy asked, eyebrows figuratively raised. "Don't tell us Haywood Sullivan came into a room, snapping his fingers and saying, 'How 'bout we play some Fine Young Cannibals between innings from now on?" Reaction from some players was favorable. "I think they did it because of me," said Steve Lyons, who had just begun his third stint with the Sox. "We've got to get out of the '40s," added Wade Boggs.[1]

Several years later, when BCN Productions was contracted to provide recorded music at Fenway Park for first time beginning with the 1998 season, Kevin Friend, the president of the company, was eager to play "Dirty Water"—one of his favorite songs—at the park. "We already had the contract with the Bruins at the Fleet Center and I had it played there pretty often—whenever I could. I mean, it is a great song, and that opening guitar riff really commands attention."[2]

Mark Chambers, the director of Game Operations & Entertainment for the Boston Bruins, confirms that the trend had indeed started at Bruins games. "We play the song after every home win. I've worked at the Garden since it opened in September 1995, and as far back as I can remember we have played the song after wins."[3] Kevin Friend was the person who was hitting the switch for "Dirty Water" at the Garden and was itching to see what the song would do to the Fenway crowds. "I really wanted to play it at Fenway because it was a perfect song. It's a Boston song even though the guys who sang it were from L.A. Besides, Fenway is right there where the Muddy River flows into the Charles and I think that is where the incident in the song was supposed to have taken place. It was a perfect song for the Park."

So before Friend had even stepped into the Fenway Park control room as the new audio production contractor on Opening Day, he had it in mind to find exactly the right moment to introduce "Dirty Water" to Red Sox Nation. That moment came very quickly, and "Dirty Water" made a most dramatic debut, instantly staking claim to become the Red Sox victory song.

1998's Opening Day fell on Friday, April 10. That year, it was coincidentally both Good Friday and Passover. In a fit of neo-Puritanism that made no sense theologically, the Red Sox decided to ban beer from the ballpark that day. But the Fenway faithful gathered, hoping for a good season. Hope always springs eternal at Fenway in April.

The ballclub had already opened the season on a West Coast road trip and returned home with a mediocre 3–5 record. Even though the team had finished the previous season with just 78 wins and 98 losses, there were higher hopes for the Jimy Williams-managed team.

Kevin Friend and Amy (Sill) Tobey, in their new roles as the music programmers at the old ballpark, were just as excited about the game and the upcoming season as anyone in the 32,805 strong crowd assembled below them. Armed with a stack of CDs, Kevin and Amy began their work. As the game progressed through the fourth inning, things were going well for the home team: the Sox jumped out to a 2–0 lead over the visiting Seattle Mariners. Seattle scored three in the sixth off Sox starter Brian Rose, though, to take the lead. The Mariners scored two more runs in the eighth on a bunch of singles off Red Sox reliever Dennis Eckersley to give them a solid 5–2 lead.

At that juncture, Amy had no thoughts of playing "Sweet Caroline" to rev up the fans in anticipation of a win, as a home opener victory did not seem likely, and things were not going "so good" at all.

It got worse for the home team in the top of the ninth. Seattle scored two more runs and the Sox were in a big 7–2 hole with just three outs remaining. They were down to their last at-bats. At this point, a bunch of players for the Sox, most of whom today's fans may not even remember, started a little Fenway magic that provided an auspicious opportunity for "Dirty Water" to be introduced into Red Sox annals.

Heathcliff Slocumb came on to pitch the ninth for the Mariners, in relief of Seattle starter Randy Johnson. Troy O'Leary led off the bottom of the ninth, pinch-hitting for center fielder Damon Buford; O'Leary singled to first. The next batter, switch-hitting reserve second baseman Mark Lemke, drew a walk, advancing O'Leary to second. Left-fielder Darren Bragg followed with a double to right field that scored O'Leary and sent Lemke to third. It was now Seattle 7, Red Sox 3.

Rookie catcher Jason Varitek had gotten the start behind the plate, so the usual starting catcher and left-handed batting Scott Hatteberg was available to pinch hit for right-fielder Darren Lewis, who was hitless on the day. But Seattle countered with left-hand specialist Tony Fossas in place of Slocumb, so Jimy Williams sent up right-hand hitting utility infielder Mike Benjamin in place of Hatteberg. Benjamin worked a walk. The bases were loaded.

Seattle skipper Lou Piniella brought in relief pitcher Mike Timlin to try to retire shortstop Nomar Garciaparra, but Nomar singled to center field driving in Lemke and it was a 7–4 ballgame. With Bragg now on third and Benjamin on second, and Nomar on first, the bases remained loaded. Next up was third baseman John Valentin, and Timlin's delivery hit him, forcing in Bragg and making it 7–5 with the bases still full and still nobody out. Piniella called on the fourth fireman of the inning, Paul Spoljaric. Boston's big slugging first baseman Mo Vaughn, in the final year of his contract, was up next. After being hit by a pitch in the first inning, Vaughn had struck out on each of his next three at-bats. Diehard Red Sox fans sensed big Mo might be due.

Kevin Friend could feel the electricity in the air. "It was a fantastic moment. The crowd was going wild. The bases were loaded, it was the home opener, and everyone believed the Sox could pull out a miraculous come from behind win if Mo Vaughn could just connect. I think Vaughn took a call strike on the first pitch and then on the next pitch he ripped one just inside the Pesky Pole in right for an astonishing walk-off grand slam to win the game, 9–7. It was an incredible, euphoric scene."

Friend knew exactly what to do at that mind-blowing moment. It was *the perfect moment* to cue up the song he'd been hoping to use. The unmistakable electric "Ah—*rum dum dum*—*dum da dum*" guitar introduction to "Dirty Water" blasted out over the public address system and another fabulous Fenway tradition was born. "Because I love that dirty water, aw-oh, Boston, you're my home."

"Dirty Water," written by Ed Cobb and sung by the Standells, has been the victory anthem of the Red Sox from that day forward.

Kevin Friend's moment of inspiration resonated with Red Sox management. It came at a time when the Sox were trying to find ways to make Fenway friendlier. Red Sox VP Larry Cancro says, "The song was suggested by a Process Improvement Team we put together to improve music. If my memory serves correctly, it was Dan Lyons who specifically recommended it and it was a favorite because of [ticket manager] Joe Helyar who told us of the true genesis of the song."[4] Lyons was involved with one of the "PIT teams"—the one that wanted to improve the music being played at Fenway. He says, "This is when the only music playing was the organ and there was no rock and roll. Our

PIT Team gathered either once a week or every other week to come up with some songs that would paint the description of that game. With the word 'Boston' being sung in 'Dirty Water,' it was only natural that the song be included in the repertoire. Our other selections included songs with the titles that mentioned days of the week, weather, baseball actions, time of the day, etc."[5]

In terms of the song becoming a regular post-victory tradition, General Manager Dan Duquette credited a seemingly unlikely man with the decision: "Jimy Williams was the driving force behind it. We were looking for a feel-good song so that people would feel good about the city and the Red Sox coming out of the ballpark after the Red Sox would win. Jimy was interested in having a tradition. A lot of the traditions that teams do before and after the games have away of preparing them for the next game. With Fenway Park's proximity to the Charles River, and the references to 'Boston, you're my home,' it was a way to feel good about the win and the city and the team, and for the fans to go home feeling good."[6]

The song gradually gained momentum as the most important song in the soundtrack of the Fenway experience. "Dirty Water" now triggers a Pavlovian response in the minds of Red Sox faithful—when the Sox win at Fenway, "Dirty Water" plays and everything is right with the world! If they should win the game with a walk-off hit it is ecstasy! And when the Red Sox win with a walk-off home run it is—nirvana!

The timing of the playing of song is naturally a critical part of its importance. There is never a long wait to hear it, *especially* if it is one of those glorious occasions when the home team has a walk-off win like they had on Opening Day 1998. It typically plays within one second of the moment of victory.

Megan Kaiser explains why she touches the "Dirty Water" button on her computer screen as fast after a win as an Olympic sprinter coming out of the blocks. "We're New Englanders. We aren't patient people. I don't wait, for two reasons. First, I find that it adds punch to the win. A home run is a punctuated moment in time. BANG! It's like that drop in the rollercoaster, that split second that can't be repeated but you remember it. That sock-it-to-me kinda fun. And it heralds the win—it's over, and in grand, Red Sox fashion. It's our anthem. Let the boys have it as they run onto the field, give them something to bang—in time—on the hero's helmet."[7]

She continued to stress the song's importance to all of the "ladies and gentlemen" and to the many young "boys and girls" who have come to the ballpark—some for the first time and others for the hundredth: "To let the fans clap along. It can't be beat. There is so much electricity in that instant! I'll never hit a walk-off in Fenway, but to play a part in adding to the magic that the fans feel is glorious. Savoring—to me—comes later. That's for the Cask, the Tavern, or as your friends retell the moment in the car home.

"Second, and the more practical reason, not everyone can see [what's going on]. The sightlines in the park aren't exactly flawless. Some people are short—and undoubtedly everyone is on their feet at that moment. Imagine holding your breath and waiting, waiting—waiting for that ball to land somewhere… did it happen? And then…you hear that unmistakable riff rip through the stadium and everyone around you—sans the brave souls that donned visitors jerseys—are in heaven. Yet another unbeatable day to be at Fenway Park."

Not limited to the friendly confines of Fenway Park, the "Dirty Water" anthem can be heard in every baseball bastion across the nation whenever the Sox are victorious. Since that auspicious launch in 1998, even in other regions, when two or more Red Sox fans are gathered together, "Dirty Water" can be heard being sung, whistled, or hummed in joyful celebration of a win by the "olde towne team," no matter where they play.

The victory anthem has even spread throughout much of the Red Sox baseball system. Todd Stephenson, Coordinator of Florida Operations for the Red Sox, runs the Fort Myers facility—home to Red Sox spring training since 1993. After every win at City of Palms Park, the Red Sox play "Dirty Water" on the park's sound system. They adopted the practice after the 2003 campaign and have been doing so since spring training 2004.

Portland Sea Dogs Director of Public Relations Chris Cameron says, "I'd say we play 'Dirty Water' eight out of ten victories. We started playing in it 2003, the year we got the Red Sox affiliation. We don't really have set exceptions, just every now and then we play something else to change things up a bit." Geoffrey Iacuessa agrees that the song is played after most Red Sox victories at Hadlock Field. Geoff is the Director of Sales and Promotions. He adds, "I think we played it here and there with little regularity in 2003. We then talked about incorporating it in for every win in 2004, which we did all season. We have had no negative feedback at all. Fans enjoy it and seem to get into it. It obviously helps that we are playing it after a win so the fans are happy. We also play 'Sweet Caroline' during some games too."

Jon Goode of the Lowell Spinners advises that the Red Sox Single-A club plays "Dirty Water" after every home victory at LeLacheur Park. They noticed how much fans at Fenway enjoy hearing the song and adopted the practice. Goode says, "It made perfect sense being a Red Sox team and playing right up the road in Lowell. It's a natural fit." Jon dates the Spinners practice to 2002.

The Pawtucket Red Sox haven't yet begun to play "Dirty Water" on a regular basis, but Vice President of Public Relations Bill Wanless points out, "We did play 'Have a Bad Day' a lot this year after losses." Let's hope there are more wins than losses in the years to come. Maybe PawSox patrons would enjoy a little Standells as they file out of McCoy.

The Standells—Four Decades Later

There have been occasional reunions for the Standells, such as at the 1999 Cavestomp Festival in New York and the Las Vegas Grind in 2000, but for the most part the band had been inactive for decades. To say that a lot of things happened in the 40 years or so after the Standells first formed would be an understatement of enormous proportions. America and the world have changed in ways absolutely unimaginable back in the early 1960s. Two generations have passed and the teenagers of that era are parents and grandparents of today. Chapters upon chapters have been added to the history books—in fact, whole history books have been written just about what has gone on since "Dirty Water" was first heard on the air, in jukeboxes, and on record players across the nation. Yet after four decades, that simple song still reverberated with new meaning for Red Sox fans from Boston to Bangkok, and the four guys who recorded it so many years ago all still resided in the Southern California communities of their younger days.

♪ ♪ ♪

Dick Dodd was sitting down in his home just south of Los Angeles watching the Red Sox on television one evening when he noticed something unusual at the end of the game. Although Dick was born and raised in California, he had become a big fan of the Red Sox and the city of Boston since the summer of 1966. The song and band were so well received in Boston that Dick, the lead singer and drummer of the Standells, became attached to and interested in all things Boston—particularly the baseball team and his favorite player, Carl Yastrzemski. Dodd also liked to "go against the grain," by rooting for a team other than his hometown Dodgers back then. "It was part of my punky image then. But I really liked the Red Sox and have always remained a big fan."

What caught his attention on television that night was what he *heard* in the background at the end of the Red Sox game, while the ESPN announcers were doing their post-game wrap-up. Faintly, but distinctly, Dick was able to pick out the familiar guitar riffs of his nearly 40-year-old Top 10 recording behind the voices of the commentators. Sure enough, when the camera panned the crowd, he could see the moving lips and then faintly, heard the voices of the fans in the ballpark singing, "...love that dirty water. Aw—oh, Boston you're my home!"

After the Standells split up in the 1970s, they all went their separate ways and had little contact with each other or, in some cases, even with the music business. Dick Dodd had found employment as a limousine driver and was living in Orange County with his wife Jane, a former Playboy Bunny—a grown-up "Dick and Jane" story, he joked.

Larry Tamblyn was still composing music, and working as a recording engineer and audio editor for a company called Audio Digest in the San Fernando Valley city of Glendale. Larry lived outside the L.A. area in Palmdale, California with his wife, actress Glenda Chism.

Tony Valentino owned an Italian restaurant in Woodland Hills called Cafe Bellissimo featuring singing waiters and waitresses. Occasionally Tony would entertain his patrons with renditions of "Volare" and other Italian favorites.

Gary Lane was now known as Gary McMillan once again—had been since he left the group—and was a barber in the community of La Cañada nestled between the Verdugo and San Gabriel mountains. Edie, his wife of 45 years, had compiled an incredible scrapbook of the band that she had kept since 1962 as tangible evidence of their years as a rock and roll couple.

Recently, personal connections had brought the Standells back together, if not as a performing group, certainly as old friends. They had been in touch with each other more frequently. They all realized how special it was to have survived the crazy days as rock stars in the 1960s and still be friends, healthy and happy in their lives. Or as Larry lightheartedly put it, "Hey, we were rock stars in the '60s, doing all of the things a traveling band did back then and here we are—amazingly still alive and still friends!"

Excited about what he was seeing on TV, Dick began to call his old band mates one by one. "You guys have got to listen to this! I mean everybody's lips in the stands are moving to our song, you won't believe it!" Dick urged them to tune into the next Red Sox game they could get. "I told the guys to watch the Red Sox. They weren't Red Sox fans, or even baseball fans *per se*, so I explained—listen, after every time they win, they play 'Dirty Water' as their victory song!"

Seeing Red Sox fans singing his band's signature song gave Dodd a big kick and it reinforced his long-time loyalty to the Boston baseball team. Occasionally, he and Jane would catch the Sox on the road at a game in Anaheim but he had never personally experienced the crowd at Fenway singing his song. He relished the thought that people in Boston and Red Sox fans worldwide still enjoyed the Standells' music and had adopted "Dirty Water" as their own. But Dick continued on with his life in southern California as a limo driver without much further thought about the new status of his old song.

"Dirty Water" and the
Magical Mystery Season of 2004

During the fabled 2004 World Series Championship run, the extraordinarily large contingent of citizens from the Red Sox Nation attending the Wild Card Series in Anaheim broke into a spontaneous *a cappella* concert singing "Dirty Water" in the stands. Kevin and Elaine Hegarty, transplants from Dorchester to San Diego, were at the October 5 game in Angels Stadium. When the couple and their friends returned to their tailgating party in the stadium parking lot after the game, Kevin turned on his car's CD player which was optimistically loaded before the game with the Standells' song—much to the irritation of the relatively laid-back Angels fans around them.

At the famous Sonny McLean's Pub in Santa Monica, California—a Boston-themed sports bar and the self-proclaimed headquarters of Red Sox Nation West—owner Jim Conners vividly recalled the excitement of being present for the beginning of the Red Sox run for the roses: "When we found out that they were coming to Anaheim it was tough to get a ticket. [Red Sox president] Tom Werner actually gave me a call and asked if we could use 40 for each game, which obviously we were all excited about. I think the tickets were gone in about 30 seconds. A lot of people managed to get off work that day.

"We went down to the game and of course we were hearing Angels fans taunting us with the chant '19–18! 19–18!' It was tough to give it back to them because they'd won it all in 2002. It was kind of tough; you just had to bite your tongue.

"Then we won the first game, and in the second game we blew them out again. Finally it felt a lot better. Now we were up two games to none, and a couple of the guys brought brooms saying that the sweep would be in Boston. It was a great feeling—especially for us Red Sox fans who were not used to sweeping anybody in the playoffs."[1]

The citizens of the far-flung Red Sox Nation finally had something to cheer about, although even in the direst of situations and in any venue away from home you can always hear, even above the cheers of the local partisans, the rally cries of true Boston fans repeated over and over: "Here We Go Red Sox, Here We Go! (Clap-Clap) Or "Let's Go Red Sox! (Clap-Clap, Clap, Clap, Clap) voiced as "Here we go Red Sawx, here we go! And "Let's go Red Sawx!" in true "Boston-ese" of course.

Even though only a few of the patrons at Sonny McLean's had personally heard "Dirty Water" in Fenway, most were very much aware of the significance of the tune through watching NESN broadcasts of the games and from stories from folks back home in New England.

"In Angels Stadium we had a bunch of folks bring signs—all kinds of different signs," recalled Conners. "One guy had a sign that read, 'Love that Dirty Water' and another guy sitting next to him had one that read, 'Boston you're "our" home.' Growing up in Boston, I heard that song always playing on the radio, so it is just a great song—it means so much to Boston sports fans everywhere—so it's a great song for the Red Sox to have.

"The bar was packed during the rest of the Anaheim series back in Boston. Everyone was hoping for the sweep so Sonny's was filled up. I sent people over to a 'Phillies' bar across the street called The Shack. They got filled up so they sent people on to an English pub down the road and then *they* filled up! There were probably 700 to 800 Red Sox fans in a single square mile area of Santa Monica, which was pretty exciting. It was a great feeling to experience all these people coming out of their homes in order to sit and cheer with a bunch of other Red Sox fans."

The euphoria of the eventual Red Sox sweep of the Angels series did not last very long, even after they finished off Anaheim in Boston with a David Ortiz 10th inning, two-run, walk-off homer. The cursed Yankees were next and the "great" feeling soon began to sour for the customers at Sonny's and all over Red Sox Nation during the course of the first three games of the American League Championship Series with the Yankees.

There wasn't much for Sox fans to sing about, as three straight losses seemed to portend another cursed season for the long-beleaguered team. "During those first three games, it was tough. Everybody was just so disappointed especially after we swept Anaheim. We really thought that with Schilling and Pedro, our offense and strong lineup—nobody expected to be down 3–0 just like that. It was just awful. After that third game a couple of buddies and I went across the street so depressed and had a few hard drinks—we only have beer and wine at Sonny's. 'Why?' we asked. 'Why do we have to do this year after year?' We were sick of saying 'wait until next year'—this *was supposed to be* the 'next year.' We hadn't had a season like it in a long, long time. People were really disappointed that once again the Yankees were poised to beat us—especially after 2003, with that home run that just killed us—here we are a year later and it looked like it was all down the drain again. It was tough."

Back on the East Coast the night of that dreadful game, author Chuck Burgess and his wife Catherine were having dinner at the home of Jim and Margaret Maguire, recent retirees to Cape Cod from New Jersey. "It was awful, just awful to have had to watch that game in the close company of a couple of Yankee fans who were also the in-laws of my oldest son," he said. "Although Jim, a true gentleman, tried to conceal his ingrained Yankee fan conceit (they really can't help themselves), I couldn't wait to finish dinner and get out of there."

That third game of the LCS, a 19–8 loss, seemed like another knockout blow for the battered Sox but in one of the most incredible comebacks in sports history, the Sox did the seemingly impossible. The Sox did what no other baseball team had done before: come back from a 0–3 deficit to win the final four games in a seven-game playoff series.

The perspective from Sonny McLean's reflected that of Red Sox fans all over the world. Conners basked in the remembrance of that reversal. "And then the turnaround came. That Game Four, the place was still busy, Sonny's was still packed. People were down, a lot of folks thought it was over but they kept on cheering. When we were losing before we scored the winning run — everyone was saying how they couldn't believe that the Yankees could sweep us. And then all of a sudden [Dave] Roberts stole second and the whole place started going crazy! Everyone was standing up and jumping around. The following three games, it was just absolute pandemonium. Unlike back east, it was pretty good for us on the west coast because it wasn't midnight or two in the morning when those games finished.

"Then Game Seven came along and the next thing you know we had about three different news stations come in and the Fox national network was broadcasting from here. We had three cop cars across the street in case we won and everyone decided to spill out into the street. That happened here before when the Pats won the first Superbowl, so I think they were getting ready for another similar happening. There was also a helicopter hovering above — I think it was a news one. Other people thought it might have been a police one, but I doubt that. So it was quite exciting and after we won it was just a *great* feeling! I call it the 'sweep' of the Yankees because the first three games were something else — maybe a bad dream — because coming back four straight was unbelievable."

After Boston beat New York in extra innings to win Game Five at home, just as they had done to win Game Four (both times on David Ortiz walk-off hits), "Dirty Water" was sung again, and again, and again at Fenway Park. It was sung again by Sox fans after Game Seven in Yankee Stadium, where a stunned and subdued New York crowd had to finally give the Red Sox fans their due as they won the American League pennant and prepared to take it home to Boston.

Red Sox Nation was on a collective high, one that few living citizens had ever experienced — not unless they were around in 1918, the last time the Sox won the World Series. And in some ways this was truly something more to savor. The dreaded arch-nemesis New York Yankees had been defeated in the most dramatic way imaginable. The Sox pulled off something no other baseball team had ever accomplished, coming from the depths of playoff despair to win four straight and to triumph. It felt like redemption redoubled, following on the disaster that had been the League Championship Series just the year before. Even Hollywood could not have scripted a more gripping come-from-behind fantasy.

The World Series and the St. Louis Cardinals were next. With barely a moment to try to digest the elation after their incredible comeback against the Yankees, some fans thought the World Series against St. Louis could be anti-climactic—but that was not the case. How could it be? This *actually* was the "next year," (as in "wait 'til next year!") that the citizens of Red Sox Nation had been dreaming about for so long! The opportunity to face the Cardinals was the opportunity to avenge Game Seven defeats in both the 1946 and 1967 World Series. The Hollywood writers were still on the case.

Interlude: The Return of "Tessie"

Even the most casual baseball observer knows that fans from New England endured an 86-year drought between the World Series victories in 1918 and 2004. The old rally song "Tessie," though, had been out of the fans' minds and off of their lips for about the last 60 of those years until the 2004 baseball season. It seemed like everyone had a theory of how to break the long, dry spell—call it the Curse. Grasping at any straw, there were some truly outlandish ideas. Fans and team officials alike were ready to try anything that might help the ballclub reach the Holy Grail. With an eye more on history than the absurd, Red Sox Executive Vice President for Public Affairs Dr. Charles Steinberg suggested that perhaps it was time to revive the old song with the hope of bringing the team the good luck and good fortune needed to regain a World Series Championship.

In the Royal Rooters tradition of altering and adapting the lyrics to fit the situation, *Boston Herald* sportswriter Jeff Horrigan penned a modern version of "Tessie." Dr. Steinberg and Jeff Horrigan were at the minor league complex in Fort Myers during the early days of spring training 2004 and Steinberg mentioned "Tessie" saying, "I don't believe anyone's ever covered the song. If someone did a good cover, we'd turn that into a staple at Fenway. I don't really know who to approach." Horrigan, fresh from having Boston-based rock band the Dropkick Murphys play at the annual wintertime Hot Stove Cool Music charity fundraiser, said, "I know just the guys. They're baseball nuts and they're looking to get into baseball."

The management of the Boston Bruins Hockey Club had been experimenting with scheduling music concerts in conjunction with their hockey games as an entertainment double header designed to attract new fans to the team. The Dropkicks had success in exciting Bruins fans with their unique style of punkish rock and roll mixed with traditional Celtic music—complete with a bagpiper as part of the band—and performed after several home games in what is now informally known as the "new" Boston Garden.

Although the general public often associates the band with Boston's heavily Irish neighborhood of South Boston, the Dropkick Murphys are a collective that hail from various locales in the Greater Boston area: Quincy, Milton, Dorchester, and Brighton, and one Canadian member from Calgary, Alberta. The band's unusual name comes from an old alcohol rehabilitation facility that was located out in the far western suburbs of Boston and operated by a former boxing promoter, John Murphy. When the boys in the band were young and were misbehaving, their parents or grandparents would often threaten to "send them" to Dropkick Murphy's facility to instill a little fear in them, much in the way some people might invoke the boogeyman to scare little children.

Lead singer Ken Casey had a faint memory that Dropkick Murphy was "a wrestler or fighter in the early 1900s, or maybe even in the '30s or '40s. He had a boxing and wrestling camp and a lot of his guys...keep in mind this has become almost folklore and you hear so many different versions I don't know what is 100 per cent true...but what I have been told, by a guy I knew that was in there and knew him is...that Murphy would have so many problems with these guys that were out there training and he would lose them when they would go out and get drunk. So he started to experiment with methods of detoxification before it was...before there was such a thing. He started to become better known for *that* than he was for his boxing camp. Soon politicians, police...everybody from the low-down to the big shots would go there if they were on a jag and had to get straight. So that is where we got the name from."[1]

According to Casey, the connection between the band and sports venues began with successes at the Bruins games-concerts as well as a show they did for the Glasgow Celtic Soccer Club in Scotland while on a European tour. Horrigan e-mailed Casey in Europe and explained that the Red Sox were interested to have someone re-do "Tessie" and Casey replied quickly, "We're in! Just get me an MP-3 of the original song."

"We had remade a lot of old traditional Irish songs," Casey said. "It was pretty obvious that we would be a perfect candidate. We were a Boston band and had the experience of taking old songs and modernizing them. We had been having success with a connection between sports and music. We were thrilled."

Horrigan found a recording of the original "Tessie" and e-mailed an MP-3 to Casey. He was candid enough in his own appraisal: "It's dreadful. It's about a woman who tells her secrets to her parrot. It's almost like an opera song." Jeff heard the story of how the band reacted, "They gather around Ken's computer and they listen to it, and they said, 'Absolutely not! We're not doing a ['effing] bird song!' So Ken e-mails me back and says, 'We're out.' I said, 'I completely understand.' But then he goes, 'Listen, if you want to come up with a new "Tessie," then we'll consider it. We can work together on it.' A couple of days later, before I went to bed, I just sat down and wrote some lyrics, basically a song about a song, using the chorus from the original song. I sent the lyrics to them and they started working on it. I think they did the original demo in Europe."[2]

Ken Casey was ready to remake an old song, but the original "Tessie" presented too much of a challenge. "When I said we remake old songs, I'm talking about taking versions of Irish songs that were recorded in the '40s and '50s, or even maybe the '60s. Now we are talking about a recording from 1903! You could barely hear it; it was a man singing accompanied by just a piano, and it was very, very 'old timey' and the lyrics were very outdated. We finally said that we'd do it if we can put a bit of a modern twist on it."

"'Tessie' happened to be in the key of B-flat, which is the only key that bag-pipes can play in. . . . So we said, 'That's a sign right there', because B-flat is not a natural key for an ordinary piano and vocal song, so to hear that it was in B-flat was kind of a very odd coincidence, we thought. The Red Sox agreed to take a more modern day stab at it and I think they were obviously happy with the product."

The group clearly brought its creative genius to bear on the song, and mar-ried Horrigan's words with tremendous energy and the kind of treatment that can rouse a sports crowd. They were smart, as well, to invite Red Sox players Bronson Arroyo, Lenny DiNardo, and Johnny Damon to join in the chorus. Charles Steinberg brought some of his staff over to the recording studio, just a block from the ballpark next to the old Baseball Tavern, and consequently the chorus featured Sox staffers Peter Chase, Mark Rogoff, Sarah Stevenson, and Dr. Steinberg, too.

Jeff Horrigan understands that Steinberg loved it so much he'd play it with his characteristic enthusiasm in the Red Sox offices—nonstop. Even Red Sox president Larry Lucchino, who originally despised the song, came around and became a convert.

The contemporary adaptation makes reference to the original, self-anointed, Royal Rooters of Boston and their leader, Michael "Nuf Ced" Mc-Greevey, owner of the "Third Base" Saloon which was located in the shadows of the old Huntington Avenue ballpark. McGreevey advertised his bar as "the last stop before you steal home," and painted on the outfield wall at the Hunt-ington Avenue Grounds was a sign for McGreevey's establishment that asked, "How Can You Get Home Without Reaching 3rd Base? Nuf Ced."

The Dropkicks took care of all the expenses of the recording. The band released an EP of "Tessie," which features a video (originally shot for the *Red Sox Stories* television show) starring Colleen Reilly as Tessie. All the proceeds go to the Red Sox Foundation.

The new version of "Tessie" debuted at Fenway Park on a day that proved auspicious—July 24, 2004. It's a day that many Sox fans will never forget: a bitter Red Sox/Yankees battle at Fenway memorialized forever by dramatic photographs of Sox catcher Jason Varitek plowing his glove into the face of Alex Rodriguez in a confrontation near home plate that resulted in four ejec-tions. Boston manager Terry Francona was ejected two innings later arguing a call. The Yankees scored six runs in the top of the sixth but Boston came right back with four in the bottom of the sixth. New York held a 10–8 lead after seven, but ace reliever Mariano Rivera melted down and Bill Mueller hit a dramatic three-run walk-off home run in the bottom of the ninth to win it, 11–10. Some feel that the spirit the Sox showed that afternoon gave them greater confidence and a spark that helped carry them to the playoffs.

The "Tessie" that is played at Fenway Park today differs greatly from the original, not only in the lyrics but also in the melody, according to Casey. "The arrangement is totally different. The only thing we really kept was the melody line of the chorus but we changed the words...we kept only a few of the original words throughout the song. Basically the only thing that we took was the tail end of the chorus...*Tessie you are the only, only, only*...that's basically the gist of the melody from the song.

"I think it is no coincidence that the song was, you know, laid to rest for 86 years and they didn't win for 86 years!" (As we have seen, the song was played in the ballpark sporadically up into the 1940s, but so infrequently that it was all but forgotten. It may not have been performed even once for the last 50 years of the 20th century, though there are suggestions that it was played occasionally, very occasionally.)

When the Red Sox introduced their version of "Tessie" during their magical-mystical 2004 World Series Championship season, the Dropkicks began their own very special connection to the many legendary events in the collective history of the Red Sox faithful. "The day the Red Sox debuted the song with us on the field at Fenway was when the Red Sox played the Yankees and had the bench-clearing brawl and the Bill Mueller walk-off home run," noted Casey.

"We recorded this song in June 2004 and after giving it to the Red Sox told anyone that would listen that this song would guarantee a World Series victory. Obviously no one listened to us or took us seriously. We were three outs away from elimination in Game Four at the hands of the Yankees and receiving death threats from friends, family, and strangers telling us to stay away from the Red Sox and any other Boston sports team and get out of town. Luckily for us things turned around for the Red Sox and the rest is history."[3]

That was the first day in the modern era that "Tessie" was played at Fenway. It would not be the last.

When working for the *Herald* at the Sox games, Jeff Horrigan typically has to run to the clubhouse to get quotes to complete his game story, so he rarely hears his lyrics sung to a joyous crowd. If there's a walk-off win, though, he is bound to his laptop just a bit longer to write a new lead for the story and he hears the song played at the end of the game—right after "Dirty Water," of course! "I love hearing people shout out 'Two...three...four!' That gives me shivers, gives me chills up and down my back."

Following "Tessie", the final song of the now-traditional trio of selections played at the end of every Fenway victory is "Joy to the World." As noted earlier, Los Angeles recording producer Richie Podolor was involved with two of the songs in the trilogy, both "Dirty Water" and "Joy to the World"—the Three Dog Night song that spent six weeks at #1 on the charts back in 1971.

Those fans still in the stands after all three songs play are typically treated to additional upbeat music from the Fenway Park organist as they make their way to the ballpark exits.

A World Series Call-Up

When the Sox took World Series Game One in Boston on a late Saturday night, the reality that this team could, finally, win it all was sinking in. After the hard-fought 11–9 victory, the melody of "Dirty Water" reverberated throughout Red Sox Nation once again: from Kenmore Square to Kennebunk, from Framingham to Fort Lauderdale, from Saugus to Santa Monica. The song was taking on near-religious overtones as the fervor-laden spiritual hymn and recessional song of the Fenway faithful. To trudge out of the ballpark after a game and not hear "Dirty Water" is a disappointing moment indeed.

Once again the feelings and emotions of Red Sox faithful everywhere can be summed up in Sonny McLean's owner Jim Conners' reflections on seeing that final out in the 2004 World Series: "The first game against St. Louis almost felt like a Yankees series—back and forth, back and forth. After Game One, you just knew that—somehow—they were going to win every game. It was such a great feeling, especially after everything we fans have gone through, you're always waiting for something to go wrong—you almost couldn't believe it. You would ask yourself, 'Is this really happening, four from the Yankees and then a sweep of the World Series?' When Foulke caught the ball and threw it over to Doug, the place went just went crazy. There were probably more tears on the floor than spilt beer, which is pretty significant during a championship game in a pub like ours! I didn't see a dry eye in the place.

"You looked around and you knew you were looking at people who wanted their grandparents, or their parents who aren't there anymore to see it. Almost everyone could be heard saying, 'I wish my father . . .' or 'I wish my mother . . .' Saying that they wished that *someone* special who had passed away could have seen this. Everybody was crying. It meant so much to everyone—it was more than just the Red Sox winning. This is how we all grew up, never experiencing something like this. To get the monkey off your back finally—no more '19-18' taunts anymore. What a great feeling!"

It was a transcendental moment for every fervent fan in Red Sox Nation.

The Standells themselves had a small but very significant role to play, one they'll never forget. Before the second (and what turned out to be the *last*) home game of the World Series at Fenway, the Red Sox management had arranged an incredible surprise for everyone in Boston that was truly worthy of the moment and will be a part of Red Sox lore forever. The return of the original Standells to Boston to perform "Dirty Water"—live before a frenzied Fenway World Series crowd!

The bandmates now knew the tradition of the Red Sox and "Dirty Water," but they never could have dreamed of what happened next during the 2004 playoffs. After an exhaustive search to find the Standells, the Red Sox finally got Dick Dodd's phone number. They didn't wait long to reach out. Dick received a surprising telephone call from the office of Sox Vice President Dr. Charles Steinberg, asking him if he and the band would be interested in coming to Boston to perform "Dirty Water" live, in front of the Fenway crowd, during the World Series!

After Boston beat up on the Yankees in the final game of the LCS, 10–3, to make the ALCS rout complete, the Sox put on a full-court press to try to locate the Standells. Dr. Steinberg explained how the idea germinated:

"As a fan of rock and roll since the 1960s, I had always known of 'Dirty Water,' and its references to Boston. And having attended more than 50 games at Fenway before joining the Red Sox, I think I knew they played it after wins.

"When we arrived in 2002, I believe it was Dave Heuschkel of the *Hartford Courant*, who, knowing my enthusiasm for music, said, 'So, are you going to reunite the Standells?'

"The planted seed stayed a seed through that year and the next. I wanted to find them for post-season 2003, just as I wanted to find the original recording of 'Tessie.' I did find that recording (too scratchy to play in the ballpark), but I didn't really try to track down the Standells.

"Then, in 2004, we started working with the Dropkick Murphys on the new version of 'Tessie,' and that rising tide lifted the sunk ship that was the idea of reuniting the Standells.

"As 'Tessie' debuted and connected with young fans, I told Sarah McKenna, our Director of Fan and Neighborhood Services (and my right hand when it comes to logistics of our grand ceremonies), that we really ought to find the Standells for postseason."[1]

Courant sportswriter Heuschkel remembers the first conversation. "I do recall asking Charles about the Standells. We're both huge fans of the Beatles. I remember asking Charles if he knew the Standells once appeared on an episode of *The Munsters* and played 'I Want To Hold Your Hand' in their living room. (It may have been the only time I stumped Charles with a Beatles question!) Knowing that Charles and the new ownership group is always open to ideas, I mentioned that it would be great if the team could locate the band and invite them to play 'Dirty Water' at Fenway. At the time I didn't think they would actually pull it off! In some ways, I guess you can thank the Munsters for that. Who would ever imagine there'd be a link between 4 Yawkey Way and 1313 Mockingbird Lane?"[2]

The Red Sox had won the pennant and, after two nights off, the World Series was due to begin on Saturday, October 23. There wasn't much time. The Sox had no idea how to reach the group, but Sarah McKenna unexpectedly received a twice-forwarded e-mail informing her how to reach Dick Dodd, who in turn contacted the rest of the band just in the nick of time to make some very special Fenway Park magic. The story of how she received that information at that particular time is one of interesting coincidences.

Although the Standells had not recorded or performed together for a very long time, their music had never gone out of fashion with fans who appreciated the roots of what has become known as "garage" music.

♪ ♪ ♪

Mark Felsot is the West Coast representative of the New York City-based radio program *Little Steven's Underground Garage*. Mark handles all affiliate relations of the nationally syndicated rock music program, a show created and hosted by musician, songwriter, and actor Steven Van Zandt. Mark's responsibilities include signing new stations to carry the show and serving as liaison with the affiliate stations. He also does a number of things that sometimes involve programming. Mark met Dick Dodd in conjunction with his responsibilities for Little Steven's show, and their relationship was a key link in the chain of events that brought the Standells once again to Boston—for one of the biggest gigs of their career.

"I had met Dick because I had gone to his house where he recorded some IDs for the *Underground Garage* radio show. We talked about the music business and also about baseball because I am a big Angels fan and he didn't live that far from Angels Stadium. We had a nice chat and became friendly. I occasionally sent him copies of Steven's radio show, especially when he was playing a Standells track. So we had a friendly ongoing relationship. During the Red Sox [World Series] run, I had sort of known that 'Dirty Water' was played at Red Sox games, but not to the extent that it was, because being on the West Coast the only time you see them is on ESPN or when the Angels play them. After the Red Sox had beaten the Yankees…I think it was a Thursday night, I came home and there was a message from Dick on my machine and he said, 'Wouldn't it be really cool if me and Little Steven went to Boston and got to sing "Dirty Water" for the World Series!' He went on to say, 'Aw you know I'm just throwing out an idea, I don't know, maybe its sort of crazy, sort of weird.' I heard this message late, maybe 11 o'clock or midnight, but I went 'Eh, that is a pretty cool idea, not a bad thought.'

"I went to bed and when I got up the next morning I played back the message and thought wouldn't it be cool if the Red Sox, who are using this song, could get the guy who sang it back to Boston to perform it. I ended up e-mailing our Boston affiliate, WROR, where I know a couple of people and said that I knew the singer from the Standells and wouldn't it be a great idea if the singer sang "Dirty Water" at one of these World Series Red Sox games. That was probably 7 A.M. Pacific time—10 o'clock Eastern time."[3]

Buzz Knight, the operations manager of Boston radio station WROR-FM, got Mark's e-mail. Buzz was also the vice president of programming for Greater Media, Inc., a management corporation for nearly 20 other broadcast outlets throughout the country. Buzz and Mark had been friends in the business for a long time. Buzz recalls getting Mark's note: "Mark said he knew it might be a long shot, but it might be fun to try. Purely on a 'why not?' kind of whim, I thought that it might not be a bad idea to get the email from Mark into the hands of someone from the Red Sox. Michael Schetzel used to be in the ticket office. I'd met Michael through a mutual friend and happened to have his e-mail. I wrote to him explaining how I received the e-mail about the Standells and wondered if it would be of interest to the Boston Red Sox."[4]

Meanwhile, back in California, Dick called Mark again—this time getting him and not his machine. "About an hour and a half later, Dick actually called me asking if I got his message from the night before. I said I thought it was a pretty good idea, and such a good idea that I had e-mailed some people I knew in Boston asking if they had any contacts with the Red Sox. While I was on the phone with Dick, my cell phone rang and it was someone from the Red Sox PR department, Sarah I think. Buzz must have contacted the Red Sox. So Sarah goes, 'We have been trying to find the band for a couple of years now.' The only clues they had were the Standells records, but the labels no longer exist. She said, 'We're not interested in just the lead singer; we're interested in getting the whole band.' I said, 'Here's the irony—I am actually talking to the lead singer on the other line. I'll give you his number and you can call him yourself.' I hung up and told Dick."

Until that moment, Dick was completely unaware that the Red Sox had wanted to reach the band He would never have imagined that the Boston Red Sox would be intrigued with what he thought to be his own off-the-wall idea to sing at Fenway Park. Little did he know that it was exactly what the Red Sox had wanted to do for some time—to have the Standells perform "Dirty Water" live at Fenway Park. The timing was such that now their performance could be during the World Series!

Sarah McKenna finally reached Dick Dodd on Friday night at 6 o'clock their time, calling from her office in Fenway Park. She asked if he thought the band could make it to Boston on such short notice. Dick said, "If you can get us there, we'll come." Dick told Sarah "they'd wear their Red Sox hats. They follow the team. They [knew] about what's happening here."[5] It became an amazing whirlwind adventure as Sarah quickly made arrangements and got them to Boston. "I felt a sigh of relief when I found out that the group all keeps in touch."[6]

Dick recalls the moment he presented this news to Larry, Gary, and Tony. "When I called up the guys I said, 'This is no joke…the Red Sox called me and they want us to do the World Series! I don't even know why I'm asking you if you want to go do this because you *are* going to do this, we *are* going to Boston, we *are* going to do this thing live, we *are* going to see the World Series, we *are* going to have a good time, and the Red Sox said we can even bring our wives! How great is that, you guys? Forty years later, we are going back to Boston...you get your old butts up—we are going to play!' I was, like, one hundred feet off the ground!"

When Gary McMillan received Dick's call, he was naturally taken aback, too. "I heard it on a Friday. Dick called me and asked, 'How would you like to go to Boston?' I said, 'Why would I want to go to Boston?' He said, 'Well, you know that the Red Sox have picked up "Dirty Water" and they play it after every win and now they want us to come and play at the World Series.' I said, 'You have got to be kidding!' He said, 'No, I am not!' That was on a Friday. Saturday at noon we were on the plane to Boston. Sunday we played, and that was just amazing."

The Red Sox brass flew the band and their companions into Boston and settled them into the Boston Harbor Hotel for their weekend stay. It is not that long a walk along Atlantic Avenue and the waterfront to the mouth of the River Charles—the river immortalized in song by the band all those years ago.

♪ ♪ ♪

Psyching the home crowd with live musical performances was an innovation the team's management introduced during the 2004 season. The Dropkick Murphys had been asked back to play the Red Sox rally song "Tessie" live in Fenway during Game Three of the American League Championship Series against the Angels, and again in the first game of the World Series. The performance of the band seemed a good omen. Ken Casey recalled that every time they played it, the Sox won in dramatic fashion. "We played it...on the field for Game Three of the series against the Angels, which David Ortiz won with a walk-off home run. And then we played it again on the field in Game One of the World Series. It was not a walk-off, but it was a [Mark] Bellhorn home run in the bottom of the eighth that won it. Every game that we have played at, the Red Sox have won with a home run in their last at-bat!"

Now it was the Standells' turn to help reverse the alleged curse that dogged the Boston baseball club for nearly four generations. It was Game Two of the World Series, and possibly the last game in Fenway Park if the Sox won and then could take two of the three games scheduled in St. Louis (they did in fact take both games in Boston and the first two in St. Louis, sweeping the Series in four games.) As much as Red Sox fans would love to see their team win it all at home in Fenway, no one wanted a protracted series with another one or maybe two games at home necessary to win the championship. Red Sox history is replete with too many things going wrong in sudden-death situations. The Nation was emotionally exhausted after living through the playoffs against the Yankees and was eager, anxious, and even desperate for the 86-year championship drought to be done with.

It was never announced publicly that the band would be performing what was now Boston's most significant song—"Dirty Water"—live at the Park that night! In this remarkable baseball season, the surprise appearance of the Standells before Game Two would border on emotional overload for the pumped-up fans. It would be a very poignant night for the Standells as well, not just because of their attachment to the Red Sox and the drama of being involved in one of the most exciting sporting events in history but also because of their own personal journeys that brought them to that night. From rising rock stars anointed as the American answer to the Beatles or as the next Rolling Stones, to obscurity as one-hit wonders with their records relegated to the cutout bins, each individual Standell had gone his own separate way for many years.

Playing at the World Series was undoubtedly the most significant performance for the band since the 1960s. A lot of time—almost 40 years—had gone by since the Standells had recorded "Dirty Water." And a lot of time had passed since the band stood center stage before thousands of appreciative fans. About the only thing the guys had in common now was their past glory. But each one acknowledged that they were happy to all still be alive and healthy, and still living in Southern California. Any conflicts they may have experienced during the dissolution of the band in the 1970s had long since been forgotten and there remained an enduring friendship between them all. It was an emotional reunion.

Now the Standells were back. Back in Boston, back in the limelight after all the years that took them down different paths and after all the time that had passed since their fling with fame and glory as rock and roll stars. It was an opportunity to experience the joy of success once again. It was a situation not unlike the one the Red Sox and their fans were having in this special season—a season of success that would erase years of frustration with euphoric delight. It was a comeback of epic proportions for the both the Red Sox *and* the Standells.

So, on that special night at Fenway before Game Two of the 2004 World Series, another vignette was added to the legend of the Red Sox. Bostonians can tell their children and grandchildren about the night the Standells played their 40-year-old hit, the victory anthem of the Red Sox nation, live at Fenway Park, during the last home game of the season, when the team wound up winning the World Series for the first time in 86 years!

Dodd fondly recalls the exciting night at the park. "We had gone out there earlier in the afternoon to get a sound check. We met James Taylor and Donna Summer, which was special. They brought us into the interior of Fenway.... It's unbelievable. People don't know what's in there. I mean the offices of all the Red Sox and stuff. John Henry was there and Dr. Charles Steinberg, and all these people...we are in the *innards* of Fenway and *they* are all going, 'It's the Standells! Oh my God, are you kidding? Are you kidding?' Really, *we* were the ones in awe. I said, 'It's just us, sorry to interrupt you,' and so on.

"Then they take us...around a wall near the left-field foul pole [now called the Fisk Pole in recognition of the home run Carlton Fisk hit that won Game Six of the 1975 World Series] there is a door there somewhere. So we come out and we are on the field. We eventually wound up in the Red Sox dugout. Here I am, I'm drooling over myself, I am so excited! I'm like a blithering idiot or something; I almost have tears in my eyes and we were sitting in *the* dugout! I said, 'Give me some sunflower seeds; because I want to spit sunflower seeds in here just like the ballplayers!' Everything was immaculate, everything was so clean, and I said, 'Oh, I just want some David's seeds. I want to spit something.'

"Then we walked out to the pitcher's mound and we met James Taylor. They said, 'You are going to be coming out there—in the pitcher's mound/ home plate area—and I just went, God...unbelievable.' Then you turn around and you are looking over home plate and, you know, it just got to me ...I got a lump in my throat...it was unbelievable!"

Deep in center field, just to the left of the Red Sox bullpen, there is a big overhead door that opens up to provide access to field from Lansdowne Street. In the alleyway behind that door a rolling portable stage was set up ready to be towed out onto Fenway's warning track where the Standells would give their most emotional and most important public performance in nearly 40 years. After both teams had finished their batting practice, the outfield door was raised and the 40-foot trailer/stage was towed out onto the playing surface and set up, much to the curiosity of the crowd in the already full and overflowing stadium. The decorative banners and the special red, white, and blue bunting signaled that this was no ordinary night at the ballpark. It was the *World Series*! The teams were lined up along both baselines as James Taylor sang the National Anthem and the Standells stood by eager to perform next.

"That night when they had all our stuff set up, right before we played, *that voice*....I don't know who he is [it was, of course, public address announcer Carl Beane, with a voice reminiscent of the great traditional delivery of legendary Red Sox stadium announcer Sherm Feller] . . .*that voice* said, 'Ladies and gentlemen, boys and girls...Fenway Park proudly presents....' As he started to introduce us, people are looking at us going like, 'Who are those old farts...who are they?"

But the fans did not wonder very long. Slowly an appreciative Fenway crowd began to realize what was going on at that special and historic occasion. One of those fans was Buzz Knight, who had played an unexpected but crucial role in the evening's event. "I was privileged to get to go to Game Two of the World Series. Little did I know that the Red Sox had actually brought the Standells to Boston. Imagine my surprise as I walk in and see the Standells getting ready to play! I said to the person I was with, 'Wow, this is cool" and I told them the story about the e-mails. I thought it must be just a coincidence. I really doubted that I actually had anything to do with what I was seeing on the field. I was curious, however, and I later got back to Mark and asked if anything had happened based upon all the e-mail interplay we did about the Standells and the World Series? Mark said, 'Yeah, a short time after I sent it to you and then you sent it to the Red Sox, they were on the phone trying to put it together.' It put a big smile on my face, needless to say."

Beane's resonant voice continued to echo throughout the ancient ballpark as he announced, "Ladies and gentlemen, boys and girls …part of Fenway Park, part of the Red Sox family—Please welcome the Standells, playing "Dirty Water."'

"We came out right on the field from inside the Green Monster," Dick recalled with a delighted expression on his face. "There is a little door and a hallway there. They had our instruments out [on stage] and everything was all set up. Nobody knew we were going to be there, you know so that made it even more exciting.…I have my Boston jacket on, my Boston jersey underneath and my Boston hat on…then the other guys…all of a sudden…they all started putting on Boston jackets, hats and everything!"

The band walked along the left-field warning track towards center field and then climbed up the six aluminum steps to the stage which was placed in front of the bullpen where the pitchers were warming up. Curt Schilling was doing his own set of warm-up exercises directly in front of the stage as the Standells were getting ready to deliver their own pitch to the psyched-up Red Sox Nation. Larry Tamblyn stepped behind his keyboard and thought, "So here we are, climbing on stage before a cheering crowd of 35,000. We had seen audiences like this before, when we appeared with the Rolling Stones at the Cow Palace in San Francisco and the Hollywood Bowl in 1966. But that was almost 40 years ago. It's amazing when you think that, until this day, we had assumed that we would never perform as a group again. As we took our respective positions, the crowd did not see a barber, limousine driver, restaurant owner, and an audio engineer, standing before them; they saw the Standells.

"As far as most of the world was concerned, we had been relegated to one-hit wonder status and had been considered long gone. But, here we were, having been asked to perform at this most prestigious event, Game Two of the 2004 World Series in Boston. Miraculously, all of the original members of the Standells were pretty darn happy, healthy and still close friends. We all had jobs and other responsibilities, which we left behind to make this trek, from one coast to the other. As the Fenway Park announcer introduced us, a thought crossed my mind. 'We've come full circle.'"

Tony Valentino made the trip to Boston accompanied by his 10-year-old daughter Brianna. She had never known her dad as a rock and roll musician; Brianna just knew Tony as her dad who owned a nice Italian café. As he had his picture taken with her in the Fenway outfield before he went on stage, Tony was thrilled that she could witness the evening. "I was anxious to get on stage and play, not nervous but excited. For a while there it was kind of bizarre as it hit me—all that green in the stadium—the grass, the stands, that wall, and then the brilliant white and red of the Red Sox uniforms on the guys as they warmed up. Then I started to get the vibes of the crowd, it was amazing, like when we were with the Rolling Stones. I looked around at the other guys and it was a time warp. It seemed like I never had left the band, the music, the tour."

For Gary McMillan, it was the completion of an unfulfilled chapter in his musical career. Gary was an original Standell—part of the line-up that recorded "Dirty Water" in 1965. He had, however, left the group just before they went on tour with the Stones and missed out on playing in the big venues before thousands and thousands of fans. Gary, acknowledged as the quietest member of the group, was the only Standell married when "Dirty Water" hit the charts in 1966. It was tough enough to be on the road for the pre-"Dirty Water" shows all over California and Nevada but a cross-country expedition of the magnitude the Stones had planned was not something he wanted to do back then. But now, in Boston, that night, things were different. "It was like a dream. Walking up to that stage, it hit me. I was going to play in front of all those great Boston fans who appreciated our song and appreciated us. I could feel the energy in the park. It really felt like home. This was the place where we were always meant to sing that song. Brother—it was unbelievable!"

Tony and Gary took their respective places on the platform and strapped on their guitars. Dick sat down on his stool, settled in behind the drums, and adjusted his microphone during the enthusiastic applause that greeted Carl Beane's introduction of the group. Larry was poised at the organ. On cue, Tony masterfully struck those unmistakable chords on his original Fender Telecaster, amplified at maximum volume—

"A-RUM, DUM, DUM—DUM, DA-DUM. AH-RUM, DUM, DUM,—DUM DA-DUM!"

Fenway Park erupted!

"When I hit that first note, they started screaming so loud I had to look down at the neck of my guitar to see if I hit the right note!" Tony smiled. "Then I just got into the groove." Everyone was on his or her feet as the signature notes of "Dirty Water" reverberated within the park and spilled out into Yawkey Way, Lansdowne, Van Ness, and Ipswich Streets.

Joyous bedlam ensued within the ancient ballpark and out in the streets. Patrons in the Monster seats and rooftop boxes strained to see the action below. People in the bleacher seats were hanging over the wall behind the stage shouting and screaming. The grandstands were rocking, and people walking in the aisles stopped dead in their tracks to witness the incredible surprise that was presented to them just before the game was set to begin.

Dick Dodd relished the moment. "The fans just went WILD! They went crazy! We started playing that thing and it was like we had just hit a grand slam, walk-off home run!" "There were flashes from cameras just everywhere … everyone was singing along with us, the people's voices were louder than what we were playing … I couldn't hear the music, I couldn't hear myself, I could only hear the roar of the voices of thousands and thousands of Red Sox fans and I just sang "Dirty Water" along with *THEM!*"

Encore—2005

Of course, the Red Sox finished their incredible 2004 season by winning the next two games in St. Louis to finally capture the World Series again, and the Standells' connection to the team, Fenway Park, the city of Boston, and Red Sox Nation was forever linked in history. The Standells returned to Fenway for an encore performance on Monday afternoon, April 11, 2005. The occasion was the Red Sox home opener, which coincidentally was against the New York Yankees. It was also the day the Red Sox raised the 2004 World Championship banner, flagpole honors being done by Johnny Pesky and Carl Yastrzemski. The Red Sox won the game with ease, 8–1. Tim Wakefield pitched seven innings, giving up just one run. After the top of the ninth, when Keith Foulke retired Posada on a fly to right, struck out Giambi, and induced Bernie Williams to pop up to shortstop, it was time for the Red Sox victory song once more. With no fanfare, without an introduction, the notes rang out through the Fenway sound system: "Ah—rum, dum, dum—dum da dum…"

The Standells, live at Fenway once again, this time performing from atop the Green Monster!

The End of Innocence—2006

The Standells had been batting 1.000. Both times they'd come to Fenway, in 2004 and 2005, they'd seen the Red Sox win. Come 2006, Dr. Charles Steinberg wanted to honor the group by celebrating the 40th anniversary of the year "Dirty Water" first became a hit by inviting the group back to Boston. The night of the invite was September 8. Kansas City was in town. We're talking about the 52–89 Kansas City Royals, some 33 games out of first place in their division. It looked like a lock.

And when Boston had visited KC a few weeks earlier, the Royals had swept them. The Sox were just $5\frac{1}{2}$ games back in the wild card race. Turnabout being fair play, if the Sox could sweep Kansas City, they could maybe pick up a game or two in the standings. And the Sox jumped off to a 3–0 lead early in the game. Unfortunately, though, the Royals came back with two, added three more, and then added a crushing three more in the top of the eighth, dealing Boston an 8–3 deficit.

The Standells were atop the Green Monster, primed and ready to play the Red Sox victory anthem. They summoned up some serious mojo and put it on the Royals and, lo and behold, the Red Sox rallied for six runs in the bottom of the eighth to take a 9–8 lead. It was exhilarating. Everyone was pumped. The Standells prepared to play their celebrated song. Gary strapped on his bass guitar, Tony tuned a string on his Fender Telecaster, Dick settled in behind the drums, and Larry fingered the keys on his organ. Just three outs to a rousing Red Sox win.

Two quick outs started things off for the Sox. Then a seemingly harmless single was followed by a hit batsman, and a blown chance to cut down the lead runner on a sacrifice bunt suddenly turned the situation into a dicey one. It was still two outs, and two on—one good pitch and the Sox could still secure a hard-fought win. Instead, a two-run double by Joey Gathright right down the first-base line gave the Royals two runs and the lead once again, 10–9. The Sox couldn't score in the bottom of the ninth, and the Standells were initiated into what Red Sox Nation is all about. It was the end of innocence. Charles Steinberg consoled the band, seeing their disappointment, "Well, now you truly know what it means to be a Red Sox fan. They can excite you and break your heart at any moment."

Closing in on midnight, an hour after the game, Steinberg was on the piano in the Crown Royal Room, a private club within the ancient ballpark's confines, with Larry giving him a few pointers on what's so deceptively distinctive about "Dirty Water" as Tony played unplugged guitar (and a little harmonica) and Dick did the vocals.

Perhaps there was an omen preceding the Standells' first experience of a loss at Fenway. In special pre-game musical entertainment, Darlene Love (of the L.A.-based girl group the Blossoms, and later of the Crystals) sang the National Anthem and Martha Reeves (of Martha and the Vandellas) kicked into "Dancing in the Streets" just before the Standells prepared to mount the portable stage set up in center field to play "Dirty Water." As Fenway Ambassador Cindi Adler went over the printed script with Dick, a red splotch landed on the white paper from above. Glancing up, they saw a hawk flying overhead with its prey dangling from its talons. It wasn't a Fenway frank; it was a Fenway rat. A dead rat which the hawk then began to consume atop the smaller electronic scoreboard over dead center field. From Schilling's bloody sock to the Standells' bloody script? Whatever, the season took a turn for the worse with the bitter loss, compounded the following night when the Royals exploded for six runs in the top of the 12th to deal the down and dying Sox yet another blow.

The Standells were philosophical. They'd known they couldn't do it all by themselves. It takes a good bullpen, too. Perhaps the silver lining, if you're looking for one, is that the band members truly did learn about the highs and lows of Red Sox baseball—one pitch to go, and then it's all snatched away.

Billboard HOT 100

For Week Ending July 9, 1966

Record Industry Association of America seal of certification as million selling single.

★ STAR performer. Side registering greatest proportionate upward progress this week.

Billboard Award

THIS WEEK	Wk. Ago	2 Wks. Ago	3 Wks. Ago	TITLE Artist (Producer), Label & Number	Weeks On Chart
Billboard Award	2	1	15	**PAPERBACK WRITER** . . . . Beatles (George Martin), Capitol 5651	5
2	3	6	10	**RED RUBBER BALL** . . . . Cyrkle (John Simon), Columbia 43589	8
3	1	2	5	**STRANGERS IN THE NIGHT** . . Frank Sinatra (Jimmy Bowen), Reprise 0470	10
4	6	15	25	**HANKY PANKY** . . . . Tommy James & the Shondells (Jeff Barry & Ellie Greenwich), Roulette 4686	6
5	5	9	12	**YOU DON'T HAVE TO SAY YOU LOVE ME** . . . . Dusty Springfield, Philips 40371	8
6	47	75	—	**WILD THING** . . . . Troggs (Page One-York Pala), Atco 6415- Fontana 1548	3
7	7	8	9	**COOL JERK** . . . . Capitols (Ollie McLaughlin), Karen 1524	11
8	11	24	41	**LITTLE GIRL** . . . . Syndicate of Sound (Gary Thompson), Bell 640	6
9	4	3	1	**PAINT IT, BLACK** . . . . Rolling Stones (Andrew Loog Oldham), London 901	9
10	19	32	44	**ALONG COMES MARY** . . . . . . Association (C. Boettcher), Valiant 741	6
11	16	21	26	**DIRTY WATER** . . . . Standells (Ed Cobb), Tower 185	12
12	31	55	93	**LIL' RED RIDING HOOD** . . . . . . Sam the Sham & the Pharaohs (Stan Kesler), MGM 13506	5
13	12	14	17	**DON'T BRING ME DOWN** . . . . Animals (Tom Wilson), MGM 13514	8
14	15	20	27	**AIN'T TOO PROUD TO BEG** . . . Temptations (N. Whitfield), Gordy 7054	7
15	50	67	82	**HUNGRY** . . . . Paul Revere & the Raiders (Terry Melcher), Columbia 43678	4
16	14	12	13	**OH HOW HAPPY** . . . . Shades of Blue (John Rhys), Impact 1007	10
17	8	5	3	**I AM A ROCK** . . . . Simon & Garfunkel (Bob Johnston), Columbia 43617	10
18	20	26	34	**HE** . . . . Righteous Brothers (Bill Medley), Verve 10406	6
19	53	—	—	**I SAW HER AGAIN** . . . . Mama's & the Papa's (Lou Adler), Dunhill 4031	2
20	10	7	7	**BAREFOOTIN'** . . . . Robert Parker (Wherly-Berly Prod.), Nola 721	12
21	26	27	33	**POPSICLE** . . . . Jan & Dean (Jan Berry), Liberty 55886	6
22	42	56	70	**THE PIED PIPER** . . . . Crispian St. Peters (David Nicolson), Jamie 1320	5
23	24	29	42	**RAIN** . . . . Beatles (George Martin), Capitol 5651	5
24	37	58	81	**SWEET PEA** . . . . Tommy Roe, ABC Records 10762	5
25	30	38	57	**I WASHED MY HANDS IN MUDDY WATER** . . . . Johnny Rivers (Lou Adler), Imperial 66175	5

APPENDIX

"Dirty Water" on the Charts

"Dirty Water" never was a national #1 song. It hit the Top 10 briefly in July 1966, by year's end ranking #54 among the year's singles, per the December 24, 1966 issue of the now-defunct *Cashbox* magazine.

In *Billboard* magazine, which still reigns as the weekly chronicle of the music industry, it never quite cracked the Top 10 but for two weeks hovered just one slot below at #11. *Billboard* ranked the single at #57 for the year.

Cashbox Charts

"Dirty Water" first broke into *Cashbox*'s singles chart the week of April 30, 1966 at #94 on the Hot 100. Other debuts on the Hot 100 that week were "It's a Man's Man's Man's World" by James Brown and the Famous Flames on Atlantic at #61 and "Double Shot (of My Baby's Love)" by the Swinging Medallions at #81. The week also saw higher debuts of "Marble Breaks and Iron Bends" by Drafi (#83), "I Love You Drops" by Vic Dana (#83), and "I Am a Rock" by Simon and Garfunkel (#89).

Finishing just below "Dirty Water" were:

"My Little Red Book" by Love (#95)
"Still" by the Sunrays (#96)
"Twinkle Toes" by Roy Orbison (#97)
"You're Ready Now" by Frankie Valli (#98)
"Oh How Happy" by the Shades Of Blue (#99)

And three singles tied at #100: "All These Things" by the Uniques, "Mame" by Bobby Darin, and "The Teaser" by Bob Kuban & the In-Men.

The charts had been fluid all year. The first weeks of the year saw "We Can Work It Out" by The Beatles in the #1 spot. The week of January 29 saw Simon and Garfunkel's "The Sounds of Silence" grab the top spot for just the one week. Another one-week chart-topper was "Barbara Ann" by The Beach Boys, followed by two weeks of Lou Christie's "Lightning Strikes." Nancy Sinatra's "These Boots Are Made for Walking" hit #1 the week of February 26, knocked off by the dominating hit "The Ballad of the Green Berets" by Sgt. Barry Sadler which held the top slot for four full weeks—only The Beatles managed a similar four-week run in 1966 (though The Monkees launched "I'm a Believer" near the end of the year and held first place not only for the last two weeks of 1966 but the first six weeks of 1967 as well.)

April was a busy month, with The Rolling Stones claiming top rank with "19th Nervous Breakdown" on April 2, The Lovin' Spoonful with "Daydream" on April 9, and then The Righteous Brothers with "(You're My) Soul and Inspiration" on both April 16 and 23. The week The Standells first hit the charts, April 30, the top five positions were held by:

"Good Lovin'" (The Young Rascals)
"Monday, Monday" (The Mamas and the Papas)
"(You're My) Soul and Inspiration" (The Righteous Brothers)
"Secret Agent Man" (Johnny Rivers)
"Kicks" (Paul Revere and the Raiders).

Other top tracks included "Sloop John B" by the Beach Boys, "Gloria" by The Shadows of Night and "Rainy Day Women #12 and 35" by Bob Dylan.

The Debut

"Dirty Water" debuted in *Cashbox* at #94 the week of April 30, climbing the following week to #88. It rose another 10 notches to #78 the week of May 14 and 10 more the week after that to #68. With Percy Sledge's "When a Man Loves A Woman" at #1, "Dirty Water" jumped up 15 slots to #51 on May 28 and, steadily climbing, to #42 the next week. The single hit #30 on June 11, #21 on June 18, and #16 on the 25th. "Paperback Writer" was #1. In its 10th week on *Cashbox*'s chart, "Dirty Water" rose to #16 on July 2.

This was a year that fell between 1965's Mississippi Summer of the civil rights movement and the year the antiwar movement took hold in earnest, 1967. President Lyndon B. Johnson was committed to halting what he called Communist aggression in Vietnam and by late April, when "Dirty Water" hit, American troop totals there had reached 250,000. Back on January 17, two American military planes crashed and three unarmed H-bombs fell on Spanish soil, with another one landing off the coast. The underwater one was found two months later.

The hippie movement hadn't yet been born as such, but there were signs: early in the year saw the first Acid Test at the Fillmore in San Francisco. In March, John Lennon was quoted in an *Evening Standard* article as noting how famous The Beatles had become: "We're more popular than Jesus now." Had there not been some truth to his statement, it would not have aroused the backlash it did.

The Standells went on tour opening for The Rolling Stones, kicked off by their Boston show on June 24, at the Manning Bowl in Lynn, Massachusetts.

Breaking into the Top 10 at #8 on July 9, the single was clearly a national sensation. The only songs above it were:

"Hanky Panky" (Tommy James and the Shondells)
"Paperback Writer" (The Beatles)
"Red Rubber Ball" (Cyrkle)
"Strangers In the Night" (Frank Sinatra)
"You Don't Have to Say You Love Me" (Dusty Springfield)
"Paint It, Black" (The Rolling Stones)
"Wild Thing" (The Troggs)

The Standells stood still at #8 on July 16, but standing still in the Top 10 is not a bad place to be.

Slippage began the following week, down to #15. "Wild Thing" was #1, but songs like "Lil Red Riding Hood," "Along Comes Mary" and "Mother's Little Helper" had leapt over "Dirty Water." When "They're Coming to Take Me Away (Ha Ha)" hit #1, "Dirty Water" dropped further to position 24. The single plunged to #60 the week of August 6, and it was gone from the Hot 100 by the following week. It had been a very good 15-week run.

Tower wasn't ready to quit yet. A new single "Sometimes Good Guys Don't Wear White" hit the charts the very next week, at #86. The single climbed respectably to #80, 69, 66, 59, but couldn't sustain itself, dropping to 62 the week of September 24 and then off the charts completely after that.

The group's singles did not translate to major album sales. The album didn't crack the year's Top 100 in *Cashbox*'s pages.

Breaking into the *Billboard* Charts

A study of the *Billboard* charts offers a more detailed look at "Dirty Water"—where the record appeared on the charts both before and after its ascendancy in *Cashbox*. The single first achieved national note in the pages of *Billboard* in the March 26, 1966 issue in the "Bubbling Under" chart appended to the Hot 100 listing. "Dirty Water" was at #132. It was on a slow boil, and climbed toward the Hot 100 by rising eight slots to #124 on April 2, another four slots to #120 on April 9, and nine more to #111 on April 16.

It was in Miami that the song first began to hit, evidenced by its being cited as a "regional breakout" there in the April 2 magazine. That week the Beach Boys' "Sloop John B" was the lone national breakout. Other regional breakout tracks were:

"Funny (Not Much)"
"Desiree"
"Elvira"
"Chain Reaction"
"Daddy's Baby"

"Real Humdinger"
"Barefootin'"
"Good, Good Loving"

Early in 1966, *Billboard* offered 15 regional Top 40 charts. The publication suspended regional reporting after its May 14 issue, but a look at these regional reports offers a sense of how the record picked up steam. The first mention of "Dirty Water" came in the March 5 issue, when it was reported at #35 in the Miami Top 40 list. It climbed to #24 on March 12, and then jumped all the way to #8 on March 19. The next week it held at #8, and that was the week it began to appear on the "Bubbling Under" section of the national chart.

One week later, in the April 2 issue, it hit #2 in Miami. The only song more popular in Miami was "Daydream" by the Lovin' Spoonful.

On April 9, "Dirty Water" remained #2 in Miami but had still not appeared on any of the other regional charts—not in Atlanta, nor Baltimore, nor Boston, nor Chicago, Cleveland, Detroit, Los Angeles, New York, Philadelphia, Pittsburgh, St. Louis, San Francisco, Seattle, or Washington DC. It may have hovered below the Top 40 on some of these; we can't know that today. The #1 song in Miami was now "Bang Bang" by Cher. "Daydream" was on the wane.

For the third week in a row, "Dirty Water" was #2 in Miami on April 16. Cher still blocked it from reaching #1. Nationally, as we have seen, it was bubbling under at #111. Tower supported the album, taking out a full page ad, which ran on page 39 of the April 16 issue.

The following week—April 23—was a big one. Boston finally took note, and "Dirty Water" crept onto the last slot on the regional chart, #40. The song displaced Cher and reached #1 in Miami, though it was still not anywhere on the charts in the band's home base of Los Angeles. On the strength of the Miami and Boston showings, "Dirty Water" cracked *Billboard*'s Hot 100, debuting at #98. There were a lot of other debuts that week. As noted above, the charts were very active in this era. Other tracks cracking the Hot 100 for the first time were:

#49—"How Does That Grab You Darlin'"—Nancy Sinatra
#79—"The 'A' Team"—S/Sgt Barry Sadler
#83—"Remember the Rain"—Bob Lind
"86—"Backstage"—Gene Pitney
#89—"You're the One"—The Marvelettes
#90—"The Cruel War"—Peter, Paul and Mary
#95—"Hold On! I'm Comin'"—Sam and Dave
#96—"Wang Dang Doodle"—Ko Ko Taylor
#97—"Double Shot (of My Baby's Love)"—Swingin' Medallions
#99—"Come On Let's Go"—The McCoys
#100—"Barefootin'" Robert Parker

"Teen-Oriented Dance Beat Material"

In the April 30 pages, the single slipped to #4 in Miami. It had enjoyed its first
and last #1 rating. "Gloria" by Them took over first place, followed by "Secret
Agent Man" and "Good Loving"—all pretty worthy competitors. "Dirty Water"
notched up one slot to #39 in Boston, but it wasn't exactly tearing the town up.
It still hadn't reached any of the other regional charts. Was it really over? Had
it had its day? Apparently not, perhaps due to lower chart action in other areas.
It climbed three positions on the national Hot 100 from #98 to #95.

May 7 showed further slippage in Miami, down to #9, and in Boston it
lapsed back to #40. The good news was that it debuted at #27 in Cleveland. It
had now broken in a third market. This, presumably combined with very
strong airplay in other areas, jumped it into the 60s on the Hot 100 and the
large leap from #95 to #69 gave it a star on the charts, indicating "greatest proportionate upward progress this week." The star of the day was the contemporary equivalent of today's "bullet" on the charts.

The Billboard charts measured radio play, not sales. They were also subject
to manipulation by savvy (or crooked) record executives and compliant, com-
plicit broadcasters. Later in May, a national payola investigation was launched
by the Federal Communications Commission and as many as 50 subpoenas
were issued to compel testimony from a variety of witnesses. "Pay for play" was
by no means unheard of at the time. Nor was the granting of special favors.
Even without money (or drugs) changing hands, a radio station might respond
to a simple "please" from a record plugger and put a track in at, say, #40 on a
regional chart, just as a simple gesture of friendship. There was but the pre-
tense that the charts were objective, not based—as they are today—on objective optical scanning at the cash registers. And they were based on airplay, not
sales, partially because at least people could hear the songs on radio. With so
many independent record stores and outlets for recorded sound across the
country, there was simply no way to obtain accurate sales reports; one would
have had to rely on the record label to cite sales figures, and there was no way
that was going to be impartial. These were the days before consolidation where
a handful of monster merchandisers became the gatekeepers for the flow of
recorded music to the consumer.

Radio at the time was quite open as well. There were no chains owning
hundreds of stations, and there was no reliance on tastemakers and radio con-
sultants. In fact, Billboard reported in its May 7 issue, radio was exceptionally
responsive to the public—now there's an idea—and "You-Asked-For-It" radio
was "booming across nation" according to a headline in the trade publication.
To what extent popular demand for "Dirty Water" boosted its prospects for success, and to what extent it was orchestrated by Tower's sales staff and distribution efforts would be difficult to discern today, and probably impossible.

In the May 14 *Billboard*, "Dirty Water" climbed to #63, largely on the strength of Cleveland and other non-reported play. It held at #9 in Miami and held at #40 in Boston.

One week later, in its fifth week on the Hot 100, the single climbed only one slot, to #62. Beginning with the May 21 issue, *Billboard* dispensed with its regional reports, so "Dirty Water" goes down in Boston history as never reaching higher than #39 on the local charts—as reported nationally. Local Top 40 sheets were often produced by radio stations in the area and offered as handouts on the counter at record stores; anyone with access to such local ephemera would be able to offer more detailed local information.

May 28—the single earned an increase of five more slots on the Hot 100, from #62 up to #57. Tower Records released an album by John Stewart and Scott Engel. And The Beatles announced a three-week concert tour of the United States. The big news, though, was "Payola Probers Plot Hush Hush Hearings."

On June 4, "Dirty Water" earned another star, with a 12-slot climb from #57 to #45.

June 11 was a major date in the evolution of a hit. Tower Records released the album *Dirty Water* (T 5027) and the release earned a Spotlight Review on the back cover of *Billboard*, with accompanying text reading: "With their 'Dirty Water' currently climbing the Hot 100, the four California boys have a top sales entry in the album of teen-oriented dance beat material. '19th Nervous Breakdown' and 'Pride and Devotion' are standout rockers."

This was the kind of boost you can't buy—or maybe you can. There's no suggestion that Tower monkeyed with the magazine for better coverage, and it's not easy today to know what friendships Tower executives might have had with the magazine moguls at *Billboard*. It was a slow week for album spotlights, anyhow. The other albums earning "Pop Spotlight" attention were:

10 Golden Years—Brenda Lee
More Highlights from An Evening at the "Pops"—Boston Pops Orchestra
Beat Group!—The Hollies
Patty—Patty Duke
The Platters: I Love You 1,000 Times—The Platters
The Best of Al Hirt, Vol. 2—Al Hirt
Children of the Morning—The Kingston Trio
Come Alive!—Joanie Sommers

The single was indeed climbing the Hot 100, as reported. It jumped from #45 all the way to #31 with a star. It was now in the Top 40 nationally. *Cashbox*, as indicated above, had it at #32 this very same week - a reassuringly equivalent number.

The week of June 18, Tower Records released an album of Ketty Lester,

T-5029. "Dirty Water" the single reached #26 with a star. The Standells album had yet to reach the LP chart.

The June 25 *Billboard* reported that Capitol Records had recalled 750,000 LPs of *Yesterday and Today* by The Beatles. The company then stripped or papered over the cover that had been deemed too controversial, showing as it had the Fab Four surrounded by "what appears to be dismembered baby dolls and butcher shop cuts of meat." The same issue showed "Dirty Water" continue its climb, from #26 to #21 while still retaining a star.

On July 2, "Dirty Water" cracked the Top 20 on *Billboard*'s singles chart and also entered the Hot LP's chart the same time, at #129 with a star. The Hot LP's chart reported the top 150 albums, and (in contrast to the singles chart) was meant to be a sales chart. Tower released another album that week, by Mae West (T-5028). *Billboard* featured a story celebrating the significance of Detroit and Los Angeles as markets that were a "happening place" for record sales. Text in the story highlighted the role of the Miami market in breaking songs. Three songs in that week's top 20 singles had first broken in Miami: "Elusive Butterfly" by Bob Lind and "Ain't Too Proud to Beg" by the Temptations were cited, along with "Dirty Water."

Just Shy of the Top 10

July 9 saw the Standells' single reach its highest chart position in *Billboard*, #11. Sad to say, it never reached *Billboard*'s top 10, though it achieved #8 in *Cashbox* both the weeks of July 9 and 16. Climbing five points from #16 to #11, it retained its star. The album broke into the list of the top 100, leaping from #129 to #93. Tower Records released an album as T-5031, listed as Goodwin "Goody" Goodload and his Frostonia Ballroom Orchestra.

The 10 tracks above "Dirty Water" on *Billboard*'s Hot 100 chart that week were:

1. "Paperback Writer"—The Beatles
2. "Red Rubber Ball"—The Cyrkle
3. "Strangers in the Night"—Frank Sinatra
4. "Hanky Panky"—Tommy James and the Shondells
5. "You Don't Have to Say You Love Me"—Dusty Springfield
6. "Wild Thing"—The Troggs
7. "Cool Jerk"—The Capitols
8. "Little Girl"—Syndicate of Sound
9. "Paint It, Black"—The Rolling Stones
10. "Along Comes Mary"—The Association

What a great week for music in America. Some 40 years later, every single one of these songs, including "Dirty Water," would fit into any station's oldies programming without a blink.

The apex of "Dirty Water" came the week of July 16. The single remained at #11 in *Billboard* and #8 in *Cashbox*, and climbed to #81 with a star on *Billboard*'s Hot LP's chart. This was the week that had the highest combination of single and LP chart success. Come the July 23 issue, the single dropped back to #16 (#15 in *Cashbox*), though the album climbed somewhat, two notches to #79, albeit without a star.

Both the single and album dropped the week of July 30, the single plunging from #16 to #31 and the LP dropping three notches, #79 to #82. Perhaps Tower realized that the album needed a boost, because they had prepared a second single. The August 6 magazine featured "Sometimes Good Guys Don't Wear White" as its lead Top 60 Spotlight pick, including it among a few singles "predicted to reach the top 60." The album recovered one notch, rising from #82 to #81, and "Dirty Water" held at #31. The new single was listed as "bubbling under" at #130.

A radio boycott of The Beatles was noted in the August 13 *Billboard*, in a bit of a delayed reaction to Lennon's "more popular than Jesus" comment. "Dirty Water" fell completely off the charts, all the way from #31 to oblivion. "Sometimes Good Guys Don't Wear White" entered the Hot 100, though, debuting at #96. The album *Dirty Water* increased significantly, from #81 to #73. The album stayed put at #73 the week of August 20, while the "Sometimes" single rose from #96 to #86. Airplay of the single began to drive album sales, and when the single earned a star while rising from #86 to #68, the LP rank edged up one level, to #72.

Tower Records announced a package of nine new albums for the fall of 1966, including the soundtrack album from *The Wild Angels* and new albums by Kay Adams, Dean Martin, Ian Whitcomb, the Louvin Brothers, and Justin Wilson. They launched a new imprint, Uptown Records, with an album of songs by Gloria Jones, and Tower released a couple of "religious and ethnic" LPs, *Canticle of the Gift* and *Jewish Songs*. The same week saw "Sometimes" climb from #68 to #61, and drive *Dirty Water* from #72 to #70.

The next few weeks show the single rise and then, inevitably, fall:

Week	Single Chart Position	Album Chart Position
9–10	61 to 53	70 to 63
9–17	53 to 48	63 to 61
9–24	48 to 43	61 to 52, with a star
10–1	43 to 50	held at its peak position of #52
10–8	dropped off chart	52 to 83
10–15	still gone	83 to 111

The week of October 22 showed both the single and the album gone. But Tower wasn't finished yet. Another single (Tower 282) was released that very week, debuting at #93. The song was "Why Pick On Me" and it improved to

The Standells!!
**YES, YOU CAN WIN THE STANDELLS TO DRIVE
YOU HOME FROM SCHOOL! AND THE SECND
PRIZE IS NEARLY AS GREAT!**

Courtesy of Edie McMillan.

#83 the week of October 29, then earned a star and a bump all the way up to #72 in its third week. The third Standells single moved up to #61 the week of November 12, held there the week that followed, then advanced again (to #54) the week of November 26. It didn't take long to drop, though, heading down the week of December 3 from #54 to #59, and then was gone entirely the following week.

In their year-end summary (covering the first 10 months of 1966), *Billboard* ranked "Dirty Water" as #43 for the year on its Top Singles chart. A separate ranking of Top Singles Artists took into account multiple singles by the same artist; The Standells had placed three singles on the Top 100 charts in 1966 but ranked #57 based on what *Billboard* obscurely called its "point system of chart ratings." The Beatles were #1 and The Rolling Stones were #2. Following them were the Lovin' Spoonful, the Beach Boys, and The Mamas and the Papas. The Standells did not make the list of Top 100 LP Artists. But they had made their mark.

Red Sox and Music

The Red Sox have had a number of musical talents in their ranks over the years. The first noted was the Red Sox Quartet. In 1911, the Red Sox held their one and only spring training in California and they took the train cross-country. As much as anything, to entertain themselves on the long trip, a barbershop-style quartet sprang up featuring Hugh Bradley and Marty McHale as tenors, Tom O'Brien as baritone, and Larry Gardner as bass. News reports indicate that team captain Heinie Wagner formed a rival quartet with Red Kleinow, Bill Carrigan, and Eddie Cicotte.

After the 1911 season was over (and it was a disappointing one, Boston finishing 24 games out of first place), the Red Sox Quartet was booked as an attraction into the Keith's vaudeville circuit, playing to packed houses and reportedly earning at least six encores at every stop.

Buck O'Brien and the Red Sox Quartet performed at Keith's Theater on November 27. O'Brien was joined by Hugh Bradley, Marty McHale, and newly-acquired pitcher Bill Lyons. "They can sing, and sing well. They compare favorably with any quartet in vaudeville," commented the *Boston Globe* a couple of days before the show. After a quartet number, each one soloed, Lyons leading off with "Any Old Port in a Storm." O'Brien then sang "The Garden of My Heart," followed by McHale's "When You and I Were Young, Maggie."

The Washington Post singled out Bradley's rendition of "O, You Beautiful Doll" and added, "The second time you hear them you like them better than the first." Bill Lyons, who took Gardner's place in the foursome, grumbled in good humor after being coached on how to bow theatrically in appreciation of audience applause, "Hold on there, I'm bowing so much now that my neck's lame." McHale reportedly cracked that Lyons couldn't play baseball all that well, but had been signed just to keep the quartet alive.

When the Sox signed Hubert "Dutch" Leonard for the 1913 season, though, they may not have known they'd tapped into another talent. Leonard, who led the league with a 0.96 ERA the following year (1914), had forsaken a career in music to play baseball. The Leonard family of Fresno was a musical family, each playing different instruments. Leonard "put over all the tricks of the trap drummer" according to the *Los Angeles Times*, and had been considering professional orchestra work when he hooked on as a ballplayer. As with Tony Conigliaro a half-century later, Leonard appears to have focused on ballplaying, not letting music get in the way.

Red Sox pitcher Mickey McDermott was known in his time (he broke in with Boston in 1948 and played for the Red Sox though 1953) as quite a good singer. As he writes in his entertaining autobiography *A Funny Thing Happened on the Way to Cooperstown*, "I loved singing almost as much as pitching." He sang duets with Eddie Fisher at Grossinger's in the Catskills, was friends with the Tommy Dorsey Orchestra, and even sang at Steuben's night club for a couple of winter off-seasons (pulling in $500 a week, which was big bucks in those days—his annual salary at the time was $7,500.) Steuben's Vienna Room was in Boston; once McDermott was traded to the Senators, he was much less an attraction on Boylston Street. One of the owners told him, "18–10 in Boston? Oh, what a beautiful voice! 7–15 in Washington? You don't sing so good no more."[1]

The one and only time he tried to sing the Anthem at Fenway Park, it was after the Ink Spots invited him to join them. The popular group had been singing at Blinstrub's. Mickey got as far as: "Oh, say can you see by the dawn's early light," when he froze. He couldn't remember any more. "Singing out there in front of tens of thousands of music fans was tougher on the nerves than listening to baseball fans boo.... Thank heavens for the Ink Spots. They carried me."

McDermott wound up his book declaring, "I wanted to be in show business as much as I wanted to play baseball. For one thing, that's where all the women are. For another, as a pitcher I was onstage only one day out of four or five, and now and then I got booed. At Steuben's Vienna Room I got applauded every night."

Johnny Pesky, DJ. In addition to being a clubhouse kid, effective rookie of the year, a sparkplug shortstop for the Red Sox, coach, manager, broadcaster, and all-around ambassador for the Red Sox, the man known as "Mr. Red Sox" also did a stint as a disc jockey during the winter of 1950. He worked for radio station WBMS and hosted a six-day-a-week broadcast ("It's a hit. It's the Johnny Pesky Show!") Johnny selected the records himself, telling the *Lynn Item*, "I play all kinds of records. Whatever the listeners request. My favorite is Glenn Miller. He's the best. Tommy Dorsey's good, too." Among Johnny's guests were ballplayers like McDermott and Birdie Tebbetts, and entertainers like Frankie Fontaine and WCOP's Sherm Feller. "Sure, I was nervous," he admitted, "especially when it came to reading commercials, but there aren't 35,000 fans watching me when I'm on the radio. They can hear me but they can't see me if I boot one.... I worry about my batting average all summer. Now I have a Hooper Rating to think about all winter."[2]

Ted Williams was a big music fan as well, particularly enjoying jazz piano by Errol Garner, Oscar Peterson, and Dave McKenna. Brian Interland, a music business veteran in the Boston area, talks about Ted's interest in Count Basie, Stan Kenton, Sarah Vaughan, Ella Fitzgerald, Frank Sinatra, and Dakota Staton as well. McKenna, a local New England pianist, even composed a couple of instrumentals in Ted's honor: "The Splendid Splinter" and "Theodore the Thumper." In 1999, a Boston company released a compilation album of swing music entitled *The Perfect Swing*. The cover was graced by a drawing of Ted Williams and Ted himself recorded a spoken intro to the music.

Impossible Dream—1967

The song "[To Dream] the Impossible Dream" became closely associated with the Impossible Dream team of that pennant-winning season. The song comes from *Man of La Mancha*, a 1965 Broadway musical centered on the life of Don Quixote. Before the '67 season opened, anyone believing the Sox had a shot at winning the pennant would have been considered not only quixotic but delusional. They had been 72–90 the previous year, finishing in ninth place, 26 games out of first. An album entitled *The Impossible Dream* was released after the season and became the best-selling sports record album of all time. For the Red Sox, 1967 was their first pennant in 21 years and the song still resonates well with those who lived through the totally unexpected triumph.

Another musical connection between the Red Sox and music comes from third baseman/trumpter Carmen Fanzone. Signed by the Sox in 1964, he broke into the majors in August 1970, appearing in 10 games for Boston and batting .200 in 15 total at-bats. He was backup to George Scott and Luis Alvarado at the hot corner for the Red Sox. Traded in late 1971 to the Cubs for Phil Gagliano, he went on to play in another 227 games with the Cubs, posting a career .224 average. The end of the 1974 season saw the end of his major league career.

He had greater talent, it appears, on the trumpet. Yes, he played the National Anthem once or twice at the ballpark, but he also played for, variously, a number of Chicago night clubs, the Baja Marimba Band at New Orleans' Fairmount Hotel, Rudy's Italian Restaurant in Waikiki, and even the Salvation Army. His specialties were jazz and classical, and he wound up playing trumpet in Los Angeles in the Tonight Show Orchestra.

He is currently listed as Assistant to the President of the American Federation of Musicians Los Angeles local, Local 47. Quite a change from backing up Boomer at third base.

Tony Conigliaro, we have covered. The Sox star most noted for music in recent years was Bronson Arroyo. An important pitcher for the World Champion Red Sox of 2004, Arroyo plays guitar and sings, and in 2005 released a compact disc recording, *Covering the Bases*. The album release party was held on July 13, 2005, behind the left-field Wall, at Avalon on Lansdowne Street. It was an album largely of covers, and the 12th and final track on the CD is "Dirty Water." As Steve Morse summed up in his July 12 *Boston Globe* review of the disc:

> The musical arrangements are sometimes rote but are modified enough
> to make it interesting. Amy Keys's soaring harmonies add a different
> flavor to Temple of the Dog's "Hunger Strike." And on unofficial Red
> Sox theme "Dirty Water" by the Standells, players Johnny Damon,

Kevin Youkilis, and Lenny DiNardo add harmonies and shout-outs to local watering holes such as Whiskey Park, the Rack, and Avalon.

But Arroyo holds it all together. When he performed at the Sox-related "Hot Stove, Cool Music" show at the Paradise last winter, he seemed somewhat tentative, but he rocks soulfully on the album, especially on Pearl Jam's "Black" and Stone Temple Pilots' "Plush," which he learned as a 15-year-old kid.

Dick Dodd flew in from Los Angeles and joined Arroyo and the mentioned Sox players (Damon, Youkilis, DiNardo) for the live performance of the song at Avalon. Arroyo was out late, despite being scheduled to pitch against the visiting Yankees the following day. He threw 5⅔ innings, giving up four earned runs. The Red Sox lost, 8–6, but only after New York scored two runs off reliever Curt Schilling in the top of the ninth.

A West Coast album release party was held at Sonny McLean's in Santa Monica on August 20 and drew celebrities including both Teri Hatcher and John Denton from *Desperate Housewives*. The Asylum Records album debuted at #2 on the *Billboard* Heatseekers chart and #123 on the *Billboard* 200. Let's not forget that Red Sox GM Theo Epstein played lead electric guitar on "Something's Always Wrong."

Dr. Charles Steinberg had a perspective on Arroyo's inclusion of the old Standells hit: "I think it's marvelous when four guys who had a hit 39 years ago find that a pitcher today, who wasn't even born then, enjoys the meaning of that song so much." Some of Arroyo's love for Boston may have soured when he was traded to Cincinnati on March 20, 2006, just two months after signing a new three-year deal with the Red Sox.

As for Red Sox GM Theo Epstein, he's a musician, too, a guitar player and closely identified these days with the annual "Hot Stove/Cool Music" benefit concerts. Launched originally with a December 4, 2000 show in Boston at the Paradise, the event grew out of conversations between sportswriters Jeff Horrigan and Peter Gammons. Before becoming a writer for the *Boston Herald*, Horrigan was a co-op student at the *Globe* back in the 1980s. There he became friendly, and talked a lot of music with Gammons. They had similar tastes in music and kept in touch even after they went their separate ways. Peter talked about doing a benefit show sometime at the Chicken Box on Nantucket, but when the idea of doing it in the city itself came up, everything began to click. Horrigan says, "When we started, we never intended it to be a series. It was a Monday night. We were hoping to just get enough people in there that we wouldn't be embarrassed. We only had about two or three weeks to prepare for it. There were three baseball-named bands: Carlton Fisk, Thurman Munson, and Slide. We never thought it would catch on like this. Kay Hanley's been at every one. She gave it credibility. When we started out, it was just a few more obscure bands, but when Kay signed on, it really built. The Push Stars joined us, which was nice. I really doubt it would have caught on as much if Kay hadn't joined us early on." Early supporters included Bill Janovitz and Buffalo Tom, who only missed the very first one because they'd already been booked out of town. Some members of The Gentlemen have been at each event.

Now the evening sells out, once the date is announced, even before the acts have been named. The event has raised well over a million dollars to date for the Jimmy Fund and for (more recently) The Foundation to Be Named Later. The success of the winter events has led to a summer date being scheduled, beginning in 2005, on a night the Red Sox have off.

Peter Gammons released his own CD, the year after being recognized by the National Baseball Hall of Fame at its 2005 induction weekend. Entitled *Never Slow Down, Never Grow Old*, the CD is a benefit for The Foundation to Be Named Later, which raises funds for disadvantaged youths in the Boston area. TFTBNL is run by Theo Epstein's brother Paul, and is one of the charities favored by the Red Sox. The CD was released on July 4, 2006 by Rounder Records, parent company to publisher Rounder Books. Red Sox knuckleball pitcher Tim Wakefield joins Bronson Arroyo on Gammons' cover of Warren Zevon's "Model Citizen." Both Gammons' guitar work (he's joined by George Thorogood on one track) and vocal stylings won critical praise. Paul Barrere of Little Feat and Theo Epstein both contribute guitar as well. The *Boston Globe* noted in its review that "practically a whole team's worth of Red Sox add backing vocals to Al Kooper's infectious, go-go powered 'Wake Me, Shake Me,' including Jonathan Papelbon, Tim Wakefield, Lenny DiNardo, Kevin Youkilis, Gabe Kapler, and Trot Nixon, plus NESN's Don Orsillo and former Sox pitcher Bronson Arroyo." Nixon was quoted in the *Chicago Tribune* as saying, "Anybody else and I probably wouldn't have done it. I don't think I'm musically inclined. . . . I knew it was for Peter, so it didn't bother me one bit. (I'll) help him that way if I can."

Even Red Sox assistant director of baseball operations Zack Scott "lays down some hot harmonica" on a track which Gammons' liner notes reveal he first heard performed by Alvin Crow in a North Dallas honky-tonk, a 1976 show he attended with Carlton Fisk. The CD offers, the *Globe* headlined, "a winning lineup of good-time rock." In September 2006, Peter won a Boston Music Award as the "Best Blues Artist" of the year.

Songs about the Red Sox

Then there are the songs about the Red Sox, or songs that mention the Sox. It would be difficult to come up with a comprehensive list, but the following provides a good start.

The first song about baseball in Boston pre-dated the Red Sox by many years. It was "The Base Ball Quadrille" by Henry Von Gudera, published in 1867. The song was "Respectfully dedicated to the Tri Mountain Base Ball Club of Boston, Champions of New England."

There were at least a couple of songs in tribute to the Boston Braves: "The Battling Boston Braves" on a Valor 78 rpm record and the track "Come Out to Braves Field" by Henry Faunce and Toots Mondello.

It was Boston's American League team that generated the most musical interest, though. As noted, "Tessie" was the first song to truly take hold, and that happened in 1903. But "Tessie" wasn't about the Red Sox. A song from that same year that was clearly about the team was the "Boston Americans Two Step" written by J. Ignatius Coveney.

The 1908 Sox were known as The Speed Boys because of their uncharacteristically fleet team. Henry E. Casey (words) and Martin Bennett (music) composed "The Red Sox Speed Boys" and Bennett published it.

Boston right fielder Harry Hooper was celebrated in 1915 by "Hoop, Hoop, Hooper Up for Red Sox" by Daniel J. Hanifen and Bernard H. Smith.

Babe Ruth has been celebrated in song for years, but one of the first (and perhaps the only one while he was still with Boston) was "Batterin' Babe (Look at Him Now)" in 1919, words and music by Jack O'Brien and Billy Timmins. The sheet music promoted the song as "The Home Run Hit Song of the Season" and "Dedicated to our own 'Babe' Ruth." It was published by the Colonial Music Publishing Co. of Boston. Though solid research by Glenn Stout seems to prove otherwise, for years it was thought that part of the decision to sell The Babe to the Yankees may have been New York theater man (and Red Sox owner) Harry Frazee's desire to raise money for his Broadway musicals.

In 1938, Moe Jaffe wrote "Root for the Red Sox" (Mills Music), but Jaffe was not likely a Red Sox fan; in the same year, Moe wrote "We're the Boys from Brooklyn" for the Dodgers, "The St. Louis Browns," "Cheer for the Cubs," etc.—some 16 songs in all, one for each of the major league clubs of the day. The songs were gathered in the folio *Batter Up.*

A lesser-known song from 1967, one which never caught on, was "Cheer for the Red Sox" by Joseph A. McOsker, copyrighted on June 14, 1967—a date the Red Sox were in fourth place and had not yet begun their run. Perhaps future researchers will determine that this song provided under-the-radar inspiration.

That same year, after the season was over, saw the release of *The Impossible Dream* and another album from the Fleetwood studio: *Curt Gowdy Talks with Carl Yastrzemski* (Fleetwood FCLP 3026.) It wasn't music, but a recorded interview with the Triple Crown winner. *The Impossible Dream* LP reportedly sold more than 100,000 copies, setting the record for a sports album at the time.

Yet another album from this busy time was *Red Sox Organ Music* by John Kiley (MG-7-201,862) which featured Rico Petrocelli on the drums.

In 1968, rock band Earth Opera recorded "The Red Sox Are Winning" on their eponymous album on Elektra, written by Peter Rowan. Author James Mote described the song's theme as "Young man tries to hold on to baseball and innocence during the Vietnam War."

Although not a song with lyrics, West Coast jazz saxophonist Sonny Criss, recorded "El Tiante," an instrumental in honor of Luis Tiant, on his Muse album *Out of Nowhere*.

The year 1979 saw the song "Be A Believer in Red Sox Fever" by The Paid Attendance, a 45 rpm record on the Homerun label written by Sonny Marrow. Like Moe Jaffe in 1938, Marrow wrote songs with virtually identical titles for the Yankees, Phillies, Giants, and Dodgers.

There was another Yaz documentary disc, *Yaz 3000* (Fleetwood 3108), an LP that featured audio recordings of Yastrzemski's 400th home run and his 3000th base hit.

The next year, 1980, Warren Zevon included the track "Bill Lee" on his album *Bad Luck Streak in Dancing School* (Elektra 509.)

In 1982, Terry Cashman released "Baseball and the Sox" (Lifesong 45106.) Cashman also wrote "Talkin' Baseball" songs honoring the Tribe, the 'Stros, the Mets, Phils, Cubs, Bucs, Braves, and O's. Yet another indiscriminate songwriter!

A true loyalist, though, was John Lincoln Wright who, in 1985, cut a tribute to Red Sox pitcher Oil Can Boyd, entitled "Oil Can." Lincoln recorded this on his own label (Lincoln 003) by John Lincoln Wright and the Designated Hitters. The other side had "Yaz's Last At-Bat."

Ted Williams' daughter Bobby-Jo cut a record herself: *A Musical Tribute: The Ted Williams Story* (sung by Bobby-Jo Williams and Wayne Edmondson).

There was even a musical—*The Curse of the Bambino*—written by David Kruh and Steven Bergman in 1997–99. It premiered on April 25, 2001, at Boston's Lyric Stage Company and had a run lasting into early June. A compact disc recording of the show was produced and sold. In December 2004, the authors rewrote the work to accommodate that year's World Series win.

In 2003, Terry Kitchen's Fenway Park song "Just Can't Seem to Give Up on the Diamond" (with the first line, "She said we'd be married when the Red Sox won the Series") was included on the *Diamond Cuts: Seventh Inning*

Stretch CD benefiting Hungry for Music, which provides musical instruments to inner city kids.

There was a band that named itself Carlton Fisk. No doubt there are other songs and other groups. The Red Sox continue to inspire.

"The Red Sox Rock" is a recent creation by a group of guys from western Massachusetts that has been getting some notice over the last season or two. The composers hope that the team might consider adopting the tune to use during the games as a rally song. According to the Red Sox Rock website, the song "is the creation of Ludlow, MA composer Ted Chmura III, with major contributions by Charles 'Chello' Vadnais, and Mike Bouchard. The song began life as a looping seven-note keyboard 'ditty' with the phrase "Red Sox Rock" sung repeatedly in 'Call and Response' style. A full three-minute version with two verses and a tasty guitar solo 'grew' around this foundation and makes up what we now call the Red Sox Rock—Radio Mix."

In 2007, the Red Sox—in collaboration with the Berklee School of Music—planned to launch a songwriting contest to produce *The Green Album: A Sox Fans Songbook*. Intended both to raise awareness and support for their community outreach programs—and just to have fun—the top five songs (selected by a panel of Berklee faculty and Red Sox players) would be included on the album, combined with other Fenway favorites. All styles of music are welcome and encouraged, with English or Spanish lyrics. We look forward to learning more about this project.

Serious discographers may want to know that other albums by John Kiley include:

John Kiley—*Majesty of Big Pipe Organ—vol. 1*—LP Spinorama S24
John Kiley—*Plays Big Pipe Organ—vol. 2*—LP Diplomat 2207
John Kiley—*Plays Gigantic Pipe Organ*—LP Spinorama MK 3024
John Kiley—*Plays Pipe Organ*—LP Parade SP 324

Other Teams, Other Songs

The Red Sox are associated with "Dirty Water" and with "Sweet Caroline" but there are other teams who have their own songs, too. The New York Yankees are well-known for playing the celebratory Frank Sinatra recording "New York, New York" after every win at the Stadium. The grounds crew has a whole routine built around the Village People's "YMCA" and over the last several years inexplicably have a berserk cowboy contorting and gesticulating on the video screen to the old country fiddle tune, "Cotton-Eyed Joe." Even most Yankees fans can't begin to explain that one.

Gene Sunnen writes: "The Giants, despite being in a very hip city, rival the Yankees in squareness by playing 'I Left My Heart in San Francisco,' although they seem to play it only after Sunday wins."

A quick, random poll of baseball fans turns up the following connections, past or present, between given songs and given teams:

"Thank God I'm A Country Boy" (John Denver)—Baltimore Orioles

"Thunderstruck" (AC/DC)—Chicago White Sox, while introducing the home team

"Hey, Hey, Kiss Him Good Bye (Steam) is commonly used when a visiting pitcher gets driven from the game. The Red Sox have started to play the "Theme from 'Mission Impossible'" or "Pressure Drop" (The Maytals) as a visiting reliever comes in from the bullpen.

"Start Me Up" (Rolling Stones) used to be played by the Oakland A's before the first pitch back in the 1980s. Bruce Brown, who submitted this bit, sarcastically adds, "They probably can no longer afford the royalties."

In the '80s and early '90s, "The Curly Shuffle" (Jump n' the Saddle) was played at Shea Stadium between the eighth and ninth innings.

James Brown's "I Feel Good" was played at Candlestick Park after each Giants game back in the late 1980s—presumably only after wins.

The Seattle Mariners used to play "Louie Louie" (The Kingsmen) during the seventh inning stretch. If the team won, they would play "That's the Way (Uh Huh, Uh Huh) I Like It" by KC and the Sunshine Band. If they lose, they'll play The Beatles' more philosophical "Obladi Oblada (Life Goes On)."

The Blue Jays play "Okay Blue Jays" during the stretch. Around the end of the 1990s, they would play "Every 1's A Winner" (Hot Chocolate), and if they lost, they'd play "I Can't Stand Losing" (The Police).

The Angels play "Calling All Angels" (Train) as the soundtrack to their video of former stars and greatest moments.

After Dodgers wins, Randy Newman's "I Love L.A." gets play.

Maybe one of the reasons the Montreal Expos lost favor lay in their choice of music. They used to play the "Theme from the 'Tonight Show'" (Paul Anka) prior to games and—for some strange reason—an instrumental version of "See the USA in Your Chevrolet" immediately afterward. A little odd for a Canadian—much less Québécois—venue. Perhaps an early example of product placement?

In Detroit, fans heard "Eye of the Tiger" before games. Phillies fans heard "Philadelphia Freedom" (Elton John).

The Cardinals, somewhat predictably, favor "Meet Me in St. Louis" and, in a bow to Anheuser-Busch ownership, "Here Comes the King."

In another city known for its beer, the Milwaukee Brewers play "Roll Out The Barrel" during their seventh-inning stretch, and have done so for decades.

The Pirates, of course, had a very special 1979 season, one that will forever be associated with Willie Stargell and the Sister Sledge song "We Are Fam-a-lee."

In eastern Pennsylvania the following year, the Phillies adopted "Ain't No Stoppin' Us Now" (McFadden and Whitehead)—and the song wound up being adopted by the Philadelphia Eagles, and to some extent by the Philadelphia 76-ers as well.

Standells Discography

1964

"Live" and Out of Sight (Sunset SUM 1136)

Side A
1. Louie Louie (Richard Berry)
2. Ooh Poo Pah Doo (Jessie Hill)
3. Shake
4. Bony Maronie (Larry Williams)
5. Peppermint Beatle

Side B
1. I'll Go Crazy (James Brown)
2. Linda Lou
3. So Fine (Johnny Otis)
4. Money (That's What I Want) (Janie Bradford and Berry Gordy Jr.)
5. Help Yourself (Jimmy Reed)

1965

Standells in Person at P.J.'s (Liberty ST-7384; also listed as Liberty LRP-3384)
Some sources list this as a 1964 release.

Side A
1. Help Yourself (Jimmy Reed)
2. So Fine (Johnny Otis)
3. You Can't Do That (John Lennon and Paul McCartney)
4. What Have I Got Of My Own (John Herring and Paul Sawtell)
5. Money (That's What I Want) (Janie Bradford and Berry Gordy Jr.)

Side B
1. I'll Go Crazy (James Brown)
2. Bony Moronie (Larry Williams)
3. Ooh Poo Pah Doo (Jessie Hill)
4. Linda Lu
5. Louie Louie (Richard Berry)

1966

Dirty Water (Tower 5027) Re-released as Sundazed CD 6019 (1994)

Side A
1. Medication (Minette Allton and Ben R. DiTosti)
2. Little Sally Tease (James Valley)

3. There's a Storm Coming (Ed Cobb)
4. 19th Nervous Breakdown (Mick Jagger and Keith Richards)
5. Dirty Water (Ed Cobb)
6. Pride and Devotion (Larry Tamblyn)
7. Hey Joe (Warren Roberts)

Side B
1. Why Did You Hurt Me? (Dick Dodd and Tony Valentino)
2. Rari (Ed Cobb)
3. Batman (Neil Hefti)
4. It's All In Your Mind (J. Cobb)
5. Love Me (Dick Dodd and Tony Valentino)
6. Medication [instrumental] (Minette Allton and Ben R. DiTosti)
7. Poor Man's Prison (Keith Colley & Knox Henderson)
8. Take a Ride (Ed Cobb)

Why Pick On Me? (Tower 5044) Produced by Bob Irwin. Re-released as Sundazed CD 6020 (1994)

Side A
1. Why Pick On Me (Ed Cobb)
2. Paint It Black (Mick Jagger and Keith Richards)
3. Mi Hai Fatto Innamorare (Tony Valentino)
4. I Hate to Leave You (Tony Valentino)
5. Black Hearted Woman (Cut Houle)
6. Sometimes Good Guys Don't Wear White (Ed Cobb)
7. The Girl and the Moon (Larry Tamblyn)

Side B
1. Looking at Tomorrow (Barry Mann and Cynthia Weil)
2. Mr. Nobody (Larry Tamblyn)
3. My Little Red Book (Burt Bacharach and Hal David)
4. Mainline (Thomas W. Chellis and Jonathan K. Huntress)
5. Have You Ever Spent the Night in Jail (Ed Cobb)
6. Our Candidate (Michael Leroy Smith)
7. Don't Say Nothing at All (Dinah Washington and Juanita Hill)
8. The Boy Who Is Lost (Larry Tamblyn)

The Hot Ones! (Tower 5049) Produced by Bob Irwin. Re-released as Sundazed CD 6021 (1994)

Side A
1. Last Train to Clarksville (Tommy Boyce and Bobby Hart)
2. Wild Thing (Chip Taylor)
3. Sunshine Superman (Donovan)

4. Sunny Afternoon (Ray Davies)
5. L'il Red Riding Hood (Ronald Blackwell)
6. Eleanor Rigby (John Lennon and Paul McCartney)
7. Black Is Black (Michelle Granger, Steve Wadey, and Tony Hayes)

Side B
1. Summer in the City (John Sebastian, Steve Boone, and Mark Sebastian)
2. You Were the One (Ed Cobb)
3. Schoolgirl (Graham Gouldman)
4. Ten O'Clock Scholar (Ed Cobb)
5. When I Was a Cowboy (Huddie Ledbetter)
6. Don't Tell Me What to Do (Tony Valentino)
7. Misty Lane (Monty Siegel)
8. Standells' Love Theme (B. McElroy and Ed Cobb)

1967

Try It (Tower 5098) Produced by Bob Irwin. Re-released as Sundazed CD 6022 (1994)

CD track list:
1. Can't Help But Love You (Donald Bennett and Ethon McElroy)
2. Ninety-nine (and a Half) Won't Do (Steve Cropper, Eddie Floyd, and Wilson Pickett)
3. Trip to Paradise (Donald Bennett and Ethon McElroy)
4. St. James Infirmary (traditional/Joe Primrose)
5. Try It (Joseph Levine and Marc Bellack)
6. Barracuda (Ed Cobb)
7. Did You Ever Have That Feeling? (Robert Safir)
8. Poor Shell of A Man (Dick Dodd)
9. All Fall Down (Dick Dodd)
10. Riot on Sunset Strip (Tony Valentino and John Fleck)
11. Get Away from Here (Larry Tamblyn)
12. Try It [alternative vocal] (Joseph Levine and Marc Bellack)
13. Animal Girl [single 398] (Michael Moore)
14. Soul Drippin' [single 398] (Dick Monda)
15. Can You Dig It? (Ethon McElroy and Ed Cobb)

2000

Ban This! Live From Cavestomp! (Varese CD 066192)
1. Riot on Sunset Strip (Tony Valentino and John Fleck)
2. There's a Storm Coming (Ed Cobb)
3. Why Pick On Me? (Ed Cobb)
4. Sometimes Good Guys Don't Wear White (Ed Cobb)
5. Rari (Ed Cobb)

6. Pride and Devotion (Larry Tamblyn)
7. Medication (Minette Allton and Ben R. DiTosti)
8. Barracuda (Ed Cobb)
9. Mr. Nobody (Larry Tamblyn)
10. Little Sally Tease (Jim Valley)
11. Try It (Joseph Levine and Marc Bellack)
12. Dirty Water (Ed Cobb)
13. Why Did You Hurt Me? (Dick Dodd and Tony Valentino)
14. Untitled

2004

In Person at P.J.'s CD MAM 30397
Same tracks as the 1965 album, but with the addition of one track:
"The Shake" by Larry Tamblyn.

More Compilations

Dirty Water/Why Pick on Me—Released 1992

Hot Hits & Hot Ones: Is This the Way That You Get Your High?—Released 1993

Hot Ones!/Try It—Released 1993

Riot on Sunset Strip/Rarities—Released 1993

Live Ones!—Released November, 06, 2001

Very Best of the Standells—Released May, 19, 1998

Anthology of Legendary Recordings, Vol. 1—Released 1981

Best of the Standells—Released 1984

Rarities—Released 1984

Films employing "Dirty Water" as part of the soundtrack include: *Fever Pitch* (2005), *Urban Legends: Bloody Mary* (2005), *The Secret Life of Girls* (1999), and *EDtv* (1999).

Text from LP Jackets

THE STANDELLS / DIRTY WATER

One thing you never find the Standells doing career-wise is standing still. With their smash hit Dirty Water secure, three teen-oriented movies to their credit, a dozen or more TV performances on the book plus a fistful of standing-room-only personal appearances, these boys are going places in a big, *big* way! What's more, old-timers and new-timers alike are predicting that where the Standells are concerned, you ain't seen nothin' yet!

What are the Standells themselves?

Meet Larry Tamblyn, 22; Dick Dodd, 21; Tony Valentino, 24; and Gray Lane, 24.

They themselves met as almost all groups do . . . by chance. Tony and Larry teamed up in 1962 when they were each earning $10 a night playing dances and record hops: Tony on guitar and harmonica; Tamblyn (now an organist) on guitar and bass.

These two traveled to Hawaii and played there during that summer. When they returned to the mainland, they joined with Gary Lane (still with the group) and Gary Leeds who has since been replaced by drummer Dick Dodd.

By mid-1964, the Standells (they decline to say where they got the name) were well on their way to show business stardom. Behind them were the afore-mentioned movies, all for MGM. They appeared in person in *Get Yourself a College Girl* while for *Zebra in the Kitchen* and *When the Boys Meet the Girls*, they supplied the big beat background music.

Those TV shows which featured their solid sound were *Shindig, Bing Crosby Show, Ben Casey, The Munsters, Dick Clark's American Bandstand, The Lloyd Thaxton Show*, and in Los Angeles, *She-bang, Shivaree, Hollywood A Go Go*, and *Hollywood Discotheque*, to mention just a few.

As for personal appearances, they've had audiences cheering for more from San Francisco's Tiger A Go Go Room to Las Vegas' Thunderbird and the likes of Hollywood's Peppermint West. And, of course, on the international scene they've captured the hearts of Central Americans and are about to embark on a special tour of Japan.

Individually, the boys line up something like this:

TAMBLYN—Brother of *West Side Story*'s Russ, Larry generally acts as spokesman for the group. California-born, he went to high school and college before tackling show business. He has studied piano and the guitar in partic-ular and has worked as a fry cook, a dish washer, a hot dog vender, and a box boy. His hobbies are watching horror movies and—like many another Cali-fornian—skateboarding and surfing.

VALENTINO—As you may gather, Tony is Italian and when he came to the United States in 1958 was already proficient on the guitar. Like the Beatles, Tony had no formal music education but learned his trade during "live" performances. A keen motorcyclist, he lists among his former occupations that of baker. Although he loves America he still prefers spaghetti to hamburgers.

⊙ ⊙ ❼ SHINDIG—Music
Jimmy O'Neill welcomes Dick and Dee Dee ("Be My Baby"); Shirley Ellis ("Name Game"); Bobby Goldsboro ("Little Things"); the Tradewinds ("New York's a Lonely Town"); Glen Campbell ("King Creole"); and the Standells ("Come Home"). Jewel Atkins sings "The Birds and the Bees," disc pick of the week. Regulars on hand include Donna Loren ("Goldfinger"); Bobby Sherman ("Hello Mary Lou"); and the Shindogs ("Baby Please Don't Go"). (60 min.)

LANE—Tall, handsome, sometimes bearded, Gary is often referred to as the statesman of the group. From Minnesota, he plays, in addition to guitar, harmonica and ukulele. Like the rest of the Standells, he is an outdoor boy when it comes to hobbies. His particular interests are fishing, archery and hunting. His personal aim: to be married with a nice family and then "live happily ever after."

DODD—Californian Dick, although the baby of the group, has the longest show business career. He started 'way-back-when as a member of TV's *Mickey Mouse Club.* He's an extremely good dancer and singer (the Standells let him sing lead more often than any other drummer now active!). His hobbies: horseback riding, surfing and driving.

A Greengrass Production Produced by Ed Cobb—arrangers: Larry Tamblyn, Ed Cobb, Tony Valentino, Dick Dodd, Gary Lane.
Photo: Ronald Young
STANDELL FAN CLUB
c/o B.J. Enterprises 9220 Sunset Blvd., Suite 330 Los Angeles Calif.
Consultant Engineers: Tom May and Kearnie W. Barton

Text from very first album, on Liberty, THE STANDELLS "LIVE" AND OUT OF SIGHT

Live And Out Of Sight. These two descriptions fit the sounds of The Standells perfectly. Over the past few years they have consistently set audiences and listeners moving with their "out of sight" sounds. They have also been consistent in enjoying numerous top ten record hits. Theirs is the sound people want.

When recording an album, one of the most ideal conditions is to do so in front of a live audience. Here, both the performer and audience can react to each other to the fullest and provide a spontaneous excitement. And in the case of The Standells, this combination of performer and audience has resulted in one of the best albums they have recorded. The scene is PJs in Hollywood, California and the place is packed as is always the case when The Standells appear there. One by one they take the stand, prepare their instruments, look to the leader, and then—the downbeat. Here are the results—Live And Out Of Sight!

Text from Tower T 5044,
WHY PICK ON ME / SOMETIMES GOOD GUYS DON'T WEAR WHITE

Today they've happened! They have hits like *Dirty Water, Sometimes Good Guys Don't Wear White*, and *Why Pick On Me* to their credit, they recently finished an all-star tour with The Rolling Stones and the Standells are way up on top!

Four years ago they had nothing going for them but talent, which is the story with most young groups just starting out. But in the case of the Standells, they were heard by a man who was so impressed by them that he decided, there and then, to channel it into the right places. This was Burt Jacobs. At the time he was not even planning to become a manager in show business, but discovering the Standells made up his mind that it was time for a change. So, the success story works two ways. Burt worked with the group, building their name and reputation as well as the tab for their performances, and the boys went along with Burt, listening to his advice, and turning all that talent into successes in personal appearances all over the world; films (*Get Yourself a College Girl*, and background music for *Zebra in the Kitchen* and *When the Boys Meet the Girls*), TV (with appearances on *Shindig, The Lloyd Thaxton Show, American Bandstand, Shivaree, Hollywood A Go Go*, and many others), and, of course, their hit albums on Tower—first "Dirty Water" and now this one.

In person, the Standells are: Larry Tamblyn, organ, plus guitar and vocals—he acts as spokesman for the group; Tony Valentino, guitar and vocals—(he wrote "Mi Hai Fatto Innamorare"); Dave Burke, bass and vocals; and Dick Dodd, drummer and lead singer.

In action, the Standells are one of the world's greatest and most exciting young quartets, and there are their latest recordings.

A Greengrass Production by Ed Cobb
Production/A&R Coordination by Ray Harris
Arrangements by The Standells and Ed Cobb
Engineer: Richie Podolor
Mastering Engineer: Tom May
Cover Photo: Howard Risk
To join the STANDELL FAN CLUB
Write c/o B.J. Enterprises
9220 Sunset Blvd., Suite 330
Los Angeles, Calif.

Text from Tower ST 5098,
TRY IT—THE STANDELLS

Part of the front cover album design was the subtitle: The most talked about record of the year!!

The album cover also featured the word BANNED! In red ink on a white background, set into the otherwise all black and white cover.

The back jacket contained very few words.

TRY IT—THE STANDELLS

TRY IT—The most talked about record of the year

TRY IT—The most controversial record of the year

TRY IT—The most asked for record of the year

TRY IT—The most exciting record of the year

TRY IT—BANNED—TRY IT

HEAR IT NOW!

A product of Green Grass Productions

Produced by: Ed Cobb

Production and A&R Coordination: Ray Harris

Arrangements by: Ed Cobb, The Standells, Don Bennett and Ethon McElroy

Engineers: R. Podolor and B. Cooper

P.S.—with love to Reb, Bill & Jim

The Standells in 16 *Magazine*

In July 1965, *16 Magazine* ran a page on the Standells where they described themselves and their interests.

Dick Dodd

FULL REAL NAME: Joseph Richard Dodd
BIRTHPLACE: Hermosa Beach, Calif.
BIRTHDATE: October 27, 1943
PARENTS: Linda Dodd
BROTHERS AND SISTERS: None.
EYES: Brown.
HAIR: Brown.
HEIGHT: 6 feet.
WEIGHT: 140 lbs.
PRESENTLY LIVING: In a house in Redondo Beach, Calif., with parents.
EDUCATION: Redondo Union High School; El Camino Jr. College
HOBBIES: Surfing, working on car.
FAVORITES—
FOOD: Fried chicken and steak.
COLORS: Black and red.
TYPE OF CLOTHES: Casual.
MOVIE ACTRESS: Barbara Stanwyck
ACTOR: Charlton Heston
SINGERS: Jackie DeShannon and James Brown
KIND OF MUSIC: Rock 'n' roll; progressive jazz.
MUSICAL INSTRUMENTS PLAYS: Drums for Standells.
TV PROGRAM: The Munsters.
TYPE OF GIRL: Plain, natural, down-to-earth girls, who don't use too much make-up. Digs long hair on a gal. Can't stand phonies of any sort—especially girls who put on false airs.
KIND OF DATE: Go to dinner, then to a show.
SPORTS: Surfing, football, basketball.
ULTIMATE AMBITION: To become an all-around entertainer.

Tony Valentino

FULL REAL NAME: Emilio Tony Bellissimo.
BIRTHPLACE: Longi, Italy
BIRTHDATE: May 24, 1941.
PARENTS: Sam and Sara Bellissimo.
BROTHERS AND SISTERS: Leon, Rita, Angela, Nino, Frank.

EYES: Brown.
HAIR: Brown.
HEIGHT: 5 feet, 9 inches.
WEIGHT: 135 lbs.
EDUCATION: In Italy—where he had almost enough credits to become a high school teacher.
PRESENTLY LIVING: In Hollywood, with parents and brothers and sisters.
HOBBIES: Motorcycle riding.
FAVORITES—
FOOD: Spaghetti and most Italian dishes, which he also likes to cook.
COLORS: Black and blue.
TYPE OF CLOTHES: Likes to get dressed up in continental-cut suits; English tweeds and boots.
MOVIE ACTRESS: Sophia Loren.
MOVIE ACTOR: Don Knotts.
SINGERS: Nancy Wilson.
KIND OF MUSIC: Jazz and rock 'n' roll.
MUSICAL INSTRUMENT PLAYS: Lead guitar for Standells.
TV PROGRAM: The Munsters.
TYPES OF GIRLS: All types! Especially attracted to very quiet, lady-like girls with long black or blonde hair.
KIND OF DATE: Likes to go to a club to watch entertainers and dance; or quiet evening at the movies.
SPORTS: Car racing. Used to drive in races, until recently. Still digs watching the races.
ULTIMATE AMBITION: To go all the way through the entertainment business. Would especially like to act.

Gary Lane

FULL REAL NAME: Gary McMillan.
BIRTHPLACE: St. Paul, Minn.
BIRTHDATE: September 18, 1940.
BROTHERS AND SISTERS: Four brothers living in California.
EYES: Brown.
HAIR: Brown.
HEIGHT: Six feet, one inch.
WEIGHT: 170 lbs.
PRESENTLY LIVING: In a bachelor apartment in Tujunga (the San Fernando Valley), Calif.
EDUCATION: Van Nuys Hr. High School; Verdugo Hills High School; Trade Tech College.
HOBBIES: Anything mechanical—especially working on Mustang car.

FAVORITES—
FOOD: Steak and baked potatoes.
COLOR: Red.
TYPE OF CLOTHES: Continental-cut suits; likes to get dressed up.
MOVIE ACTRESS: Sophia Loren
MOVIE ACTOR: Kirk Douglas.
SINGERS: Nancy Wilson and James Brown.
KIND OF MUSIC: Rock 'n' roll; popular; jazz.
MUSICAL INSTRUMENTS PLAYS: Guitar and bass guitar.
TV PROGRAM: The Munsters.
TYPE OF GIRL: Short, preferably blond—although it really doesn't matter as long as she is warm, understanding and down-to-earth. Pet peeve is a loud girl—in voice or action or dress.
KIND OF DATE: Go out to dinner, then to see a play—especially a comedy. Also digs all kinds of movies.
SPORTS: Baseball—to play and watch.
ULTIMATE AMBITION: To save up enough money to buy some property and eventually go into business (preferably away from the entertainment field) for himself.

Larry Tamblyn

FULL REAL NAME: Lawrence Arnold Tamblyn.
BIRTHPLACE: Inglewood, Calif.
BIRTHDATE: Feb. 5, 1943
BROTHERS AND SISTERS: Russ Tamblyn (the movie actor) and Warren.
EYES: Brown. HAIR: Brown.
HEIGHT: Five feet, eleven inches.
WEIGHT: 150 lbs.
PRESENTLY LIVING: In a Van Nuys, Calif. apartment with mother and stepfather.
EDUCATION: Sun Valley Jr. High; Polytechnic High; Valley College (one semester); Don Martin Trade School, where he originally studied to be a disc jockey.
HOBBIES: Playing guitar and drums, collecting records.
FAVORITES—
FOOD: Hamburgers.
COLOR: Red.
TYPE OF CLOTHES: Very casual—hates to have to get dressed up; digs lounging around in khakis and sweaters.
MOVIE ACTRESS: Donna Reed.
MOVIE ACTOR: George C. Scott.
SINGERS: Ray Charles and Morgana King.
KIND OF MUSIC: Likes and collects all kinds of records except Hillbilly.

MUSICAL INSTRUMENTS PLAYS: Guitar, bass and drums.

TV PROGRAM: No particular favorites; likes to watch TV and go by who's in a show and the story.

TYPE OF GIRL: An intelligent gal with a good sense of humor. Looks are secondary to personality; likes a date to be able to carry on a good discussion and to make him feel comfortable around her.

KIND OF DATE: Go to dinner and then a movie; or sit around, listening to records and talking.

SPORTS: Baseball and basketball.

ULTIMATE AMBITION: To stay with music for the rest of his life. Eventually, to produce records.

Standells Timeline

1962
Larry and Emilio form the Standells
Oasis Club, Honolulu—Emilio now known as Tony
Fresno gig

1963
Club Esquire Jan/Feb 1963—Eureka
Royal Room May 1963—West Los Angeles
Tykes August 1963—Pasadena
Trophy Room/Sacramento early September 1963
Marusia's Peppermint West September 1963 (cover of *Key* magazine Sept 12–
    19 issue)
November—Larry Tamblyn released "Patty Ann"/"Dearest" (Faro 601)

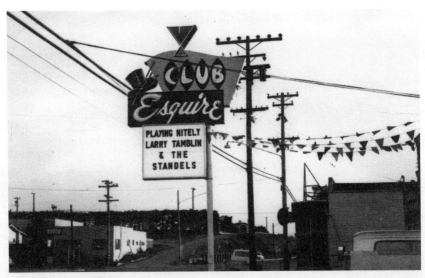

Courtesy of Edie McMillan.

1964
January—recording "You'll Be Mine Someday"/"Girl in My Heart" (Linda
    112)—released as by "Larry Tamblyn and The Standells"
February—Larry Tamblyn "The Lie"/"My Bride to Be" (Faro 603)
February 6—Tamblyn, Valentino, Gary McMillan (Lane), and Gary Leeds
    sign record contract with Liberty

March—"The Peppermint Beatle"/ "The Shake" (Liberty 55680) prod. Dick Glasser

March—Thunderbird Lounge/Las Vegas (Gary Leeds/drummer.) At one point, a press release indicated that the Standells were going to travel to England to challenge the Beatles. The band never intended to go there. This was a PR ploy by the Thunderbird.

March—booked as house band at P.J.'s

March issue of *Variety* featured an advertisement placed by Liberty, which ran as a banner ad across the bottom of the front cover, reading "SOUL MUSIC FOR SWINGERS"

In between gigs at P.J.'s, the band played the Haunted House on Hollywood Boulevard.

April—Larry Tamblyn single "This Is the Night"/"Destiny" (Faro 612)

July—"Help Yourself"/"I'll Go Crazy" (Liberty 55722) prod. Dick Glasser

July—Dick Dodd joins the group

September—Standells trip to Nicaragua—about 12 days in all

September—*The Standells In Person at P.J.'s* (Liberty LRP-3384/LST-7384) Album produced by Dick Glasser

October 17—"Linda Lou"/"So Fine" (Liberty 55743) noted as a slice from their live LP from PJ's Produced by Dick Glasser

November 24—TV show with Clarissa

December 5—Sammy Lee's Westlake, Chatsworth CA—"Teenage Dance"

December 22, 1964 issue of *Variety* lists the following appearances by The Standells:

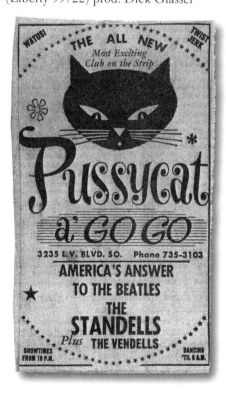

Courtesy of Edie McMillan (both clippings).

Courtesy of Edie McMillan (all clippings).

Dec 22—third return to P.J.'s

Dec 23—MGM release *Get Yourself A College Girl*

Dec 26—Vee-Jay Records release "The Boy Next Door" produced by Sonny Bono

Dec 31—"That Regis Philbin Show"—The Standells performed "I Want to Hold Your Hand" and another song.

At some point in mid to late 1964, the Standells played the Peppermint Tree in San Francisco. The Byrds were the next act booked.

1965

January 2—Sam Riddle's Ninth Street West

January 7—opening New Tiger A-Go-Go Room, Hilton Hotel, SF

January 16—Country-a-Go-Go

January 18—Title tune *Zebra in the Kitchen* MGM

January 18—*TV Guide* lists "Bugged by the Love Bugs" episode on Bing Crosby's ABC-TV show

February—*Get Yourself A College Girl* motion picture soundtrack (MGM SE-4273)

March 18—*The Munsters* episode "Far Out Munsters"

March 20—"American Bandstand" with Brenda Holloway

March 25—*TV Guide*—"Shindig," with Dick and Dee Dee, Shirley Ellis, Bobby Goldsboro, the Tradewinds, and Glen Campbell.

March 29—*Ben Casey* episode entitled "Three Little Lambs"

April—"Zebra in the Kitchen"/"Someday You'll Cry" (MGM 13350)

April—Tiger-A-Go-Go (San Francisco Airport Hilton) return engagement advertised as the "return of the Wild Standells"

ca. April—Harvey's Gold Street Club/Garden Grove, CA—met Chuck Berry

May 28—Standells play at Garden Grove's Alamitos Intermediate School "Swing into Summer" assembly, a show that also featured the Bruce Brown movie *Barefoot Adventure.*

June—"The Boy Next Door"/"B. J. Quetzal" (Vee-Jay 643) produced by Sonny Bono

June—played Gene Weed's TV Show *Shivaree* with Sonny & Cher, Bobby Goldsboro and others.

July 12—*Hollywood Discotheque* TV show hosted by Reb Foster, also featuring Ketty Lester, Eddie Hodges, and others. The Standells appeared fairly regularly on the show into November.

August—"Don't Say Goodbye"/"Big Boss Man" (Vee-Jay 679) produced by Sonny Bono

November—"Dirty Water"/"Rari" (Tower 185) produced by Ed Cobb, as are all later Standells releases

November—Pussycat a Go Go—Las Vegas four week gig

1966

February—nightly gig at San José club called Troll A-Go-Go

April 2—*Billboard* has "Dirty Water" listed as a regional breakout in Miami

April 23—*Cashbox* has "Dirty Water" as #1 pick of up and coming records. "Dirty Water" hits #1 in Miami, per *Billboard*. The song first enters the Boston regional chart at #40, and breaks into *Billboard*'s national Hot 100 chart at #98.

May 20—Birmingham High School, Van Nuys—the Standells appeared with the Jefferson Airplane, The Doors, the Sunshine Company, and the Nitty Gritty Dirt Band.

June 11—"Dirty Water" breaks into *Billboard*'s Top 40, at #31.

June 1966—*Dirty Water* (Tower ST5027) LP release

June 1966—"Sometimes Good Guys Don't Wear White"/"Why Did You Hurt Me" (Tower 257)

June 24—Stones tour opens at Manning Bowl, Lynn, MA

The following dates of the fifth North American tour of the Rolling Stones featured The Standells, McCoys, and the Tradewinds on each show, along with other varying acts.

   25—Civic Center Arena—Pittsburgh, PA
   26—Urhlien Arena (Washington Coliseum) Washington, DC—afternoon
   26—Baltimore Civic Centre—Baltimore, MD—evening show
   27—Dillon Stadium—Hartford, CT
   28—War Memorial Auditorium—Buffalo, NY
   29—Maple Leaf Gardens—Toronto, ONT
   30—Forum—Montreal, QUE

July 1—Steel Pier—Atlantic City, NJ
   2—Forest Hills Tennis Stadium—Queens, NY
   3—Convention Hall—Asbury Park, NJ
   4—Virginia Beach Dome—Virginia Beach, VA
   5—OFF
   6—War Memorial Hall—Syracuse, NY
   7—OFF
   8—Cobo Hall—Detroit, MI
   9—Indiana State Fairgrounds Coliseum—Indianapolis, NY
   10—Arie Crown Theater, McCormick Place, Chicago, IL
   11—Sam Houston Coliseum—Houston, TX
   12—Kiel Covention Hall—St Louis, MO
   13—OFF
   14—Winnipeg Stadium—Winnipeg, MAN
   15—Omaha Civic Auditorium—Omaha, NE
   16—18 OFF
   19—Pacific National Exhibition Forum Park—Vancouver, BC
   20—Seattle Coliseum—Seattle, WA
   21—Memorial Coliseum—Portland, OR
   22—Sacramento Memorial Auditorium—Sacramento, CA
   23—The Davis County Lagoon—Salt Lake City, UT
   24—Bakersfield Civic Auditorium—Bakersfield, CA
   25—Hollywood Bowl—Los Angeles, CA
   26—Cow Palace—San Francisco, CA
   27—OFF

28—International Sports Centre—Honolulu, HI (Brian Jones' last North American show)

July 2—*Billboard* has "Dirty Water" break into the Top 20 and enters the Hot LPs chart for the first time at #129 with a star.

July 9—"Dirty Water" reached #11, the highest position it achieves on *Billboard*'s singles chart. It is #8 in *Cashbox*, similarly its high point.

July 16—the top week of all. The single retains #8 in *Cashbox*, #11 in *Billboard*, and the LP reached #81 in *Billboard*. The LP would reach higher, but this week saw the highest combination of single and LP chart success.

August—"Ooh Poo Pah Doo"/"Help Yourself" (Sunset 61000)

September—"Why Pick On Me"/"Mr. Nobody" (Tower 282)

September—*Why Pick On Me*—*Sometimes Good Guys Don't Wear White* (Tower ST5044) ALBUM

October—appearances on television show "Where the Action Is" extend for several months, well into 1967

November—*The Hot Ones!* (Tower ST5049) ALBUM

Sometime late in 1966, Liberty's Sunset label released the album *Live and Out of Sight* (Sunset SUM-1136/SUS-5136)

1967

February—"Try It"/"Poor Shell of a Man" (Tower 310)

February—one week engagement at the Ice House, Glendale, CA

March—"Don't Tell Me What to Do"/"When I Was a Cowboy" (Tower 312)—released as by "The Sllednats"

May—"Riot on Sunset Strip"/"Black Hearted Woman" (Tower 314)

May—*Riot on Sunset Strip* motion picture soundtrack (Tower ST5065) A later version with a different mix was released as Tower ST5098. Note: it is interesting that Ed Cobb had prior film experience when he appeared as one of the Four Preps in the 1959 film *Gidget*.

May 27—The Standells appear on Art Linkletter's TV show "Let's Talk," debating radio mogul Gordon McLendon, who was leading a campaign to ban music with "objectionable" lyrics.

July 23—"Shebang" TV show, with Brenton Wood. Hosted by Casey Kasem. There were several other appearances on "Shebang."

July—controversy begins to build over "Try It" and Gordon McLendon's campaign to ban it.

September—first week of September, return one-week engagement at the Ice House in Glendale.

October—"Can't Help But Love You"/"Ninety-Nine and A Half" (Tower 348)

November—*Try It* (Tower ST5098) ALBUM

November 7—appearance on TV show "Groovy" with the Sunshine Company

November 9—TV appearance on "Pat Boone in Hollywood" with Bill Dana and others

December—guests on television's "Joey Bishop Show"

At some point in 1967, the Standells reappeared on "American Bandstand" and performed "Try It!"

1968

January—another week at the Ice House

February 10—show at the Guitar Center, Hollywood

April—*The First Evolution of Dick Dodd* (Tower ST5142) ALBUM

April—Ice House, Glendale

June—"Animal Girl"/"Soul Drippin'" (Tower 398)

In 1968, Dick Dodd released two singles, one on Attarack ("Guilty"/"Requiem 820") and "Little Sister" (Tower 447)

July—Larry Tamblyn released "Summer Clothes"/"Summer Clothes" (instrumental) Sunburst

September—Ice House, Glendale

October 27—Artists and Models Ball, Century Plaza, with Taj Mahal, others

1970s

Tony led the group into the 1970s before it disbanded.

1980s to Present

August 1983—The new Standells perform at Club Lingerie in Hollywood, the Golden Bear in Huntington Beach, and a weeklong engagement at Harrah's in Reno.

July 19 & 20, 1986—Summerfest/Return to the Sixties, Glen Helen Regional Park, San Bernardino, California

November 1987—Dick Dodd impersonator arrested in Austin, Texas at the Big Mamou nightclub. (See sidebar.)

1999 Cavestomp Festival in New York

June 30, 2000—Las Vegas Grind

October 24, 2004—Standells play before Game Two of the World Series

April 11, 2005—Standells play at Fenway Park

September 8, 2006—Standells play at Fenway Park

Standells Impersonator Arrested

One of the stranger situations of Standells history occurred in November 1987 when Dick Dodd and the Standells were due to appear at Big Mamou, a South Austin nightclub located on South Congress Street in the Texas capital. Dan Forte, a writer who'd recently interviewed George Harrison for *Guitar Player* magazine, was leaving an interview at radio station KLBJ when he heard that Dodd was on his way in to the station to do some advance promotion for his forthcoming show. Dan had met Dick the previous June at a reunion of surf bands, and looked forward to renewing his acquaintance.

Forte was taken aback when a total stranger came up to him. "He shook my hand and said, 'Hi, I'm Dick Dodd,'" Forte testified later in court. The guy looked nothing at all like Dodd, "not even close" in Forte's words. Realizing that something was amiss, Forte "bit his tongue," in the words of KLBJ program director Jeff Carrol. Forte called Big Mamou's owner Steve Chaney and told him, "I've got news for you. That's not Dick Dodd, and I can prove it." Forte explained that he'd met Dodd in person and then showed Chaney a couple of Standells album covers. They got Dick's phone number from Eddie Bertrand of the Belairs and called Dick, who assured them that the Standells were not active, not playing any gigs. The only work Dick was doing was with his weekend band, Dick Dodd and the Dodd Squad, playing a club in Huntington Beach. It seemed pretty clear there was some misrepresentation afoot, that someone was impersonating Dick Dodd and trying to cash in on his name and that of the Standells.

The Austin police were alerted, and they set up a sting. They needed to catch the Dodd impersonator performing for money, and so waited for the night of the show. Dick was working as a car salesman for Santa Ana Mazda at the time, but at the request of the police, he and his wife Jane flew in from California before the show. It was a Saturday night and Big Mamou's was packed. Among the audience were the Dodds and about a dozen undercover police officers. The (fake) Standells took the stage at about 11:30 P.M. and kicked into "Good Guys Don't Wear White."

"It was like a thing from 'Cops,'" Dick remembers. "The lights went on and the police came out from the side of the stage and over the front.... That was the whole thing. They had to introduce them, and then they had to start playing, and while they were playing, then we had to go up on stage." The police arrested lead singer (and Dodd impersonator) Jimmy Lee Deen, 36, and Robert Devine, 34, both of Austin. There was some drug paraphernalia found as well. Deen and Devine were led off in handcuffs and later charged with one count of attempted misdemeanor theft. The other two band members were questioned and released. They were playing for a guarantee of $400 as against 90% of the gate. Deen was out on parole for auto theft at the time.

Even though they'd been treated to an unusual on-stage bust, Dick felt bad for the fans who had come to see the Standells. "They were going to be ripped off. I didn't want them to have me there and be all mad. There was another band there, so we got together with the club owner and they backed me up for like an hour. We just did a whole bunch of classic rock and roll stuff, but we did do 'Dirty Water.' I didn't even play drums. I just fronted the band."

Another odd thing about Deen. He may not have realized that Dick was the drummer in the Standells. Deen played guitar and used a Telecaster, on which he'd written "Dick Dodd" with a black marker. Dick returned to Austin for the trial. "He got some time," Dick says. "Not a lot."

The ersatz Standells had booked some other dates, including another one in Oklahoma City. Dick only heard that one first song, but were they any good? "No, they were just some bar band."

"Dirty Water" Today

Once the song began getting played every time the Red Sox or Bruins won, its popularity began to increase once more—and not just among Boston sports fans. There has definitely been an uptick in covers of the song in recent years, and it has been used in a number of television shows and employed in several motion pictures:

TELEVISION
Saturday Night Live
Late Night with Conan O'Brien
American Dreams
Queer Eye for the Straight Guy
Crossing Jordan

FILM
The Secret Life of Girls
EDtv
Fever Pitch
Stateside
Urban Legends: Bloody Mary

There was also a storyboard created to use "Dirty Water" in a Bud Light commercial; the ad agency licensed the track but never broadcast the commercial. Scrubbing the commercial may have been a result of Anheuser-Busch being contacted by attorneys representing the Standells, and may be because of second thoughts regarding using a song named "Dirty Water" to advertise a popular beverage.

There's even an improv revue which took on the name Dirty Water. The show is based in Chicago but features five cast members, four of whom come from Massachusetts. They have performed over 150 shows since 2005 and toured Boston, New York, Toronto, Seattle, and Red Sox Spring Training. Their PR materials describe them as "a hilarious improvised comedy about the fun-loving wise-cracking regulars of the Dirty Water Pub in South Boston." No less than the *Chicago Tribune* rated them "Best of the Fringe" in the city. Their website offers more information, at www.dirtywaterimprov.com.

"Tessie"—the Rest of the Story

In the days when "Tessie" was born, the team played on a site where the Northeastern University campus stands today. The Sox played at the Huntington Avenue Grounds from 1901 through the 1911 season; they moved into brand-new Fenway Park in 1912. In 1993, Northeastern installed a larger-than-life bronze statute of immortal Red Sox pitcher Cy Young to commemorate the spot where he once toed the rubber on the pitcher's mound.

The history of Boston sport songs and chants extends even further back. A couple of rally chants were noted at the 1897 Temple Cup, the precursor of the World Series, which saw the National League Boston Beaneaters beaten by the Baltimore Orioles, four games to one. The Boston fan base was there with its chants, though. Two cheers for '97, written for the Roxbury Rooters by humorist Augustus Howell, a fellow rooter, went as follows:

"Hit er up, hit er up, hit er up again, B-O-S-T-O-N"

"Boston, Boston, Rah, Rah, Rah"

The raucous singing of the popular songs of the day by the fans in the ballpark, regardless of the song's relevance to baseball, was a common practice at the time. Partisan supporters would often hire a local band and bring the professional musicians into the ballparks to accompany the singing spectators. Sometimes the lyrics of the song would be adapted to attempt to rattle the opposition. In the case of "Tessie," the practice seems to have paid off and the incessant singing of the song may well have proved a factor in the 1903 Series itself, helping swing things in Boston's favor.

To look at the lyrics, you wouldn't think a song with words like this could affect a World Series. To hear the song sung, your first impression would only be strengthened. The lyrics:

Tessie is a maiden with a sparkling eye,
Tessie is a maiden with a laugh,
Tessie doesn't know the meaning of a sigh,
Tessie's lots of fun and full of chaff,
But sometimes we have a little quarrel, we two,
Tessie always turns her head away,
Then it's up to me to do as all boys do,
So I take her hand to mine and say,

Chorus:
Tessie you make me feel so badly
Why don't you turn around,
Tessie you know I love you madly,
Babe, my heart weighs about a pound;

Don't blame me if I ever doubt you,
You know I wouldn't live without you,
Tessie, you are the only, only, only.

Tessie has a parrot that she loves quite well,
Polly's just a learning how to woo,
Tessie tells him ev'rything she has to tell,
Polly thinks he knows a thing or two,
Tessie gave a party at her home one night
Polly said he'd like to sing a song,
Tessie thought she's never seen a bird so bright,
When Polly started off in accents strong

Chorus

Both lyrics and music are by Will R. Anderson, and the sheet music was first published in 1902 by the New York firm M. Witmark & Sons. The first edition featured a photograph of singer Horace Wright on the front cover, along with the information that the song was in "John C. Fisher's Stupendous Production *The Silver Slipper.*" The show was a musical that had a good run of 160 performances at the Broadway Theatre in New York, from October 27, 1902 to March 14, 1903, and was indeed produced by John C. Fisher.

Anderson himself composed music for a few other Broadway shows: "Lonesome Town," "The Girls of Gottenberg," and "Take It from Me." He did not appear to have a particularly illustrious career, and little is known about him today.

A second printing of the song's sheet music depicted a subsequent performer. The song was now being "Sung with Great Success by Mr. Stanley Hawkins" in the same "Stupendous Production." Finally, a third edition of sheet music was printed, this one graced by the image of vocalist Joseph S. Welsh on the cover. Again, the song was attributed to Fisher's show. The price of the sheet music was 60 cents.

The song was actually recorded almost immediately, in 1902, on a Columbia brown wax cylinder, by a very early recording pioneer, singer Dan Quinn. The song was recorded again in 1903 by Victor.

"Tessie" was popular enough to have attracted at least two recorded versions and the three printings of sheet music. There's a good chance that some of the players would have known the song from one of the recordings. One or more may have even taken in the Broadway show during the prior off-season, as might have some of Boston's Royal Rooters. Peter Nash, author of *The Royal Rooters*, considers it a well-known song of the time. "From what I gather," he writes, "the Tessie song was very popular at that time with the general public. It's probably the equivalent of an [baseball public address] operator putting on "Who Let the Dogs Out" or "The Macarena" in their day."[1]

How this sheet music ended up in the hands of a Boston fan and why it resonated as a candidate to upset the Pirates is something we'll likely never know. Nonetheless, this improbable song "Tessie" became the original fight song of the Boston Americans.

The Boston Americans had won the 1903 pennant handily, with a record of 91 wins to 47 losses, putting them 14½ games ahead of Connie Mack's Philadelphia Athletics, the second-place finisher. Buck Freeman led the league both in runs batted in with 104 and in home runs with 13. Patsy Dougherty was the team's leading hitter for average (.331), in third place behind Lajoie (.344) and Crawford (.335). Dougherty led the league in both hits and runs scored. Cy Young (who hit pretty well himself, for a .321 average that year) led the league in wins and winning percentage, posting a record of 28–9 with a 2.08 ERA and a total of 34 complete games. The team had two other 20-game winners in Big Bill Dinneen (21–13) and Long Tom Hughes (20–7).

They faced the Pittsburgh Pirates, who led the National League with a 91-49 record, good enough to finish 6½ games ahead of John McGraw's New York Giants. Pittsburgh shortstop Honus Wagner led the NL in batting with a .355 average, followed closely by team captain Fred Clarke's .351. Ginger Beaumont led his league in both hits and runs scored. Sam Leever was Pittsburgh's best pitcher (he won 25 games and lost just seven, with a league-leading 2.06 earned run average), but Charles Louis "Deacon" Phillippe wasn't far behind (25–9, 2.43 ERA.)

The post-season competition between the two pennant winners from the two rival leagues came in the third year of the upstart American League, and is considered to be the first World Series ever played. There were earlier post-season playoffs, but this was the first between the two leagues that have endured to this day.

The Series was meant to be a best-of-nine and opened in Boston, at the Huntington Avenue Grounds, on October 1. Pittsburgh won, 7–3, scoring all the runs it needed—four of them—off Cy Young in the top of the first inning. Deacon Phillippe got the win.

Game Two saw Bill Dinneen throw a three-hit shutout on October 2 and beat Sam Leever, 3-0. Dougherty hit two home runs for the Americans.

The third game was in Boston as well, and Phillippe collected another win despite just one day of rest. He won Game Three over Tom Hughes and Cy Young, 4–2, on October 3.

Both teams took the train to Pittsburgh where they played Game Four at Exposition Park on October 6. Ball was never played on Sundays in those days, and Monday's game was postponed due to rain. Some 125 Boston fans had traveled to Pittsburgh on Sunday on the Boston & Albany railroad and they were a lively crew. As Stout and Johnson write regarding the Royal Rooters in *Red Sox Century*, the rabid Boston fan group "traditionally sang and cheered as a group during the games." They sang spiritedly throughout Game Four: "Won't You Come

Home, Bill Bailey?" and "What a Difference a Few Hours Make" and "I've Got Mine, Boys, I've Got Mine." After Boston tied the game 1–1 in the top of the fifth, the band struck up "In the Good Old Summer Time."

Historian Louis P. Masur writes, "Some fans thought that the Royal Rooters were putting up a better show than the Boston players." Masur adds that noted Rooter Michael "Nuf Ced" McGreevey "climbed on the roof over the Boston bench and danced a 'hornpipe and a jig and a breakdown.' The Rooters 'jumped up in the air and waved handkerchiefs and hats and screeched until their red faces became purple and their horns curled up in envy.' Even the Pittsburgh fans applauded."[2]

What the Rooters didn't have was a win. Boston was down 5–1 after eight full innings, and seemingly beaten. Then "Tessie" intervened.

On Monday evening, one of the Rooters had come back to the Monongahela House Hotel with sheet music to the song from a music store in the city. Creative wags among the cranks parodied the lyrics and McGreevey and others had printed up song sheets and distributed copies to the assembled Rooters.

When Boston manager Jimmy Collins approached the batter's box to lead off the ninth, the Royal Rooters pulled out all the stops. The loyal contingent of Boston fans erupted with three loud cheers. The 50-piece Italian band they had hired for the occasion struck up the tune "Tessie" and the Rooters loudly sang the song with their newly-barbed lyrics.

Rogers Abrams in his wonderful book *The First World Series and the Baseball Fanatics of 1903* provides a couple of quotations from the *Pittsburgh Dispatch* to indicate how fully the Boston fans were transformed. The Royal Rooters became "howling maniacs, overjoyed to a delirious stage." As the comeback built, "the Boston rooters had simply lost control of themselves, war dances, cheers, yells and songs resounding clear across the Allegheny River."[3]

Whatever forces were at play, Collins singled, Chick Stahl singled, Buck Freeman singled, and before the inning was over, Boston had scored three runs on five hits, leaving two men on base, and putting a scare into the Pirates, who'd just held on to eke out the 5–4 win. Phillippe won again (he was now 3–0 in World Series play in a span of just six days), but he no longer seemed invincible. Phillippe had been gotten to. "Tessie" seemed to have worked as a rally song.

Still, it wasn't looking good for Boston, now down three games to one, with the next three games all scheduled in Pittsburgh. Game Five, though, proved the turning point. Boston was ready with Cy Young. Pittsburgh countered with pitcher Brickyard Kennedy, and the Royal Rooters countered with lyrics to "Tessie" intended to upset Kennedy:

Kennedy, you seem to pitch so badly
Take a back seat and sit down.

Kennedy, you are a dead one
And you ought to leave the town.
Pittsburgh needs a few good pitchers,
Such as Boston's pennant lifters.
Phillipi, you are the only, only, only one.

There were other customized lyrics as well. The ones directed at Honus Wagner ran thus:

Honus, why do you hit so badly
Take a back seat and sit down.
Honus, at bat you look so sadly.
Hey, why don't you get out of town?

Wagner, the league's batting champ, hit .222 in the 1903 World Series.

Juvenile? Sure. But the words packed punch, according to Pittsburgh third baseman Tommy Leach. Interviewed years later by Lawrence Ritter for his book *The Glory of Their Times*, the memory of "Tessie" still stuck in Leach's craw. The Rooters played the song incessantly. Probably any song played over and over, and over again, would get under the skin of the listeners. It was deliberate. McGreevey said the purpose was to "charm the Pittsburgh players so that when they hear [the lyrics] their eye will lose its keenness and their arms their brawn. I believe in the power of music."[4]

Coming down on Kennedy, suggesting that Pittsburgh had but one good pitcher, was intentionally divisive, and carried more than a kernel of truth. Kennedy was just 9-6 on the season, the fourth pitcher on the team (16-game winner Ed Doheny had suffered severe mental problems and had to leave the team late in the season.) Kennedy didn't have a good game. Boston won 11–2, scoring six times in the sixth and four times more in the seventh. And the "half-crazy antics of the Boston rooters" were noted. After singing the final parodied line "Hey, why don't you get out of town?" they would stomp their feet three times, shouting an accompanying "Bang! Bang! Bang!" and then voice the refrain again: "Hey, why don't you get out of town?" They had energy! In fact, Roger Abrams informs us that Pittsburgh owner Barney Dreyfuss even "ordered supporting beams erected under Section J, lest the Royal Rooters' 'frenzied enthusiasm' break down the park's grandstand."[5]

Leach admitted that the song, and its delivery, was effective. He said, "I think those Boston fans won the Series.... We beat them three out of four games, and then they started singing that damn Tessie song.... Sort of got on your nerves after awhile."

Boston went on a tear, winning Game Six by a 6–3 score, Dinneen over Leever. Boston held a 5–0 lead after the top of the fifth. The Royal Rooters were in rhapsody and simply wouldn't stop signing "Tessie."

The Pirates had already been unnerved by the song in previous games, and tried to battle back. Some Pirate fans formed their own group, dubbed both the Loyal Rooters and the Champion Rooters. They hired a band to play for them, the same band the Royal Rooters had hired for Game Four. Masur reports, "The band's one object, fans claimed, would be to 'drown the strains of "Tessie"' which the Boston band had played throughout the sixth game once the Americans scored their first run. Pittsburgh fans believed that the song was the Pirates' 'death knell,' and they instructed the band to perform a 'program of antidotes.'"[6] There's a long story we won't go into here about the Guenther band suing the Royal Rooters for not hiring them for Games Five and Six, but that is beyond our purview here. It's interesting to note—perhaps an incipient nod to diversity—that the Rooters hired an Italian band for Game Four, a German band for Game Five, and an Irish band for Game Six.[7]

Imitation may reflect flattery, but the greater passion seemed to be with the Boston contingent. When Boston's band began to play "Tessie," the rival band tried to drown it out by playing "Yankee Doodle." They tried a few other songs as well. The antidotes didn't do the trick. Game Seven ended with the same 7–3 score as Game One, but this time it was Cy Young who gave up the three, while Phillippe surrendered seven. And some of the Pittsburgh fans grew very tired of hearing "Tessie" which, by one count, was played 24 times throughout the game. After four games in Pittsburgh, with the totals now showing four wins for Boston against three for the Pirates, the Series went back to Boston for the eighth and possibly ninth games.

No ninth game was necessary. The Royal Rooters marched to the park behind the Boston Letter Carriers Band and everyone took their places, the band stationed on the field in front of the box seats and the Rooters in a special section behind. They figured they had a good luck charm. One Rooter told the *Boston Globe*, "'Tessie' did the trick. Ever since we began to sing that song the boys have played winning ball." The first song played at the October 13 game was "Tessie" and then the Rooters chanted, "Higgeldy piggeldy, ainst we nice / The Pittsburgh bunch will cut no ice." After a playing of "The Star-Spangled Banner" (which would not be designated the National Anthem until 1931), the game commenced. Big Bill Dinneen shut out the Pirates 3–0, while Phillippe (in his fifth start) took the loss. The Letter Carriers Band played "Tessie" endlessly, it seemed, in celebration of the World Championship. It wasn't the last time the song would be played in Boston.

Did "Tessie" truly make a difference? The dean of the day among Boston sportswriters was former ballplayer Tim Murnane, who wrote for the *Globe*. He concluded:

> "Tessie," an obscure maiden whom somebody loved in a ragtime melody, wasn't much in the place which the librettist and the composer built for her. But she has a place in history. She will go tunefully tripping down the ages as the famous mascot that helped the Boston

Americans win three out of four in Pittsburgh, capture the final game in Boston and with it the title—champions of the world.

Sang by the thundering ensemble at the Huntington baseball grounds yesterday afternoon, "Tessie" was there when anything worth doing was done. "Tessie" was never caroled for any four-flush proposition; her chaste salutes were only for that which wins the royal wreath.

Just as the claim of the heroine is to a high place on the first page of the history of the most famous post-season series, the words of the song have about as much to do with baseball as they did to the operation of stoking in the roundhouse across the field. But the effect in the thing; so "Tessie" is a four-time winner.[8]

The song truly had gotten under the Pirates' skin, as this amusing footnote illustrates:

May 13, 1904: A group of firemen traveled from Reading, Pennsylvania to Pittsburgh to catch a Pirates game against Brooklyn, and they hired a band to march into the ballpark with them. A clever Brooklyn fan passed the unsuspecting bandleader a request to play a tune called "Tessie," and he was only too glad to accommodate. The first few notes ignited an immediate outburst of angry shouts of "Kill them!" and "Throw them out!" Some bleacherites left their seats and began to approach the band in a threatening manner before the band grasped that the musical selection somehow affected the crowd as a red flag affects a bull, and stopped in mid-performance. Brooklyn won, 2–0.[9]

Regarded as a good luck song, "Tessie" stuck and for a good many years it served as at least the occasional rally song for the team that became known as the Red Sox from the 1908 season onward. When the Sox hit the World Series in 1912, 1915, and 1916, "Tessie" bowed in again—though apparently not during the 1918 World Series. Was it perhaps the abandonment of the maiden with the sparkling eye—and not the subsequent sale of Babe Ruth—that condemned the Sox to despair for the next 86 years? We'll never know for sure. John B. Holway suggested as much in a book published in 2000, *The Baseball Astrologer and Other Weird Tales*. Holway wrote: "Curse of the Bambino? I don't think so. It's been Tessie all these years, pining away on a cloud up there and pouting that Boston doesn't love her any more." Come new ownership to the Red Sox in 2002, and at the suggestion of Executive Vice President for Public Affairs Dr. Charles Steinberg, "Tessie" was revived in midsummer 2004. And the Red Sox won another World Series, all in the space of a few months.

There were other "Tessie" sightings after 1903—plenty of them. Just the following year, 1904, the team that would become the Yankees and the team that would become the Red Sox were locked in a battle for the pennant that came down to the last day of the season. A doubleheader was to be played in New

York. Should Boston win either game, they'd take the flag. The Royal Rooters decamped for New York, their band played "Tessie" on their arrival, and their team won the first game, beating New York's 41-game winner Jack Chesbro.

It was back to New York in 1912, to play in the World Series against the New York Giants. The Series opened in New York and the strains of "Tessie" were heard once more. Smoky Joe Wood won the first game, beating Jeff Tesreau, 4–3. It was a long and hard-fought Series, running eight games (Game Two ended in a 6–6 tie), and only ended after New York scored once in the top of the 10th in the final game, but saw Boston come back and score twice.

Boston's other team, the Boston Braves, won it all in 1914, leaping from last place on July 4 to win the pennant by 10 games come the end of the season. The "Miracle Braves" earned the allegiance of the Royal Rooters, who were Boston baseball boosters above all else. Their World Series games were played at the newer (and larger) Fenway Park, and sure enough, "Tessie" reappeared. Three hundred Royal Rooters had traveled to Philadelphia for the first two games, singing the song and declaring it once more their official song for the Series. The *New York Times* game account for Game One noted, "If you ask them why they don't get a new tune they will tell you that they have never sung 'Tessie' behind a losing team."[10] The next day's paper reported that the fans were still singing "Tessie" after another win in Game Two, as they took the train back to Boston.

After taking the third game, 5–4, in 12 innings, one of the *Boston Globe*'s summary stories on October 14 was headlined "Royal Rooters Mad with Joy; 'Tessie' Never Lets Up in Extra Innings." The news story reports that "Tessie" was played before the game and played at the end of every half inning. The *Globe* argued:

Perhaps "Tessie" had nothing whatever to do with the sensational win of the Braves yesterday; perhaps the strains of the antiquated song were devoid of inspiration to the players; no doubt the world's champions [the Philadelphia Athletics, who had won in 1913] were unperturbed when the band played the air until the players gasped for breath throughout the 10th, 11th, and 12th innings, but you can't make the 300 loyal Royal Rooters believe anything of the sort."

The Braves swept the Series in four, the first time any team had done so.

In 1915, the Sox opened the regular season playing the Athletics, and won the home opener on April 22. Philadelphia's second baseman Nap Lajoie committed five errors and, in the ninth inning, third baseman Danny Murphy dropped an easy two-out popup. Two runners scored, giving the Sox the winning 7–6 margin. Some suggest that incessant playing of the song "Tessie" rattled Lajoie. Red Sox owner Joseph Lannin went so far as to declare that "the Rooters and 'Tessie' won the game, and not the Red Sox."[11]

The Red Sox returned to Series play in 1915, against Philadelphia's other team, the Phillies. The maiden returned and *Globe* sportswriter Lawrence J.

Sweeny commented after the Sox took their second straight 2–1 game, Dutch Leonard over Grover Cleveland Alexander: "Perhaps 'Tessie' did not figure in the downfall of the great Aleck, but Philadelphians who managed to get sandwiched in the same sections, or adjacent to the Royal Rooters, proclaimed that 'Tessie' would unnerve a stone, and Alexander, even at his best, is no more immune from the 'rattles' than any other great hurler."[12]

The very next year, the Red Sox were back again, with another pennant and winning another World Series in just five games. During Game Two, the band suddenly started up playing as the Sox were at bat in the 11th. Not even the most ardent Royal Rooter would have wanted the band to play while Boston was batting, and the group could not determine who ordered it up. It was immediately stopped when an emissary of Brooklyn president Ebbets shouted, "Cut that out!" It was reported to be "the first time in the history of a World's Series that the musicians were forbidden to play whenever they chose." Some Boston fans wondered why the ban had not applied to Brooklyn fans who "beat their dish-pan accompaniment while Boston was at bat" on a couple of other occasions.[13]

But could it be that Boston fans were becoming blasé? In the final game, sure enough, "Tessie" was played between innings, and "in a masterly way."[14] Of course, it wasn't permitted during the action. The special to the *New York Times* said of the crowd "they had rather soured on 'Tessie' as the game drew to a close. They yearned for something novel. They had celebrated the advent of the ninth inning [the score was Boston 4, Brooklyn 1] with 'This Is the End of a Perfect Day.' The multitude's outburst of joy at the game's triumphant close inspired them to even greater heights, and they marched forward to the ringing notes of 'Glory, Glory, Hallelujah!'"[15] This despite the acknowledgement that "Tessie" was as a "symphony orchestra to the ears of Boston fans" and that the band was so adept in its rendition it can play "this well-worn selection while lying on their backs and juggling barrels with their feet." Maybe "Tessie" had had its run—and what a run it had been. John Holway reckons the results as follows:

Year	With Tessie	Without Tessie
1903	4–0	1–3
1904	1–0	
1912	3–2	1–1
1914	4–0	
1915	4–1	
1916	4–1	

The Red Sox were to win one more World Series in the 20th century. The 1918 Series started in September (due to the war in progress) and was played at Braves Field (then the larger of the two Boston ballparks.) Though there was some mention prior to Game One that "Tessie" might be "taken out of camphor for the sake of its winning prestige," apparently it was not. Edward F. Martin wrote in the *Globe* that, "While there was no material evidences [sic] of 'Tessie,' she must have been there in spirit. It is the first time that any Boston club has been in a series that 'Tessie' was not heard from good and proper."[16] Maybe not "good and proper," but there might have been at least one Tessie moment. Peter Nash writes, "In 1918 a group of rooters made the trip to Chicago and serenaded the Chicago players and fans with 'Tessie' at the Hotel Brunswick. So, Tessie did appear during the 1918 World Series."[17]

This wasn't quite the end of "Tessie" but it was nearly so. The Red Sox languished for a couple of decades, cellar dwellers for almost every year in the 1920s.

"Tessie" returned to Braves Field in 1930 for the *Boston Post* Old Timers Day. Nuf Ced McGreevey was in attendance. Band leader Jimmie Coughlin played "Tessie" for Cy Young, Candy LaChance, Jimmy Collins and others, who were escorted into the stadium on a Hansom carriage. Honus Wagner was there, too, and was again taunted by the band.

There were other baseball songs that came along during this era, most notably Jack Norworth's "Take Me Out to the Ballgame." Ironically Norworth, who was not a baseball enthusiast by any means, wrote the popular song in 1908 about a young lady named Miss Katie Casey who declined her suitor's offer of an evening out at the theater by suggesting that he could instead:

"Take me out to the ball game
Take me out to the crowd...."

Though written by a man who'd never been to a baseball game, it caught the public's fancy and has never gone out of fashion. But "Tessie" did gradually slip out of favor in Boston and in time was forgotten by all but the most dedicated baseball historians and enthusiasts. The song went into a slump almost as severe as the one the Red Sox suffered between World Series championships.

Roger Abrams reports that it was played on Opening Day at Fenway Park in the 1940s, but with little apparent success. Author Alan Foulds located a *Boston Post* article from August 19, 1940 which reported on the 1903 debut of the song, and added, "Years later Jimmy Coughlin's Band was still playing it at Opening Day at both Fenway Park and Braves Field."

Foulds also tells of meeting John Kiley just before Christmas once year around 1986 or 1987. John was playing Christmas Carols on the organ at Lafayette Place where the Jordan Marsh department store used to be. "There being virtually no audience at the time," Foulds writes, "I spent a few minutes speaking with him during a break. Our brief discussion led to his talking about playing 'Paree' for the Bruins and 'A Great Day for the Irish' for the Celtics. I asked if he had ever played 'Tessie' at Fenway Park. He answered, 'I did a few times in the early '60s, but no one remembers the song anymore.'"[18]

Abrams adds that a scratchy rendition was played on local radio once during the 1946 World Series. Should the Sox have fully revived it for the 1946 World Series, perhaps history would have been different. We'll never know.

In 1986, Red Sox historian Glenn Stout urged fans to bring back "Tessie." It didn't happen. The Red Sox had to wait 18 years for another shot.

Was "Tessie" somewhat instrumental in bringing about the World Series win in 2004? We'll leave it to others to make that determination.

NOTES

First There Was "Tessie"

1. E-mail communication from Peter Nash, August 12, 2006. Peter J. Nash is author of *Boston's Royal Rooters* (Arcadia, 2005).

The website http://www.fightmusic.com/ claims to offer the largest collection of recorded college fight songs in the world. The phenomenon of the fight song is by no means limited to America, however. Team anthems are common in other English-speaking countries; for instance, the site The website http://www.fightmusic.com/ claims to offer the largest collection of recorded college fight songs in the world. The phenomenon of the fight song is by no means limited to America, however. Team anthems are common in other English-speaking countries; for instance, the site http://www.geocities.com /himnos_es/Lenguas/espanol.html offers a selection of "himnos equipos" (team songs in Spanish) from soccer clubs around Spain.

Note: in 1903, the city of Pittsburgh was spelled without the "h" but we have included it here throughout.

2. To hear the 1903 recording of the song, visit the site www.royalrooters.com and select either the MP3 or RealAudio format. The recording is from the collection of the National Library of Canada, recorded on October 5, 1903 in Camden, NJ by the Victor Talking Machine company. It presents a rendition of the song by John Bieling and Harry Macdonough. Though the recording was made on a day between the third and fourth games of the World Series, this was almost certainly coincidental. Cylinder recordings had been offered to the public by Edison since 1887 and many homes had devices to play the recordings. Clearly, the song had achieved a degree of success.

3. Ritter, Lawrence, *The Glory of Their Times* (NY: Harper, 1992), p. 27.

John Kiley and the Organists

1. Interview with Ray Totaro by Chuck Burgess, August, 2006
2. Bill Gilman, *Leominster Champion*, April 7, 2006.
3. Interview with Richard Giglio by Bill Nowlin, May 20, 1999.
4. Interview with Ray Totaro, *op. cit.*

The National Anthem and Boston's Star-Spangled Tenor

1. E-mail communication from Larry Cancro, August 12, 2006.
2. E-mail communication from Marty Ray, August 12, 2006.
3. E-mail communication from Jim Healey, August 12, 2006.
4. Interview with Rene Rancourt by Chuck Burgess, June 7, 2006

"Sweet Caroline" in the Can—Good Times Never Seemed So Good

1. Interview with Megan Kaiser by Bill Nowlin, June 14, 2006.
2. Nowlin, *Day by Day with the Boston Red Sox, op. cit.*, p. 410.
3. Interview with Kevin Friend by Chuck Burgess, June 15, 2006.
4. Interview with Amy Tobey by Chuck Burgess, June 15, 2006.
5. Interview with Megan Kaiser, *op. cit.*

Tony Conigliaro—The Red Sox' Singing Slugger

1. Communication from Fred Lynn, October 16, 2006.
2. Interview with Brian Interland by Bill Nowlin, August 15, 2006.
3. Interview with Ed Penney by Bill Nowlin, August 15, 2006.
4. David Cataneo, Tony C: *The Triumph and Tragedy of Tony Conigliaro* (Rutledge Hill Press, 1998), p. 76.
5. Communication with Ernie Campagna, October 9, 2006.
6. Interview with George Denham by Chuck Burgess, July 12, 2006.
7. Interview with Ed Penney, *op. cit.*
8. *Ibidem.*

Dick Dodd—The Early Years

2. Dalley, Robert J., *Surfin' Guitars*, p. 267.
3. *Ibidem.*

Ed Cobb and the Four Preps

1. Peter Van Houten, "Smooth Transitions," *Appaloosa*, June 1990.
2. *Ibidem.*
3. Interview with Elaine Shipley by Bill Nowlin, October 15, 2006.
4. Quotations in the book from Ray Harris, Bruce Belland, members of Ed Cobb's family, Ray Harris, Lincoln Mayorga, Armin Steiner, and others come from interviews conducted in 2006.
5. Van Houten, *op. cit.*
6. Interview with Lennie Sorensen Cobb by Bill Nowlin, November 1, 2006.
7. Interview with Lincoln Mayorga by Chuck Burgess, October 4, 2006.
8. Interview with Ray Harris by Chuck Burgess and Bill Nowlin, August 23, 2006.
9. Interview with Armin Steiner by Bill Nowlin, October 28, 2006.
10. Droney, Maureen, "Armin Steiner," *Mix*, May 1, 2001.

Burt the Bookie, and America's Answer to The Beatles

1. Jerry Heller September 2006 interview with www.AllHiphop.com, promoting his book *Ruthless: A Memoir* (Simon Spotlight Entertainment).
2. Interview with Floyd Sneed by Chuck Burgess, February 12, 2007
3. Larry had known Scott Engle as a kid in Demoulay. Larry dropped a note about Gary (Leeds) Walker:
"As a member of the Standells, Gary did not sing (nor did he have any desire to). He was solely a drummer. Yet, with the Walker Brothers, according to his bio he did not play drums on their recording sessions. I wonder what he DID do. He later formed a rock group, Gary Walker and the Rain, in which he wrote and sang some

of the lead songs. He also did the same in the Walker Brothers reunion. To say Gary was an odd fellow is like saying the Pope is Catholic. He was always involved in zany antics like the time he dressed as a girl (he's not gay) and went out on a date with his friend Bongo Wolf. Bongo was a few fries short of a Happy Meal. Gary-in-drag was introduced to Bongo as Tony's cousin from Italy. Thus she couldn't speak English. Bongo was immediately attracted to this rather tall Italian bombshell. During the date, Bongo tried to make several passes at Gary who socked him really hard each time, in one instance sending Bongo crashing to the floor.

"Gary also had some pretty bizarre ideas for the direction of the group. Fortunately, he was not the leader. After we signed with Liberty Records, he wanted us to change our name from the Standells to "The Children" and bleach our hair blond. He had seen the movie *Village of the Damned* and was inspired by the alien children in it. Of course, we passed on Gary's idea and I think this is what led him to form the Walker Brothers and exit the Standells. If you notice early photos of them, their hair was all bleached blond.

"As you know, John Walker (Maus) was part of the Walker Brothers. John and Judy Maus (his sister) preceeded the Standells in Hawaii (our first gig.) They were also booked by McConkey. This was a year before Gary Leeds joined the group. As far as I know, John and Gary Leeds did not know each other at the time." [Communication from Larry Tamblyn, November 30, 2006]

4. Larry Tamblyn in *Goldmine*, April 8, 1988.

Creating "Dirty Water"
1. Interview with Matt Cobb by Bill Nowlin, September 11, 2006.
2. Interview with Armin Steiner by Bill Nowlin, October 20, 2006.

Selling the Song
1. Communication from Chris Durman, October 7, 2006.
2. E-mail communications with Bill Vermillion, August 27 & 28, 2006.
3. Interview with Peter McDermott by Chuck Burgess, November 10, 2006.
4. Communication from Dennis O'Malley, November 10, 2006.
5. Interview with Stew Ross by Chuck Burgess, November 10, 2006.
6. Interview with Kearney Barton by Bill Nowlin, October 28, 2006.

One Hit Wonders
1. *Goldmine*, op. cit.
2. See Aguilar's full interview at www.richieunterberger.com.
3. Shade, Will, "From LA to Boston to Nicaragua to Cavestomp," *Soundviews* 2001, found at http://members.aol.com/Shake6677/DFstandells.html.
4. *Los Angeles Times*, May 18, 1967.
5. *Washington Post*, July 25, 1967, Davison was responding to Mopsy Strange Kennedy's "Put Another Record on the Pornograph,"—see the *Los Angeles Times*, July 23, 1967.
6. *Los Angeles Times*, August 20, 1967.
7. *Los Angeles Times*, November 19, 1967.
8. E-mail communications from J. J. Rassler, January 26, 2006.

9. Strauss, Neil, "Raiding Memory Lane," *The New York Times*, November 3, 1999.

10. Will Shade, *op. cit.*

Breakup, Blame, and Bitterness

1. Interview with Paula Jacobs by Chuck Burgess, February 6, 2007
2. Will Shade, *op. cit.*
3. *Ibidem.*
4. Ibidem.
5. Interview with Lennie Sorensen Cobb by Bill Nowlin, November 1, 2006
6. Interview with Barrie Edwards by Bill Nowlin, December 1, 2006

Red Sox Nation Loves that "Dirty Water"

1. Nowlin, *Day By Day with the Boston Red Sox*, op. cit., p. 255.
2. Interview with Kevin Friend, *op. cit.*
3. Communication from Mark Chambers, August 16, 2006.
4. Communication from Larry Cancro, January 29, 2006.
5. Communication from Dan Lyons, February 9, 2006.
6. Interview with Dan Duquette by Bill Nowlin, February 10, 2006.
7. Interview with Megan Kaiser by Bill Nowlin, June 14, 2006.

"Dirty Water" and the Magical Mystery Season of 2004

1. Interview with Jim Conners by Chuck Burgess, September 5, 2006.

Interlude: The Return of "Tessie"

1. Interview with Ken Casey by Chuck Burgess, February 3, 2006.
2. Interview with Jeff Horrigan by Bill Nowlin, August 15, 2006.
3. From the liner notes of the Dropkick Murphy album *The Warrior's Code*. The track is a hidden track on the album. It was later included in the soundtrack to the movie *Fever Pitch*.

A World Series Call-Up

1. Communication from Dr. Charles Steinberg, February 11, 2006.
2. Communication from Dave Heuschkel, February 14, 2006.
3. Interview with Mark Felsot by Chuck Burgess, October 15, 2006.
4. Interview with Buzz Knight by Chuck Burgess, October 17, 2006.
5. Quoted by Dave Heuschkel, *Hartford Courant*, October 25, 2004.
6. Communication from Sarah McKenna, October 26, 2006.

"Tessie"—the Rest of the Story

1. E-mail communication from Peter Nash, August 12, 2006.
2. Louis P. Masur, *Autumn Glory* (New York NY: Hill and Wang, 2003), pp. 102, 103.
3. Roger Abrams. *The First World Series and the Baseball Fanatics of 1903* (Boston: Northeastern University Press, 2003), p. 116.

4. *Ibidem*, pp. 135, 136. As to the "power of music," the doctoral research of Dr. Costas I. Karageorghis of Brunei University, U.K., "Music in Sport and Exercise: Theory and Practice" offers insights. The good doctor's study of psychophysical responses to music determined that the "right" music can have a "very positive impact on sport and exercise performance." He learned:

First, during submaximal repetitive exercise such as running, music can narrow a performer's attention and as a consequence, divert attention away from sensations of fatigue.

Second, music alters arousal levels and can therefore be used as a form of stimulant prior to competition or as a sedative to calm over-anxious athletes.

Third, music is beneficial as a result of the similarities between rhythm and human movement; hence, the synchronization of music with exercise consistently demonstrates increased levels of work output among exercise participants.

Fourth, in relation to the previous point, the rhythmical qualities of music also emulate patterns of physical skills; therefore, music can enhance the acquisition of motor skills and create a better learning environment.—*The Sport Journal*, Volume 2, Number 2, Spring 1999.

5. *Ibid.*, p. 118.
6. Masur, *op. cit.*, p. 180.
7. Abrams, *op. cit.*, p. 117.
8. *The Boston Globe*, October 14, 1903.
9. Bill Nowlin, *Day by Day with the Boston Red Sox* (Cambridge MA: Rounder Books, 2006), p. 157.
10. *The New York Times*, October 10, 1914.
11. Nowlin, *op. cit.*, p. 120.
12. *The Boston Globe*, October 12, 1915.
13. Nowlin, *op. cit.*, p. 495.
14. *The Boston Globe*, October 13, 1916.
15. *The New York Times*, October 13, 1916.
16. *The Boston Globe*, September 10, 1918.
17. E-mail communication from Peter Nash, August 12, 2006.
18. E-mail communication from Alan Foulds, March 3, 2007.

Other Teams, Other Songs

1. McDermott, *A Funny Thing Happened on the Way to Cooperstown*, pp. 87, 255. McDermott's best season was his 18-10 year with the Red Sox.
2. Nowlin, *Mr. Red Sox: The Johnny Pesky Story*, p. 250. The Hooper Ratings were like today's Nielsen's.

Standells Timeline

Sources: Interview with Dick Dodd, November 1, 2006.
"Would the real Standells please…," *Goldmine*, April 8, 1988.
Frank Mickadell, "'Scamdells' make arresting debut," *Orange County Register*
Patrice Gravino, "Performer finds himself facing the music in court," *Austin American-Statesman.*

INDEX

220

Not indexed: portions of the appendix: "Dirty Water" on the Charts, Songs About the Red Sox, Other Teams, Other Songs, Standells Discography, Text from LP Jackets, The Standells in *16 Magazine*, Standells Timeline, and portions of "Tessie"—The Rest of the Story.

Chuck Burgess and Bill Nowlin, hoping to hear "Dirty Water" after the game. Photograph by Jamison Cormier.

CHARLES "CHUCK" BURGESS attended his first game at Fenway Park in 1953 at age 7 and bought his first rock and roll record—"Tutti-Fruiti" by Little Richard— when he was 10. In addition to a long career in education, Chuck had a 20-year gig as an "Oldies" disc jockey. In the 1980s he hosted WJCC radio's "Reflections," which featured his personal interviews with scores of pop music stars—from Chubby Checker to Bobby Vinton. He has emceed dozens of concerts and shows starring the Skyliners, Frankie Valli, Joey Dee, the Searchers, the Coasters, the Crystals, the Platters, and other rock and roll legends. Chuck has written numerous articles on sports and entertainment, is a member of the Golf Writers Association of America, and is the author of *Golf Links*, published by Rounder Books (2005).

BILL NOWLIN's first record was Rusty Draper's C&W single "The Railroad Runs Through the Middle of the House" b/w "Pink Cadillac," followed shortly by Elvis's "Hound Dog"/"Don't Be Cruel." His first concert was a 1959 Ray Charles show at the Orpheum in downtown Boston. His first LP was Lloyd Price's *Mr. Personality*. A lifelong love of music led to founding Rounder Records with Ken Irwin and Marian Leighton in 1970. The independent label has produced and released more than 3,000 record albums. A former professor of political science, Bill began to write about baseball in the mid-1990s and has more than 15 books to his credit, including *Ted Williams At War* and *Day by Day with the Boston Red Sox*. The first time he saw The Standells was in 1966.

LOVE THAT DIRTY WATER